Beacon
Hill and
West End

North End
and the
Waterfront

Old Boston
and the
Financial
District

Chinatown
and the
Theater District

**NORTH END AND
THE WATERFRONT**
Pages 68–79

**OLD BOSTON AND THE
FINANCIAL DISTRICT**
Pages 56–67

EYEWITNESS TRAVEL GUIDES

BOSTON

EYEWITNESS TRAVEL GUIDES

BOSTON

Main contributors:
TOM BROSS, PATRICIA HARRIS, AND DAVID LYON

DK PUBLISHING

LONDON • NEW YORK • MUNICH
MELBOURNE • DELHI

Project Editor Marcus Hardy
Art Editor Nicola Rodway
Editor Simon Hall
U.S. Editor Mary Sutherland
Designers Elly King, Nikala Sim
Map Co-ordinators Dave Pugh, Casper Morris
DTP Maite Lantaron
Picture Researcher Brigitte Arora
Production Michelle Thomas

Contributors
Tom Bross, Brett Cook, Patricia Harris, Carolyn Heller,
David Lyon, Juliette Rogers, Kem Sawyer

Photographers
Demetrio Carrasco, Linda Whitwam

Illustrators
Stephen Conlin, Gary Cross, Richard Draper,
Chris Orr & Associates, Robbie Polley, John Woodcock

Maps
Ben Bowles, Rob Clynes, Sam Johnston,
James Macdonald (Colourmap Scanning Ltd)

Reproduced by Colourscan, Singapore
Printed and bound by South China Printing Co. Ltd., China

First American Edition, 2001
03 04 05 10 9 8 7 6 5 4 3 2

Published in the United States by DK Publishing, Inc.,
375 Hudson Street, New York, New York 10014

Reprinted with revisions 2003

Copyright © 2001, 2003 Dorling Kindersley Limited, London

Published in Great Britain by Dorling Kindersley Limited.

A cataloging in publication record is available
from the Library of Congress.

ISSN 1542-1554
ISBN 0-7894-9559-7

Throughout this book, floors are referred to in accordance with
American usage, i.e., the "first floor" is at ground level.

See our complete product line at
www.dk.com

◁ **Rowes Wharf, part of new development along Boston's waterfront**

Contents

How To Use This Guide 6

Tiffany window in the Arlington Street Church, Back Bay

Introducing Boston

Putting Boston on the Map 10

The History of Boston 14

Boston at a Glance 24

Boston Through the Year 36

Federal-style houses, Beacon Hill district (see pp44–7)

View of the Back Bay skyline, with the John Hancock Tower *(see p99)*

Clambakes, including lobster and clams, a New England specialty

SURVIVAL GUIDE

Pumpkins for sale, a regular sight in the fall

Memorial Church steeple, Harvard Yard *(see pp112–3)*

TRAVELERS' NEEDS

Trinity Church, Back Bay *(see pp96–7)*

HOW TO USE THIS GUIDE

THIS GUIDE WILL HELP you get the most from your visit to Boston, providing expert recommendations and detailed practical information. *Introducing Boston* maps the city and sets it in its geographical, historical, and cultural context, and the quick-reference timeline on the history pages gives the dates of Boston's significant historical events. *Boston at a Glance* is an overview of the city's main attractions.

Window at First Baptist Church *(see p94)*

Boston Area by Area starts on page 40 and describes all the important sights, using maps, photographs, and detailed illustrations. The sights are arranged in two groups: those in Boston's central districts, and those a little farther afield. Hotel, restaurant, and entertainment recommendations can be found in *Travelers' Needs*, while the *Survival Guide* includes tips on everything from transportation and telephones to personal safety.

FINDING YOUR WAY AROUND THE SIGHTSEEING SECTION

Each of the six sightseeing areas is colorcoded for easy reference. Every chapter opens with an introduction to the area it covers, describing its history and character. For central districts, this is followed by a

Street-by-Street map illustrating a particularly interesting part of the area; for sights farther away, by a regional map. A simple numbering system relates sights to the maps. Important sights are covered by several pages.

1 Introduction to the Area
For easy reference, the sights are numbered and plotted on an area map, with "T" stations shown where helpful. The key sights (historic buildings, churches, museums, and open-air sights) are listed by category.

A locator map shows where you are in relation to other areas of the city center.

Color-coded thumb tabs mark each area.

Locator map

The area shaded in pink is shown in greater detail on the Street-by-Street map.

2 Street-by-Street Map
This gives a bird's-eye view of interesting and important parts of each sightseeing area, with accurate drawings of all the buildings within them. The numbering of the sights ties in with the preceding area map and with the fuller descriptions on the pages that follow.

A list of star sights recommends the places that no visitor should miss.

Suggested walking route

BOSTON AREA MAP

The colored areas shown on this map *(see inside front cover)* are the five main sightseeing areas of central Boston (excluding the *Farther Afield* section.) Each is covered in a full chapter in the *Boston Area by Area* section *(pp40–119)*. The areas are also highlighted on other maps throughout the book. In *Boston at a Glance (pp24–39)*, for example, they help you to locate the most important sights that no visitor should miss. The maps' colored borders match the colored thumb tabs at the top corner of each page.

Numbers refer to each sight's position on the area map and its place in the chapter.

Practical information lists all the information you need to visit every sight, including a map reference to the *Street Finder* maps *(pp176–181)*.

3 Detailed information on each sight
All the important sights are described individually. They are listed to follow the numbering on the area map at the start of the section. The key to the symbols summarizing practical information is on the back flap.

A visitors' checklist provides the practical information you will need to plan your visit.

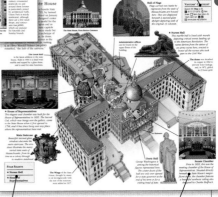

Story boxes provide details on famous people or historical events.

4 Boston's Major Sights
These are given more extensive coverage, sometimes two or more full pages. Historic buildings are dissected to reveal their interiors; museums and galleries have color-coded floor plans to help you find important exhibits.

Stars indicate the most interesting sights.

Captions provide more detailed information about specific sights.

INTRODUCING
BOSTON

Putting Boston on the Map

BOSTON IS SITUATED along the United States' northeastern Atlantic coast on Massachusetts Bay. Founded in the early 17th century around a large natural harbor at the mouth of the Charles River, the modern city now covers an area of 49 sq miles (127 sq km) and has a population of 600,000. Boston is the capital of Massachusetts and a major center of American history, culture, and learning.

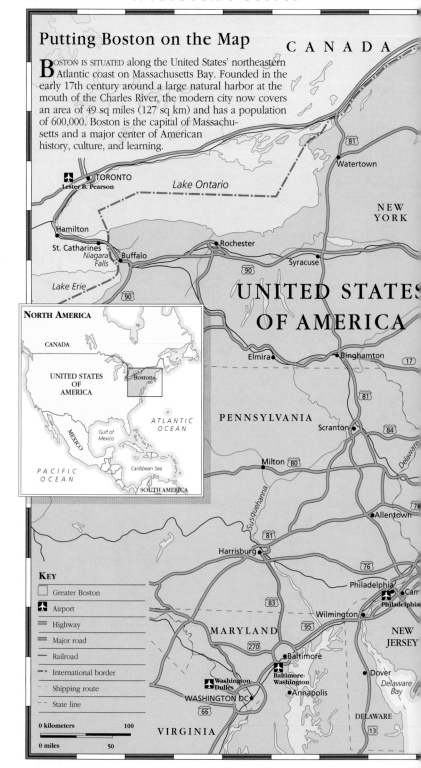

CANADA

Lake Ontario

TORONTO
Lester B. Pearson

Watertown

NEW YORK

Hamilton

St. Catharines
Niagara Falls
Buffalo

●Rochester

Syracuse

Lake Erie

90

UNITED STATES OF AMERICA

NORTH AMERICA

CANADA

UNITED STATES OF AMERICA

Boston

ATLANTIC OCEAN

MEXICO

Gulf of Mexico

PACIFIC OCEAN

Caribbean Sea

SOUTH AMERICA

Elmira●   ●Binghamton

17

81

PENNSYLVANIA

Scranton

84

Delaware

Milton   80

Susquehanna

81

Allentown●

Harrisburg●

76

KEY

☐	Greater Boston
✈	Airport
═	Highway
━	Major road
─	Railroad
‒ ‒	International border
─ ─	Shipping route
‑ ‑	State line

Philadelphia
Philadelphia

83   Cam

Wilmington●

NEW JERSEY

MARYLAND

270

95

●Baltimore

Dover

Delaware Bay

Washington-Dulles
Baltimore-Washington

WASHINGTON DC

●Annapolis

66

VIRGINIA

DELAWARE

13

0 kilometers   100
0 miles   50

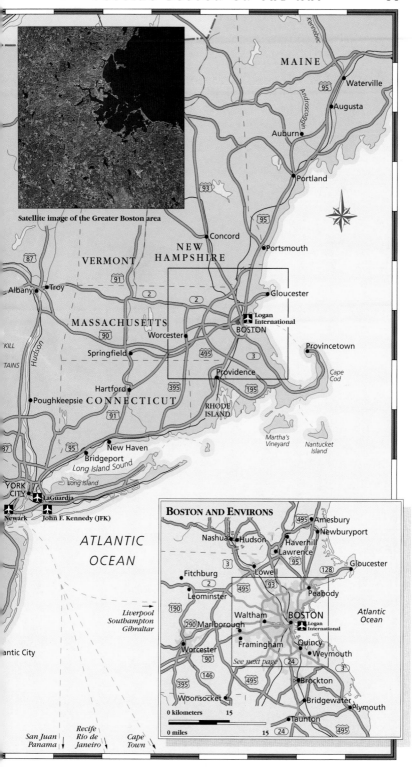

Satellite image of the Greater Boston area

MAINE

Waterville
95
Augusta
Androscoggin
Auburn

Portland

Kennebec

93
95

Concord
Portsmouth
NEW
HAMPSHIRE
VERMONT

87
Albany
Troy
91
2
2
Gloucester
Logan
International
BOSTON

MASSACHUSETTS
90
Worcester
Springfield
495
3
Provincetown

Cape
Cod

Hudson

KILL

TAINS

395
Hartford
Poughkeepsie CONNECTICUT
91
RHODE
ISLAND
Providence
195

Martha's
Vineyard
Nantucket
Island

37
95
New Haven
Bridgeport
Long Island Sound
Long Island

YORK
CITY
LaGuardia
Newark
John F. Kennedy (JFK)

ATLANTIC
OCEAN

Liverpool
Southampton
Gibraltar

antic City

San Juan
Panama
Recife
Rio de
Janeiro
Cape
Town

BOSTON AND ENVIRONS

495
Amesbury
Newburyport
Nashua Hudson
Haverhill
Lawrence
95
128
Gloucester
3
Fitchburg
Lowell
2
495
93
Peabody
Leominster
190
Waltham
BOSTON
Logan
International
Atlantic
Ocean

290 Marlborough
Framingham
Quincy
Weymouth
Worcester
90
24
3
See next page
395
146
495
Brockton
Woonsocket
Bridgewater
Plymouth
Taunton
24
495

0 kilometers   15

0 miles   15

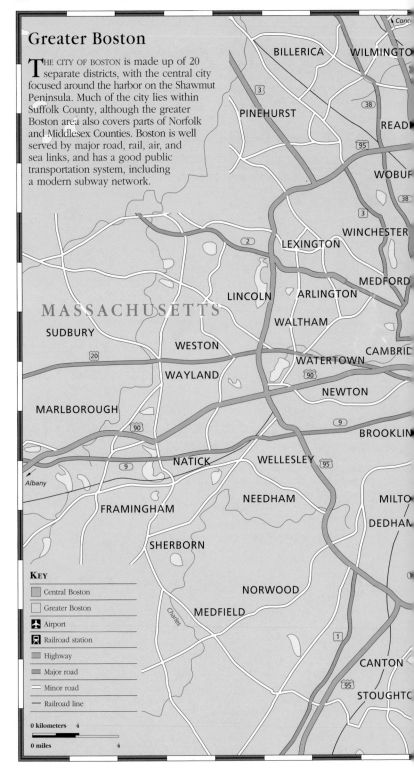

Greater Boston

THE CITY OF BOSTON is made up of 20 separate districts, with the central city focused around the harbor on the Shawmut Peninsula. Much of the city lies within Suffolk County, although the greater Boston area also covers parts of Norfolk and Middlesex Counties. Boston is well served by major road, rail, air, and sea links, and has a good public transportation system, including a modern subway network.

BILLERICA

WILMINGTO

Conc

PINEHURST

READ

WOBUF

WINCHESTER

LEXINGTON

MEDFORD

MASSACHUSETTS

LINCOLN   ARLINGTON

WALTHAM

SUDBURY

WESTON

WATERTOWN   CAMBRID

WAYLAND

NEWTON

MARLBOROUGH

BROOKLIN

NATICK   WELLESLEY

Albany

NEEDHAM   MILTO

FRAMINGHAM

DEDHAM

SHERBORN

NORWOOD

MEDFIELD

CANTON

STOUGHTO

KEY

	Central Boston
	Greater Boston
✈	Airport
Ⓡ	Railroad station
	Highway
	Major road
	Minor road
	Railroad line

0 kilometers   4

0 miles   4

Charles

THE HISTORY OF BOSTON

VIDENCE OF HUMAN OCCUPATION *in Massachusetts dates from around 7500 B.C. By around A.D. 500 Algonquin Indians were widespread in the region. Hunter-gatherers, they fished, farmed beans and pumpkins, and hunted moose and deer. They were made up of seven tribes, the closest geographically to present-day Boston being the Massachusetts, Wampanoags, and Nipmucks.*

Other tribes in the region included the Nausets around Cape Cod, the Pennacooks farther north, and Pocumtucs and Mohicans to the west. Their dialects came from the same language, and their physical features were similar. Each tribe lived in close-knit communities of approximately 250 people.

Artist's impression of the
Viking Leif Ericsson's ship

THE FIRST EUROPEANS

During the Age of the Vikings, Norsemen from Scandinavia adventured far from home, reaching North America. The coastal land of Vinland discovered by Leif Ericsson in around A.D. 1000 may well have been on the Massachusetts coast. French and Spanish fishermen fished here in the mid-15th century and the Italian-born explorer John Cabot led an English expedition to the New England coast once in 1497 and again in 1498. A few years later Miguel Cortereal sailed from Portugal to Massachusetts, where his ship was wrecked. His name was found carved on a granite rock with the year 1511. Throughout the 16th

century, the English, French, Portuguese, Spanish, and Italians explored the East Coast, whaling, fishing, and trading with the natives. In 1602 the Englishman Bartholomew Gosnold sailed to Massachusetts, landing on the peninsula he called Cape Cod and traversing the island he would name Martha's Vineyard after his daughter. He returned to England with furs from the natives and sassafras to be used medicinally. In 1607 James I of England offered land in the New World to two companies. What is now Virginia he gave to the London company, led by Captain John Smith. To a group from Plymouth, England, he assigned New England and land as far south as what is now Delaware. The Plymouth Company set out in 1607 to found a colony along the Kennebec River in present-day Maine, but the harsh winter led the company to return to England. John Smith's Virginia expedition was more successful. In May 1607 he arrived in Jamestown, where he founded a permanent colony.

TIMELINE

Viking casket

1497 John Cabot leads English expedition to New England coast

1608 Puritan separatists flee England for the Netherlands

A.D. 500	1000	1500

500 Algonquin tribes inhabit land stretching from Canada to Florida

1000 Viking explorer Leif Ericsson is thought to have reached Massachusetts

1511 Portuguese Miguel Cortereal explores Massachusetts

1602 English explorer Bartholomew Gosnold names Cape Cod and Martha's Vineyard

1607 James I assigns land to Plymouth Company

◁ **Inhabitants of Boston watching the Battle of Bunker Hill** *(see p18)*

The first Thanksgiving at Plymouth, Massachusetts, celebrated by the Pilgrim Fathers in 1621

THE PILGRIM FATHERS

In 1614 John Smith traveled to the northeast and published his findings in a book entitled *A Description of New England*. This land would become a haven for people who were victims of religious persecution, especially Puritans, who did not adhere to all the beliefs and rituals of the Church of England. One group of Puritan separatists had already left England to seek greater freedom in The Netherlands, but had faced economic hardship there. Lured by Captain Smith's reports, they returned to England to seek a grant for land in the New World. Joining other Puritans led by William Bradford, they set out from Plymouth in two ships, the *Mayflower* and the *Speedwell*. Quickly discovering that the *Speedwell* was leaking, they returned to Plymouth, crammed into the *Mayflower*, and set sail again on September 16, 1620.

Two months later the 102 Pilgrims arrived at Cape Cod. Before disembarking, they formulated the "Mayflower Compact," agreeing to govern themselves democratically with "just and equal laws... for the general good of the colony." The Pilgrims named their new home Plymouth and soon made friends with the natives. On April 1, 1621, Governor John Carver and Chief Massasoit signed a peace treaty. They celebrated the first Thanksgiving that year sharing provisions with their native hosts.

Meeting of John Winthrop with local native in around 1630

FOUNDING OF BOSTON

Charles I assigned land 40 miles (65 km) north of Plymouth colony, near the Charles River, to the Massachusetts Bay Company, a large group of Puritans. In the spring of 1630 over 1,000 Puritans departed in 11 ships bound for Massachusetts. Some settled in Salem and other communities along the Massachusetts Bay. The vast majority,

TIMELINE

1614 Captain John Smith explores the Northeast

1630 John Winthrop and Puritans settle in Boston

1636 Harvard University is founded

1652 First American coin produced in Boston

Pine-tree shilling, the first U.S. coin

1686 James II appoints Sir Edmund Andros as governor

| 1610 | 1630 | 1650 | 1670 |

1620 The Pilgrims land at Plymouth

1621 Governor John Carver and Chief Massasoit sign peace treaty

1635 Boston Latin School opens

1640 First English-language book printed in America

1638 Anne Hutchinson banished from Boston for religious beliefs

1660 Quaker Mary Dyer hanged on Boston Common

1684 Charles II nullifies the Massachusetts Bay Charter

however, followed John Winthrop, their newly appointed governor, to the mouth of the Charles River. Across the river lived a recluse, an Anglican clergyman, William Blackstone. He learned that disease was rampant among the Puritans due to the scarcity of fresh drinking water, and invited them to move their settlement over the river. Winthrop and his followers were quick to accept. They first called this new land Trimountain, but soon renamed it Boston after the town in England they had left behind. In 1635 they established the Boston Latin School, the first public school in the British colonies. A year later the Puritans founded a university, named subsequently after John Harvard, who had bequeathed it his library.

Mary Dyer with other condemned Quakers, before being hanged in 1660

Although the Puritans had come to Massachusetts in pursuit of religious freedom, they often proved intolerant of others. Anne Hutchinson was driven out of Boston in 1638 for not conforming to the Puritan tradition. Many Quakers were also beaten, fined, or banished. The Quaker preacher Mary Dyer was hanged for religious unorthodoxy on June 1, 1660 on Boston Common. In 1692 after several girls in the town of Salem accused three women of witchcraft, mass hysteria broke out throughout Massachusetts, and many innocents were tried, and hanged. No one felt safe until Governor William Phips put an end to the trials in 1693.

SEEDS OF REBELLION

The British had passed the Navigation Acts to encourage the colonists to trade only with them, but when the colonists refused to obey, Charles II withdrew the Massachusetts Bay Charter in 1684, putting the colony under the control of the king. His successor James II appointed Sir Edmund Andros as royal governor. After James II lost power, the colonists arrested their governor and in 1689 established their own government. But in 1691 William and Mary granted a new charter to the Massachusetts Colony, combining the Massachusetts Bay and Plymouth colonies and recognizing a bicameral legislature. Later, the British and French started a long series of battles over New World territory. France finally ceded control of Canada and the American West, but the cost of war had taken its toll on the British, and the colonists were asked to pay their share in taxes. The seeds of rebellion were sown.

View of the commercial port of Boston in about 1730

Revolutionary Boston

Samuel Adams

IT WAS IN BOSTON, the most important city in the 13 British colonies, that ideas for independence were nurtured and the American Revolution born. The colonists' main quarrel with Britain lay in taxation. The Stamp Act of 1765, and the later Townshend Acts, which placed duties on imports, inflamed colonists because they had no vote. "No taxation without representation" became a common cry. The so-called "Sons of Liberty," led by Samuel Adams, demanded and received the repeal of the Stamp Act. However, attempts to enforce the Townshend Acts led to the Boston Massacre, a tragedy which signaled increasingly poor relations between Britain and colonies.

The Boston Tea Party (1773)
In protest at taxation, Boston patriots boarded three British East India Company ships and threw their cargoes of tea into Boston Harbor (see p77).

THE BOSTON MASSACRE (1770)
At the time of the Townshend Acts, British troops were sent to Boston to protect customs commissioners. Bostonians often scoffed at the soldiers and threw stones. On March 5, 1770 the jeering got out of hand. Shots were fired and five Americans fell.

Old State House (*see pp62–3*)

Five Americans were killed when British troops shot into the crowd.

The Battle of Bunker Hill (1775)
In June 1775, militiamen from all over New England had traveled to Boston to wrest control of the city from the British. The Americans lost the ensuing battle, the bloodiest of the Revolution.

TIMELINE

1765 British Parliament passes the Stamp Act

British Revenue stamp

1773 Tea Act gives British East India Company monopoly. Boston Tea Party

1765		1770

1767 Townshend Acts place duties on imports

1770 Five Americans killed in Boston Massacre

1766 Repeal of the Stamp Act

Evacuation of Boston 1776
Following the Battle of Bunker Hill, Boston remained under British control. For almost a year American troops lay siege to the city, until in March 1776 George Washington masterminded a strategy that led the British finally to evacuate.

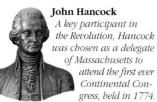

John Hancock
A key participant in the Revolution, Hancock was chosen as a delegate of Massachusetts to attend the first ever Continental Congress, held in 1774.

British soldiers were sent to protect customs commissioners.

Declaration of Independence (1776)
Events surrounding the Battle of Bunker Hill and the evacuation of Boston inspired insurrection throughout the 13 colonies. This led, in July 1776, to the signing of the Declaration of Independence. Freedom from Britain finally came in 1781.

PAUL REVERE'S RIDE

On April 18, 1775 the British planned to march to Lexington to capture Samuel Adams and John Hancock, and then on to Concord to seize arms. To warn of the arrival of British troops, sexton Robert Newman hung lanterns in the tower of the Old North Church *(see p73)* and, so legend has it, Paul Revere undertook his "midnight ride." Revere's ride is immortalized in Longfellow's epic 1863 poem *Tales of a Wayside Inn*. During the ensuing skirmish at Lexington Green, eight American militiamen were killed – the first battle of the American Revolution had been fought.

Warning lights in the Old North Church

1774 Intolerable Acts passed; Boston Harbor is closed

1776 Siege of Boston ends. Declaration of Independence adopted by Continental Congress

1781 General Cornwallis surrenders at Yorktown, Virginia

1775

1780

1775 Midnight ride of Paul Revere

1777 U.S. victory at Battle of Saratoga is the turning point of the war

Grand Union, America's first national flag

1783 U.S. and Britain sign Treaty of Paris

ATHENS OF AMERICA

With the end of the Revolutionary War, Boston's population began to grow and its economy flourish. Its port boomed, and trade, with China in particular, flourished. Some Bostonians made their fortunes at sea; others started profitable textile mills. A number of old Boston families – the Cabots, the Lowells, the Lodges – rose to great prominence boasting of their lineage, their wealth, and their Yankee independence. The United States elected not one but two members of the Adams family (both Boston residents) to the presidency: John Adams (1797–1801) and his son John Quincy Adams (1825–1829). John Adams' wife Abigail, one of the nation's most revered first ladies, made an early call for women's rights when she admonished her husband to "remember the Ladies," for "we ...will not hold ourselves bound by any law in which we have no voice, or representation."

Abigail Smith Adams (1744–1818)

Boston soon earned a reputation as the intellectual capital of the new United States. The Boston Athenaeum *(see p51)*, both a museum and library, was first organized in 1807 "for the promotion of literary and scientific learning." Eminent Bostonians *(see pp28–9)* at this time included the essayist Ralph Waldo Emerson, who formed the Transcendental Club, naturalist Henry David Thoreau, novelist Nathaniel Hawthorne, poet Henry Wadsworth Longfellow, whose epic poem made famous the midnight ride of Paul Revere *(see p19)*, James Russell Lowell, the first editor of the *Atlantic Monthly*, and poet, diarist and educational reformer Oliver Wendell Holmes *(see p47)*. The Boston Public Library, the oldest free library in the U.S., was founded in 1852.

Initially most of Boston's European settlers came from England, but from 1846 Boston attracted thousands of immigrants driven out of Ireland by the potato famine. When the Irish first arrived they settled in overcrowded tenements along the city's waterfront and faced discrimination from the city's residents, especially its social elite, the Boston Brahmins *(see p47)*. Signs went up

The Boston Athenaeum, first organized in 1807 but later housed in this building, which was designed in 1846

TIMELINE

1787 Constitutional Convention held in Philadelphia

1789 Inauguration of George Washington as president

1812 War with England

1825 William Ellery Channing founds American Unitarian Association

1800

1820

1786 Daniel Shay's rebellion

1796 John Adams elected as second president

1807 Boston Athenaeum is founded

George Washington (1732–99)

Irish immigrants, who poured into mid 19th-century Boston

around the city with the words "No Irish Need Apply." But despite these obstacles, the Irish rose in stature and by the end of the 19th century would dominate Boston politics and other areas of the city's life.

THE ABOLITION MOVEMENT

Some of America's most vehement anti-slavery sentiment originated in Boston. William Lloyd Garrison *(see p28)* published the first issue of *The Liberator* on January 1, 1831 calling for the unconditional abolition of slavery: "I will not equivocate ... I will not excuse ... I will not retreat a single inch ... and I will be heard." Not all Bostonians sympathized with his cause. To escape from angry mobs he once had to seek safety for the night in a Boston jail. Garrison and other abolitionists (Charles Sumner, Wendell Phillips, Frederick Douglass) gave rousing anti-slavery speeches in Faneuil Hall *(see p65)*, and accounts of their fiery oratory spread across the United States. The city also played an active role in the underground railroad. Fugitive slaves were assured a safe haven,

and popular stopping-off points were the Second African Meeting House, the home of Lewis Hayden (a former slave), and John J. Smith's barbershop on the corner of Howard and Bulfinch Streets. When the first shots of the Civil War were fired on Fort Sumter on April 12, 1861, President Abraham Lincoln immediately asked volunteers to enlist. The state of Massachusetts answered the call first, sending 1,500 men within four days. As soon as African Americans were admitted to the Union forces, black soldiers started training in Boston. The Boston Brahmin, Colonel Robert Gould Shaw *(see p28)* led these men (the 54th Regiment of the Massachusetts Volunteer Infantry) in an assault on Fort Wagner, South Carolina – Shaw and 62 members of the regiment lost their lives. The battle is still remembered for the role played by African Americans, and a monument *(see p49)* to it on Boston Common was dedicated on May 31, 1897.

Attack on Fort Wagner by black soldiers of the 54th Massachusetts

1846 First influx of Irish immigrants into Boston

1852 Boston Public Library founded

1861 First shots at Fort Sumter begin Civil War

1840

1860

1831 First issue of William Lloyd Garrison's abolitionist newspaper, *The Liberator*

Mural in the Boston Public Library

1863 The 54th Massachusetts leads assault on Fort Wagner

1865 General Robert E. Lee surrenders. The Union is preserved. President Abraham Lincoln is assassinated

GROWTH AND DESTRUCTION

The end of the Civil War in 1865 led to a decline in shipping, but the Industrial Revolution, specifically in cotton and wool manufacturing, enabled Boston to thrive again and grow both in size and population. The Back Bay had been filled and some of the neighboring towns already annexed. However, on November 9, 1872, Boston suffered a terrible setback as flames from a fire that started in a dry goods store spread to warehouses downtown, destroying 765 buildings. Newspaper headlines declared a loss of $250 million with "rich men beggared in a day." The city recovered quickly, though, rebuilding and revitalizing textile and shoe manufacturing.

The Great Fire of Boston, November 9, 1872

Public institutions also continued to flourish. The Museum of Fine Arts *(see pp106–9)* was opened in 1876, and the Boston Symphony Orchestra *(see p150)* founded in 1881. The first subway in the United States, the "T," opened in 1897. In Boston and the surrounding areas educational establishments such as Harvard, Radcliffe, the Massachusetts Institute of Technology (M.I.T.), the New England Conservatory of Music, and Boston University all played their part in making the city a mecca for young students. The renowned collector of art Isabella Stewart Gardner *(see p105)*, a rich, famously outspoken, and well-connected woman, opened her house to the public on New Year's Day, 1903.

THE EARLY 20TH CENTURY

Following World War I, changing political and cultural attitudes across the U.S. increasingly left government clashing violently with the wishes of the people. Life in Boston was no exception. The Boston Police Strike of 1919 marks one of the most dramatic chapters in the U.S. Labor movement. As many as 1,290 policemen filed complaints over low wages, unsanitary stations, and lack of overtime compensation and sought affiliation with the American Federation of Labor (A.F.L.). When the strike started, mobs smashed windows and looted stores. After a skirmish with state militia, in which two were wounded and nine killed, A.F.L. president Samuel Gompers persuaded the police to return to work.

However, this was not just a time of conflict, but also

Harvard University students rowing on the Charles River, 1896

TIMELINE

1872 The Great Fire of Boston	1884 First Irish mayor, Hugh O'Brien, elected	1897 The "T," the U.S.'s first subway, opens.	1905 "Honey Fitz" elected mayor	1919 Boston Police Strike results in riots

1875	1900	1925

1876 Museum of Fine Arts opened	*Museum of Fine Arts exhibit*	1912 Fenway Park opens	1914 James Michael Curley elected mayor for the first time

1881 Boston Symphony Orchestra formed

1903 Isabella Stewart Gardner opens her house as a museum

one when popular culture came to the fore. One way this manifested itself was in spectator sports, which began to enjoy unparalleled popularity. Fenway Park in Boston, home to the Boston Red Sox, had opened on April 20, 1912. The Boston Red Sox won the World Series four times before 1918. However, since selling Babe Ruth, the so called "home-run king," to the New York Yankees, they have not won the World Series again.

Prominent politicians from this time included John F. Kennedy's grandfather, John F. Fitzgerald, or "Honey Fitz," as he was known, who was elected mayor in 1905. The flamboyant James Curley, son of Irish immigrants, who became mayor, congressman, and governor, and spent time in jail for fraud, became a legend in his own lifetime.

Babe Ruth (1895–1948) in an ad for chewing gum

John F. Kennedy, perhaps the most famous of all American politicians, born of Boston Irish stock

CITY RENAISSANCE

Following economic decline during the 1950s, Boston's economy shifted to finance, high-technology, medicine, and higher education. The resulting prosperity revitalized the city's cultural life and led to the gentrification of entire Victorian neighborhoods that had been spared the wrecker's ball during postwar "urban renewal." The preservation of human-scale living areas has helped Boston emerge as one of the United States' most appealing cities.

POST-WAR POLITICS

The most famous Boston-born politician was John F. Kennedy, the great-grandson of an Irish potato famine immigrant. In 1960 he became the U.S.'s first Catholic, and youngest elected, president. His brother, Robert, served as attorney general and U.S. senator for New York. The Irish, however, were not the only immigrants to enter politics. Michael Dukakis, the son of Greek immigrants, was elected governor in 1974, becoming Democratic presidential candidate in 1988.

The late 20th century saw immigrants arrive from countries such as Puerto Rico, Vietnam, India, and Cambodia, all of whom continue a tradition of making their mark on the city.

Spending leisure time in boats on the Charles River, evidence that Boston is prospering

1960 John F. Kennedy elected president

1988 Governor Michael Dukakis becomes Democratic presidential candidate

1993 John F. Kennedy Library and Museum (see p104) opens

1950   **1975**   **2000**

1962 Edward Kennedy elected to U.S. Senate

1963 John F. Kennedy assassinated

Michael Dukakis, Democratic presidential candidate in 1988

BOSTON AT A GLANCE

ALTHOUGH IT IS a small, compact city, Boston offers a wealth of attractions that draw visitors from all over the world. Indeed the range of attractions can exceed that of much larger cities in the U.S. The sights in the center and a little way out of Boston are covered in the *Area by Area* section of the book. There are historic neighborhoods, such as Beacon Hill and Back Bay; examples of some of the best Federal architecture in the U.S., such as the Massachusetts State House; and beautiful examples of late 19th-century opulence such as Trinity Church. The treasures of the Museum of Fine Arts and the Harvard Museums are also shown. A selection of Boston's best is featured below.

BOSTON'S TOP TEN ATTRACTIONS

Beacon Hill
See pp44–7

Old State House
See pp62–3

Massachusetts State House
See pp52–3

Museum of Fine Arts
See pp106–109

New England Aquarium
See pp78–9

Trinity Church
See pp96–7

John Hancock Tower
See p99

Old North Church
See p73

Harvard
See pp112–17

Boston Common
See pp48–9

◁ Trinity Church, reflected in the John Hancock Tower

Boston's Best: Museums

THE CITY OF BOSTON'S Athenian self-image is manifested in dozens of museums, galleries, and archives. Wealthy 19th-century patrons stocked art museums that have now become world-class collections, the best example being the Museum of Fine Arts. Likewise, Boston's leadership in scientific inquiry has created first-rate natural history and science collections. Museums such as the John F. Kennedy Library and Museum provide insight into some of the city's most compelling and influential historical figures, while a strong architectural heritage means that some of the museum buildings are also very beautiful.

Museum of Science
*A favorite family destin-
ation, this museum
has more than 1,000
interactive exhibits,
that explain the laws
of nature and the
science of computers.*

**Harvard
University Museums**
*These museums house a
diverse range of collections:
European Art, archaeology,
natural history, and Asian
and Near Eastern Art.
This, the Sackler Museum,
is housed in a modern
building by James Stirling,
noteworthy in its own right.*

**Isabella Stewart
Gardner Museum**
*This Venetian-style palazzo
stands as Isabella Gardner
left it – filled to the brim
with fine old masters and
modern paintings. Her
taste in art was considered
by many to be impeccable.*

Museum of Fine Arts
*One of the largest museums in North
America, the MFA is famous for its
Greek, Roman, and Egyptian art,
and French Impressionist paintings.*

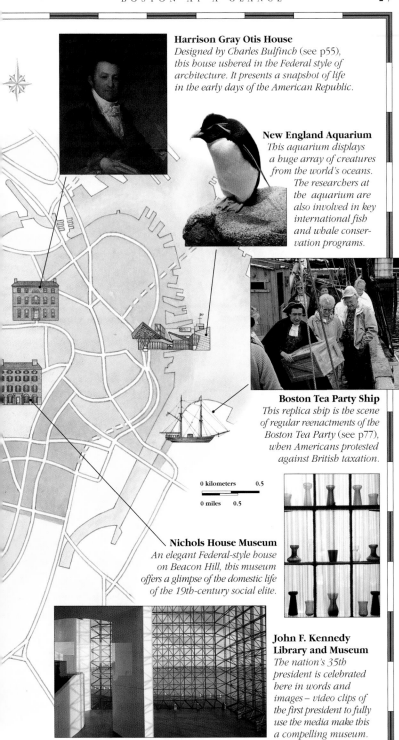

Harrison Gray Otis House
*Designed by Charles Bulfinch (see p55),
this house ushered in the Federal style of
architecture. It presents a snapshot of life
in the early days of the American Republic.*

New England Aquarium
*This aquarium displays
a huge array of creatures
from the world's oceans.
The researchers at
the aquarium are
also involved in key
international fish
and whale conser-
vation programs.*

Boston Tea Party Ship
*This replica ship is the scene
of regular reenactments of the
Boston Tea Party (see p77),
when Americans protested
against British taxation.*

0 kilometers 0.5

0 miles 0.5

Nichols House Museum
*An elegant Federal-style house
on Beacon Hill, this museum
offers a glimpse of the domestic life
of the 19th-century social elite.*

**John F. Kennedy
Library and Museum**
*The nation's 35th
president is celebrated
here in words and
images – video clips of
the first president to fully
use the media make this
a compelling museum.*

Eminent Bostonians

Phillis Wheatley (1753–84)

FOUNDED AS A REFUGE for religious idealists, Boston has always been obsessed with ideas and learning. Mark Twain once observed that "In New York they ask what a man is worth. In Boston they ask, 'What does he know?'" This insistence on the power of ideas has made Boston a magnet for thinkers and doers, and a hotbed of reform movements and social revolution. Education has always been one of the city's leading industries. Consequently, Boston is disproportionately represented in the honor roll of American intellectual life. Bostonians are generally considered to be liberal minded, and tend to occupy the left flank of American political thought.

Malcolm X (1925–65), one of Boston's many famous residents

REFORMERS, RABBLE ROUSERS, AND REVOLUTIONARIES

EVEN WHILE Boston was still in its infancy, Bostonians began to agitate to do things differently. Anne Hutchinson (1591–1643) was exiled for heresy in 1638 (she moved south to found Portsmouth, Rhode Island), while friend and fellow religious radical Mary Dyer died on the Boston Common gallows for Quakerism in 1660 *(see p17)*. Spokesman for the Sons of Liberty and part-time brewer Samuel Adams (1722–1803) incited Boston to revolution in the "Boston Tea Party" *(see p77)*. The city bubbled over with 19th-century reformers, including Dorothea Dix (1802–87), who championed the welfare of the mentally ill, and William Lloyd Garrison (1805–79), publisher of *The Liberator*, who was one of America's most strident voices calling for the abolition of slavery. Malcolm Little (1925–65) spent his adolescence in Boston before converting to Islam in prison and emerging as the charismatic Black Muslim leader Malcolm X. Like Malcolm X, Nguyen Tat Thanh (1890–1969) spent part of his youth in Boston, working for a time in the restaurant of the Omni Parker House Hotel *(see p60)*. Traveling much of the world in his 20s, he was later to assume the name Ho Chi Minh.

Abolitionist William Lloyd Garrison (1805–79)

BOSTON BRAHMINS

IN 1860 Oliver Wendell Holmes (1809–94) dubbed Boston's prosperous merchant class the "Boston Brahmins … a harmless, inoffensive, untitled aristocracy" *(see p47)*. Any suggestion that the Brahmins were unaccomplished, however, could not be farther from the truth. Julia Ward Howe (1819–1910) was a prominent abolitionist and later a crusader for women's rights. She also penned the Unionists' Civil War marching song, "The Battle Hymn of the Republic." Brahmin Colonel Robert Gould Shaw (1837–63) led the all-Black 54th Massachusetts Regiment in the Civil War, and Major Henry Lee Higginson (1834–1919) survived the war to found the Boston Symphony Orchestra in 1881.

Many famous authors were also Brahmins, notably the Lowell clan: James Russell Lowell (1819–91) was the leading literary critic of his day, Amy Lowell (1874–1925) championed "free verse" and founded *Poetry* magazine, and Robert Lowell (1917–77) broke the barriers between formal and informal verse in American poetry. The Brahmins' greatest chronicler was the noted historian Samuel Eliot Morison (1887–1976).

The Brahmins persist through business partnerships, family trusts, and intermarriage, as highlighted in their ditty: "And this is good old Boston, The home of the bean and the cod, Where the Lowells talk to the Cabots, And the Cabots talk only to God."

INVENTORS AND ENTREPRENEURS

INNOVATION HAS always been a way of life in Boston. Donald McKay's (1810–80) East Boston clipper ships revolutionized international sea trade in the 1850s. Working in his Cambridge

Edwin Land (1909–91), inventor of Polaroid instant photography

workshop, Elias Howe (1819–67) created the modern sewing machine, radically altering both the clothing trade and the shoe industry. Alexander Graham Bell (1847–1922) had offices in Cambridge and Boston, and later joined the faculty of Boston University. This was part of a trend of academic affiliation that became almost the rule for Boston's inventors. Edwin H. Land (1909–91) experimented with polarized light in his Harvard lab before inventing Polaroid instant photography. The innovators Bolt, Beranek, and Newman also made academic affiliations with the Massachusetts Institute of Technology, when they sent the world's first electronic mail message in the 1970s.

THINKERS

IN ADDITION TO showing the world how to do things, Bostonians have always been adept at explaining why. In his many essays and poems, Ralph Waldo Emerson (1803–82) first laid the philosophical groundwork for an American school of transcendental religious thought. Meanwhile, his friend and fellow Harvard graduate Henry David Thoreau (1817–62) wrote many seminal works of natural philosophy. A professor at Harvard, William James (1842–1910) not only taught

psychology and physiology, but also promulgated philosophical pragmatism, the concept that the worth of an idea is based on its usefulness. His student, George Santayana (1863–1952) blossomed as the 20th-century's chief philosopher of aesthetics.

More pragmatically, the Harvard economist John Kenneth Galbraith (born 1908) investigated the sources of societal affluence and advocated social policies to put that affluence to work for the common good.

POLITICAL LEADERS

BOSTON'S MOST infamous politician was the "rascal king" James Michael Curley (1874–1958), who served many terms as mayor and U.S. Congressman, winning his last election from a jail cell. His life was to serve as the model for the novel *The Last Hurrah*. Boston also gave the country four presidents: John Adams (1735–1826) and his son John Quincy Adams (1767–1848); the tight-lipped ex-governor Calvin Coolidge (1872–1933), who rose to prominence by crushing the Boston police strike in 1919; and John F. Kennedy, infamously assassinated in Dallas in 1963. Kennedy's brothers were also prominent on the national stage: Robert F. Kennedy (1925–1968) served as attorney general and then as senator, when he, too, was assassinated. Edward M. Kennedy (born 1932) continues to serve as the senior warhorse for social justice in the U.S. Senate. His good friend, Thomas P. "Tip" O'Neill (1912–94), served as U.S. Speaker of the House.

John F. Kennedy campaign button

AUTHORS

AMERICA'S FIRST published author was Boston's Anne Bradstreet (1612–72). The first published African American author was Phillis Wheatley (1753–84), born in Africa, enslaved, then freed in Boston. Her 1778 volume, *Poems on Various Subjects, Religious and Moral*, echoed Boston authors' moral concerns. Henry Wadsworth Longfellow (1807–82) made his fortune from best-selling verse epics such as *Evangeline* and *Hiawatha*, but made his mark translating Dante. Although associated with nearby Concord, popular novelist Louisa May Alcott (1832–88) also lived on Beacon Hill and was active in Boston reform movements. New York-born Henry James (1843–1916) was educated at Harvard and often returned to Boston from his London home, spending a lifetime contrasting American and European culture. Nobel laureate poet and playwright Derek Walcott (born 1930) teaches at Boston University, as does the U.S. poet laureate Robert Pinsky (born 1940). When not in Hollywood, playwright David Mamet (born 1947) can usually be found writing in Harvard Square cafés. The popular Boston-based fictional detective Spenser is the creation of Robert Parker (born 1932).

Author Louisa May Alcott (1832–88), part of Boston's reform movement

Boston's Architecture

BUILDINGS FOLLOWED British styles through the 1790s, when the first American architect of note, Charles Bulfinch, defined the Federal style. In the 19th century, Bostonians evolved a local Victorian style, which first embraced Greek Classicism, then French and Italian styles. Two styles of the late 19th century, Renaissance Revival and Richardsonian Romanesque, remained influential through World War I. In the 20th century, Harvard University and Massachusetts Institute of Technology (M.I.T.) attracted many leading modern and post-modern architects, all of whom left their mark.

Freestanding Federal-style Harrison Gray Otis House

FEDERAL

CHARLES BULFINCH and his protégé Asher Benjamin adapted British Georgian styles to create Boston's first signature architectural style. Typical of this style are freestanding mansions and town houses, with symmetrical brick façades adorned by shuttered windows, and ground-floor windows set in recessed arches. Entrances are often cut from granite slabs, featuring gently fluted columns. The largest and most elegant rooms of Federal homes are usually found on the second floor.

Some of the grander examples of Federal domestic architecture, found mainly on Beacon Hill, feature ornamental ironwork and are often crowned with octagonal cupolas. Chestnut Street on Beacon Hill *(see pp44–5)* represents the greatest concentration of Federal-style row houses in Boston. Individual examples of the style include the Harrison Gray Otis House *(see p54)* and the Hepzibah Swan Houses *(see p47)*.

BOSTON GRANITE

THE GRANITE outcrops found around Boston Harbor provided stone for the city's waterfront development in the early 19th century. Technological advances had made it possible to cut entire columns from single blocks of granite. Freed from the constraints of soft limestone or sandstone, Alexander Parris and other architects adopted granite as a principal material for markets and warehouses, as can be seen for example at Charlestown Navy Yard *(see p117)* and Quincy Market *(see p66)*. Although the basic style is an adaptation of Greek Revival, it also includes modern innovations such as iron tension rods and laminated wooden ribs to support copper domes.

Granite Greek Revival façade of Quincy Market

Distinctive, multicolored, square tower of Trinity Church

Renaissance Revival interior of the Boston Public Library

RENAISSANCE REVIVAL

CHARLES MCKIM'S 1887 design for the Boston Public Library *(see p98)*, conceived as a "palace of the people," established Renaissance Revival architecture as a favorite American style for monumental public structures. Evenly spaced windows and arches, adorned by inscriptions and sculptural details, define the style. Soaring, barrel vaulted interiors are also featured. Boston's Renaissance Revival structures make extensive use of New England and Italian marbles, carved stucco ceilings, and carved wood in staircases and walls. Many of the Italian artisans who were brought over to execute this work stayed in Boston, forming an elite group within the Italian immigrant community by around 1900.

RICHARDSONIAN ROMANESQUE

AMERICA is far too young to boast a true Romanesque style, but Henry Hobson Richardson effectively created one from European inspirations and American stone. By the 1870s, the wealthy city of Boston demanded more elaborate churches than the existing sparsely designed "boxes with a spire." Gothic styles, however, were associated with medieval Catholicism and were unacceptable to the Protestant heirs of the Puritans. Richardson's churches provided a pleasing alternative. Often, the building's main components were massed around a central tower, as can be seen in Boston's most important example of the style, Trinity Church *(see pp96–7)*, as well as in the First Baptist Church *(see p94)*. In sharp contrast to the Boston Granite style, which used many similar materials and sharp angles, Richardson used stones of contrasting colors and rounded off virtually every square edge.

Italianate interior detail of the Victorian Gibson House Museum

upper Newbury Street and Massachusetts Avenue reflect a more mature synthesis: raised granite entrances, slate-shingled mansard roofs, and dormer and bay windows. Nowhere is the transition from early to late Victorian styles so evident than on the walk westward, from the center of Boston, along Commonwealth Avenue *(see p95)*.

Art Deco

Most of Boston's Art Deco buildings are clustered around Post Office Square in the Financial District, with the former Post Office *(see p67)* and the Verizon Building *(see p67)* being the finest examples. Essentially tall buildings of light gray granite, they are constructed with vertical strips and slit windows that elongate their forms. Elaborate geometric steps and surface ornament on the upper stories help

Romanesque-style front portico of the First Baptist Church

Victorian

Boston's Victorian style largely eschews the pointed Gothic lines of English Victorian in favor of French Academic, French Empire, and various Italianate influences. The variations are displayed in an almost chronological march of styles in the Back Bay and South End *(see pp90–101)*, paralleling the decade-by-decade creation of filled land in those neighborhoods in the second half of the 19th century. Earlier buildings tend to reflect their stylistic influences more accurately; for example, the Italianate Gibson House Museum *(see p94)* on Beacon Street, which would have been among the first wave of Back Bay development. The later town houses of

relieve their mass. Boston Art Deco tends also to make great use of Greco-Roman geometric friezes and stylized, vegetable-inspired ornament. Some Financial District Art Deco buildings also feature bas-relief murals of historic and heroic themes. Back Bay was once the site of many Art Deco storefronts with stylized Parisian pilasters and grill-work, but only the jewelry store Shreve, Crump & Low Inc. on Boylston Street *(see p98)* remains intact.

Modernist interior of the Kresge Chapel, built in the 1950s

Modernism

The willing embrace of modernism at Boston and Cambridge colleges has graced the Boston area with a wide range of outstanding 20th-century buildings where simplicity of form is favored over ornament, and expressive lines grow out of function. When Bauhaus founder Walter Gropius fled the Nazis for the safety of Harvard University, he served as a magnet for some of the mid-century's great designers and architects. The range of styles in Boston's modernist buildings is diverse: the poetic sculptural grace of Eero Saarinen's Kresge Auditorium and Chapel at M.I.T. *(see p111)*; Le Corbusier's Carpenter Center for the Visual Arts *(see p113)*; and Josep Lluis Sert's International-style Holyoke Center, both near Harvard Yard *(see pp112–13)*.

Art Deco exterior of the the Verizon Building, overlooking Post Office Square

The Freedom Trail

From Boston Common to Paul Revere House

Boston has more sites directly related to the American Revolution than any other city. The most important of these sites, as well as some relating to other freedoms gained by Bostonians, have been linked together as "The Freedom Trail." This 2.5-mile (4-km) walking route, marked in red on the sidewalks, starts at Boston Common and eventually ends at Bunker Hill in Charlestown. This first section weaves its way through the central city and Old Boston.

Elegant Georgian steeple of Park Street Church

Nurses Hall in Massachusetts State House

Central City

The Freedom Trail starts at the Visitor Information Center on Boston Common ① *(see pp48–9).* This is where angry colonials rallied against their British masters and where the British forces were encamped during the 1775–76 military occupation. Political speakers still expound from their soapboxes here, and the Common remains a center of much activity.

Walking toward the northwest corner of the Common gives a great view of the Massachusetts State House ② *(see p52)* on Beacon Street, designed by Charles Bulfinch as the new center of state governance shortly after the Revolution. Along Park Street, at the end of the Common, you will come to Park Street Church ③ *(see p50),* built in 1810 and a bulwark of the antislavery movement. The church took the place of an old grain storage facility, which in turn gave its name to the adjacent Granary Burying Ground ④, one of Boston's earliest cemeteries and the final resting place of patriots John Hancock and Paul Revere *(see p19).* Continuing along Tremont Street you will come to King's Chapel and Burying Ground ⑤ *(see p60).* The tiny cemetery is Boston's oldest, containing, among others, the grave of city founder John Winthrop. As the name suggests, King's Chapel was the principal Anglican church in Puritan Boston, and more than half of its congregation fled to Nova Scotia at the outbreak of the Revolution. The box pew on the right just inside the front entrance was reserved for condemned prisoners to hear their last sermons before going to the gallows on Boston Common.

Heart of Old Boston

Head back along Tremont Street and turn down School Street, where a hopscotch-like mosaic embedded in the sidewalk commemorates the site of the First Public School ⑥, established in 1635. At the bottom of the street is the Boston Globe Store ⑦ (see p61), a landmark more associated with Boston's literary emergence of 1845–65 than with the Revolution.

The Old South Meeting House ⑧, a short way to the south on Washington Street, is a graceful, white-spired brick church, modeled on Sir Christopher Wren's English country churches. As one of the largest meeting halls in Revolutionary Boston, "Old South's" rafters rang with many a fiery speech urging revolt against the British. A few blocks along, the Old State House ⑨ presides over the head of State Street. The colonial government building, it also served as the first state legislature, and the merchants' exchange in the basement was where Boston's colonial shipping fortunes were made. The square in front of the Old State House is the Boston Massacre Site ⑩, where British soldiers opened fire on a taunting mob in 1770, killing five and providing ideal propaganda for revolutionary agitators.

Follow State Street down to Congress Street and turn left to reach Faneuil Hall ⑪, called the "Cradle of Liberty" for the history of patriotic speeches made in its public meeting hall. Donated to the city by Huguenot merchant Peter Faneuil, the building was built primarily as Boston's first central marketplace.

The red stripe of the Freedom Trail comes in handy when negotiating the way to the North End and the Paul Revere House ⑫ on North Square. Boston's oldest house, it was home to the man famously known for his "midnight ride" (see p19).

TIPS FOR WALKERS

Starting point: Boston Common. Maps available at Boston Common Visitors' Center.
Length: 2.5 miles (4 km).
Getting there: Park Street Station (T Green and Red lines) to start. State (Orange and Blue lines) and Haymarket (Orange and Green lines). T stations also on route. Follow red stripe on sidewalk for the full route.

Faneuil Hall, popularly known as "the Cradle of Liberty"

Old State House, the seat of colonial government

WALK

Boston Common ①
Boston Globe Store ⑦
Boston Massacre Site ⑩
Faneuil Hall ⑪
First Public School Site ⑥
Granary Burying Ground ④
King's Chapel and Burying Ground ⑤
Massachusetts State House ②
Old South Meeting House ⑧
Old State House ⑨
Park Street Church ③
Paul Revere House ⑫

0 meters 250
0 yards 250

KEY

••• Walk route
Ⓣ Subway
ℹ Tourist information

The Freedom Trail

From Old North Church to Bunker Hill Monument

DISTANCES BEGIN to stretch out on the second half of the Freedom Trail as it meanders through the narrow streets of the North End, then continues over the Charles River to Charlestown, where Boston's settlers first landed. The sites here embrace two wars – the War of Independence and the War of 1812.

View from Copp's Hill terrace, at the edge of Copp's Hill Burying Ground

The North End

Following the Freedom Trail through the North End, allow time to try some of the Italian cafés and bakeries along the neighborhood's main thoroughfare, Hanover Street. Cross through the Paul Revere Mall to reach Old North Church ⑬ *(see p73)*, whose spire is instantly visible over the shoulder of the statue of Paul Revere on horseback. Sexton Robert Newman famously hung two lanterns in the belfry here, signaling the advance of British troops on Lexington and Concord in 1775. The church retains its 18th-century interior, including the unusual box pews.

The crest of Copp's Hill lies close by on Hull Street. Some of Boston's earliest gallows stood here, and Bostonians would gather in boats below to watch the hangings of heretics and pirates. Much of the hilltop is covered by Copp's Hill

Gravestone at Copp's Hill Burying Ground

Burying Ground ⑭. This was established in 1660, and the cemetery holds the remains of several generations of the Mather family – Boston's influential 17th- and 18th-century theocrats – as well as the graves of many soldiers of the Revolution. Boston's first free African American community, "New Guinea," covered the west side of Copp's Hill. A broken column marks the grave of Prince Hall, head of the Black Masons, distinguished veteran of the Revolution, and prominent political leader in the early years of the Republic. The musketball-chipped tombstone of patriot Daniel Malcolm records that he asked to be buried "in a stone grave 10 feet deep" to rest beyond the reach of British gunfire.

CHARLESTOWN BRIDGE

COMMERCIAL STREET

PRINCE STREET

SNOWHILL STREET

SALEM STREET

⑭

⑬

HANOVER STREET

Unusual box pews inside Old North Church

WALK

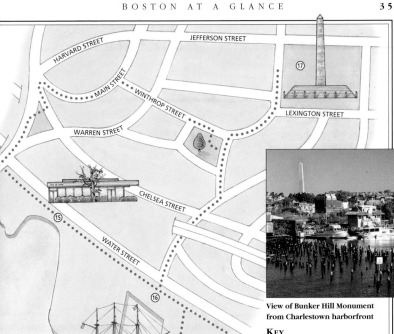

View of Bunker Hill Monument from Charlestown harborfront

KEY

• • • Walk route

0 meters   250

0 yards   250

Charlestown

The iron bridge over the Charles River that links the North End in Boston with City Square in Charlestown dates from 1899. Across the bridge, turn right along Constitution Road, following signs to Bunker Hill Pavilion ⑮, a privately sponsored multimedia show about the first pitched battle of the Revolution, fought here in 1775. The visitors' center for the nearby Charlestown Navy Yard ⑯ shares the building, and it is worth visiting to get an overview of the site. The colonial navy had been no match for the might of Britain's naval forces during the Revolution, and building a more formidable naval force became a priority. This was one of several shipyards that were set up around 1800. Decommissioned in 1974, the yard is now maintained by the National Park Service.

Lion carving, *U.S.S. Constitution*

Lying at her berth alongside Pier 1, the *U.S.S. Constitution* is probably the most famous ship in U.S. history and still remains the flagship of the U.S. Navy. Built at Hartt's shipyard in the North End, she was completed in 1797. In the War of 1812, she earned the nickname "Old Ironsides" for the resilience of her live oak hull against cannon fire. Fully restored for her bicentennial, the *Constitution* occasionally sails under her own power.

The granite obelisk that towers above the Charlestown waterfront is Bunker Hill Monument ⑰, commemorating the battle of June 17, 1775 that ended with a costly victory for British forces against an irregular colonial army that finally ran out of ammunition. British losses were so heavy, however, that the battle would presage future success for the colonial forces. As a monument to the first large-scale battle of the Revolution, the obelisk, based on those of ancient Egypt, was a prototype for others across the U.S.

Defensive guns at Charlestown Navy Yard with view of the North End

BOSTON THROUGH THE YEAR

PERHAPS MORE THAN in any other city in the U.S., Boston's cultural life tends to follow the academic calendar, with the "year" beginning when classes commence at its many colleges and universities in September, and winding down a little with the start of the summer recess in May and June. In between is so-called "ice cream" season, when the warm weather causes most activities to shift out of doors, and reading lists favor

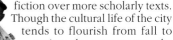

Model of a saint, North End Italian Feast Days

fiction over more scholarly texts. Though the cultural life of the city tends to flourish from fall to spring, the summer months do feature many of Boston's major carnivals, festivals, parades, and free outdoor concerts at the Hatch Shell *(see p94)*. After the students' return to their studies in the fall, the busy performing arts season begins, with symphony concerts, theater, and ballet continuing into the following spring.

Springtime tulips in full bloom, Boston Public Garden

SPRING

WHEN THE WEATHER warms, Boston bursts into bloom. Thousands of tulips explode in the Public Garden, and the magnolia trees of Commonwealth Avenue are sheathed in pink and white. Spring is a season of remembrance, with commemorations of events leading up to the American Revolution. It also marks the start of the season for the Boston Red Sox.

MARCH

New England Spring Flower Show *(mid-Mar)*, Bayside Expo Center. Oldest annual flower exhibition in the United States.
Reenactment of Boston Massacre *(Mar 5)*, Old State House. Marks watershed event that turned Bostonians against their British rulers.
St. Patrick's Day Parade

(Sun before Mar 17), South Boston. Annual parade also commemorates the British evacuation of Boston during the Revolutionary War.

APRIL

Baseball *(first week)*, Fenway Park. Major league season starts for Boston Red Sox.
Annual Lantern Celebration *(Apr 18)*, Old North Church. Commemorates the hanging of signal lanterns in the steeple to warn revolutionaries.
Patriots Day Parade *(third Mon)*, from City Hall Plaza to Paul Revere Mall, where the start of Paul Revere's Midnight Ride is reenacted.
Boston Marathon *(third Mon)*, Hopkinton to Back Bay. America's oldest marathon.

MAY

May Fair *(first Sat)*, Harvard Square. International street fair.
Walk for Hunger *(first Sun)*, 20-mile (32 km) walk, one of

the oldest and largest pledge walks in the country, raises funds for food banks.
Ducklings Day Parade *(second Sun)*, Boston Common. Parade retracing the route of the ducklings in Robert McCloskey's classic children's storybook, *Make Way for Ducklings*.
Harvard Square Book Festival *(early-mid May)*, Cambridge. Week-long series of readings, book signings, and luncheons.
Hidden Gardens of Beacon Hill *(third Thu)*, Beacon Hill. Garden tours organized.
Lilac Sunday *(third Sun)*, Arnold Arboretum. More than 400 lilac bushes are in bloom.
Street Performers Festival *(late May)*, Faneuil Hall Marketplace. Street musicians, jugglers, acrobats and other performers.
Boston Pops *(May–Jun)*, Symphony Hall. Season features light Classical repertory and American popular music.

Runners at the finish of the annual Boston Marathon, held in April

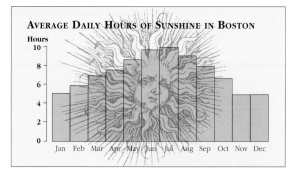

AVERAGE DAILY HOURS OF SUNSHINE IN BOSTON

Hours: 10, 8, 6, 4, 2, 0

Jan Feb Mar Apr May Jun Jul Aug Sep Oct Nov Dec

Sunshine Chart
This chart shows the average daily number of hours of sunshine in Boston each month. The city enjoys long and light summer days from June to August, with July being the sunniest month. Fall has more sunshine than spring, but while spring is mild, fall becomes quite chilly. Winter days are shorter, but many are still clear and bright.

SUMMER

WHEN SUMMER'S heat finally arrives, Bostonians head outdoors to relax on the grassy banks of the Charles River, along the harbor, and in the city's many parks. The Hatch Shell on the Esplanade becomes the scene of many free open-air concerts. The grandest celebration occurs on the Fourth of July, with one of the country's greatest fireworks displays, following an invariably rousing performance by the Boston Pops Orchestra.

Fourth of July fireworks lighting up the sky over the Charles River

Summer outdoor concert at Hatch Shell, Charles River Esplanade

JUNE

Performing Arts Series at the Hatch Shell *(Wed & Fri–Sun, Jun–Aug)*, Hatch Shell, Esplanade. Free outdoor concerts and movies.
Boston Common Dairy Festival *(Tue–Thu of first full week)*, Boston Common. Farm show with displays and zoo.
Scooper Bowl *(Tue–Thu of first full week)*, City Hall Plaza. One of the largest ice cream festivals in the nation.
Bunker Hill Weekend *(weekend before Jun 17)*, Charlestown. Costumed re-enactments, demonstrations, a parade, and guided tours at Bunker Hill Monument.
Dragon Boat Festival *(second Sun)*, Charles River. Traditional, Asian dragon boat races.
Cambridge River Festival *(mid-Jun)*, multicultural festival on the banks of the Charles River.
Italian Feast Days *(mid-Jun–Aug)*, North End. Religious processions with music and food take place almost every weekend.
Boston Globe Jazz and Blues Festival *(late Jun)*. Free and ticketed performances throughout the city.

JULY

Boston Harborfest *(week of Jul 4)*. Features children's events, a fireworks display over Boston Harbor, and a Chowderfest on City Hall Plaza.
Boston Pops Annual Fourth of July Concert and Fireworks *(Jul 4)*, Esplanade. The largest of the free Boston Pops concerts in July.

Bastille Day *(Fri before Jul 14)*, Back Bay. Block party on Marlborough Street.
Annual Festival Betances *(third weekend)*, South End. Annual Puerto Rican festival with music, dance, and food.

AUGUST

Annual Civil War Encampment *(first weekend)*, Georges Island. Fort Warren hosts 300–400 people in period costumes.
Boston Caribbean Carnival *(third weekend)*, Franklin Park. Extravagant costumes, music, food, and dancing.

July 4th parade, Government Center

AVERAGE MONTHLY TEMPERATURE

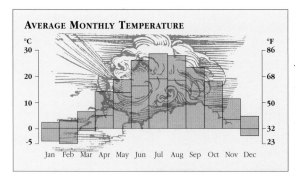

°C
30
20
10
0
-5
Jan Feb Mar Apr May Jun Jul Aug Sep Oct Nov Dec

°F
86
68
50
32
23

Temperature Chart
This chart shows the average minimum and maximum temperatures for each month in Boston. The highest temperatures of the year are in July and August, when it is hot and humid. Winters are cold, and while they can be clear and bright, they are also often stormy, resulting in wind-chill temperatures well below freezing point.

FALL

AFTER LABOR DAY, Boston's massive student community returns. This time also sees the start of seasons for the performing arts and for basketball and hockey. The vivid colors of New England's deciduous fall trees attract thousands of people to Boston, on their way to backcountry tours. Mid-November brings cold weather and the beginning of the holiday season.

Famous fiery colors of New England's fall foliage

SEPTEMBER

Arts Festival of Boston *(first week)*. Events include gallery exhibitions, arts and crafts pavilions, and outdoor musical performances.
Feast of Saints Cosma & Damiano *(second weekend)*, East Cambridge. Italian festival with parade.
Boston Blues Festival *(late Sep)*. Musicians emerge from cozy bars and nightclubs around the city to perform along the banks of the Charles River.
Art Newbury Street *(third weekend)*, Back Bay. Open

houses at art galleries and live music on the street.
South End Open Studios *(third full weekend)*. Artists' studios open to visitors, including those at the Boston Center for the Arts.

OCTOBER

Boston Symphony Orchestra Season *(Oct–Apr)*. Orchestra performs in historic Symphony Hall.
Basketball *(Oct–Apr)*, Fleet Center. NBA (National Basketball Association) season begins for the Boston Celtics.
Hockey *(Oct–Apr)*, Fleet Center. NHL (National Hockey League) season begins for the Boston Bruins.
Harvest Moon Festival *(first Sun)*, Harvard Square. Festival at Charles Square features New England produce, chefs, and microbreweries.
Gallop's Island Applefest *(early Oct)*, Boston Harbor Islands. Islands' apples are

transformed into cider, ice cream, and caramel apples.
Boston Ballet Season *(mid-Oct–May)*, Wang Center and Shubert Theater. Professional repertory company performs.
Head of the Charles Regatta *(second to last Sun Oct)*, Cambridge. Rowing event featuring 1,400 boats and 3,000 athletes.
Ellis Memorial Antiques Show *(late Oct)*, Cyclorama Building, South End.

NOVEMBER

Ice Skating on Frog Pond *(early Nov–March)*, Boston Common.
Fort Point Arts Community Open Studios *(first weekend)*. Features more than 100 artists in 23 buildings.
Boston International Antiquarian Book Fair *(mid-month)*, Hynes Convention Center. One of oldest and largest in the U.S.
Enchanted Village *(late Nov–Jan 1)*, City Hall Plaza. This Boston tradition is a Christmas-themed village for children with live performers.

Outdoor musical performance

AVERAGE MONTHLY PRECIPITATION

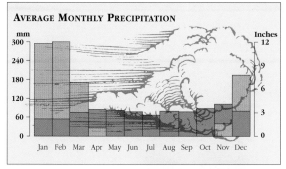

Rainfall Chart

This chart shows the average monthly rain and snowfall in Boston. Precipitation levels are fairly constant throughout the year, at around 3–4 inches (8–10 cm) per month. During the winter much of this falls as snow, which stays on the ground until March.

■ Rainfall (from baseline)

■ Snow (from baseline)

WINTER

TREE-LIGHTING CEREMONIES and decorated store windows help make Boston's cityscape magical at Christmas. As the old year ends, the entire city, from downtown to the most remote neighborhoods, erupts with the joy of First Night, a worldwide institution launched in Boston. When the frigid weather arrives in mid-January, Bostonians get geared up to a busy season of performing arts and food and wine expositions.

DECEMBER

Crafts at the Castle *(first full weekend)*, Park Plaza Castle. Top-quality crafts exhibition rated by judges.
Reenactment of the Boston Tea Party *(Sun closest to Dec 16)*. Begins at Old South Meeting House and proceeds to the Tea Party Ship and Museum, where this key historical event is replayed.

First Night ice sculpture

First Night *(Dec 31)*. The original city-wide New Year's Eve celebration, now an international phenomenon.

JANUARY

Chinese New Year *(late Jan to Mar depending on lunar calendar)*, Chinatown. Celebration includes parade, dragon dances, and firecrackers.

FEBRUARY

Boston Wine Expo *(first weekend Feb)*, World Trade Center. Two arduous days of international wine tastings and cooking demonstrations.
Beanpot Tournament *(mid-Feb)*, Fleet Center. Annual college hockey tournament between Boston College, Boston University, Northeastern University, and Harvard University *(see pp112–13)*.
Longfellow Birthday Celebration, *(late Feb)*, Cambridge. Tours of Longfellow House, poetry readings, and wreath-laying at the illustrious poet's grave.
Harvard's Hasty Pudding Club Parades *(variable)*, Cambridge. Outrageous Harvard theatrical club presents Man and Woman of the Year Awards to Hollywood celebrities after cross-dressing parades through Harvard Square.

PUBLIC HOLIDAYS

New Year's Day (Jan 1)
Martin Luther King Day (3rd Mon, Jan)
Presidents Day (mid-Feb)
Evacuation Day (Mar 17) (Boston only)
Patriots Day (3rd Mon, Apr) (Middlesex and Suffolk counties, including Boston and Cambridge)
Memorial Day (end May)
Bunker Hill Day (Jun 17) (Boston only)
Independence Day (Jul 4)
Labor Day (1st Mon, Sep)
Columbus Day (2nd Mon, Oct)
Election Day (1st Tue, Nov)
Veterans Day (Nov 11)
Thanksgiving (4th Thu, Nov)
Christmas Day (Dec 25)

Christmas lights on a snowy Boston Common in December

BOSTON
AREA BY AREA

BEACON HILL AND WEST END

BEACON HILL was developed from pastureland in the 1790s. The south slope, facing Boston Common, became the main seat of Boston wealth and power, while the north slope and the land rolling down to the mouth of the Charles River, known as the West End, became populated by tradesmen, servants, and free blacks. South-slope Beacon Hill

Stained glass, Massachusetts State House

retained its cachet into the late 19th century, while the north slope and West End degenerated. Urban renewal in the 1950s and 1960s cleared away the slums and coherent neighborhood of the West End, while gentrification of the north slope made even the most modest homes on Beacon Hill highly desirable, and this neighborhood one of Boston's most picturesque.

SIGHTS AT A GLANCE

Historic Streets and Squares
Beacon Street **6**
Charles Street **1**
Louisburg Square **2**
Mount Vernon Street **3**

Historic Buildings, Churches, and Museums
African Meeting House **12**
Boston Athenaeum **10**
Harrison Gray Otis House **13**
Hepzibah Swan Houses **5**
Massachusetts General Hospital **15**
Massachusetts State House pp52–3 **11**
Museum of Science and Science Park **16**
Nichols House Museum **4**
Old West Church **14**
Park Street Church **8**

Parks and Cemeteries
Boston Common and Public Garden pp48–9 **7**
Old Granary Burying Ground **9**

GETTING THERE
This area is well served by public transportation. Park Street, Boylston, and Arlington "T" stations are closest to the main sights. The area is also served by Charles/ M.G.H. and Science Park. Buses 43 and 55 go to Boston Common.

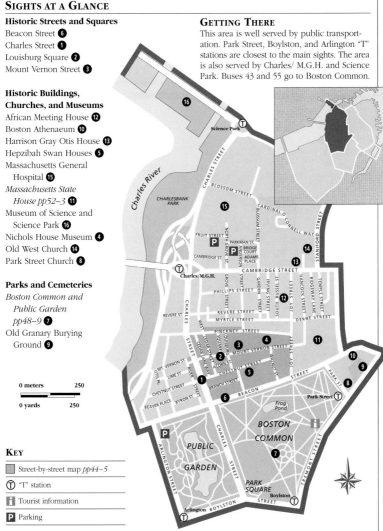

KEY
	Street-by-street map *pp44–5*
T	"T" station
i	Tourist information
P	Parking

0 meters 250
0 yards 250

◁ **Front view of the Massachusetts State House, seen from Boston Common**

Street-by-Street: Beacon Hill

Lion door knocker, Beacon St.

FROM THE 1790s TO THE 1870s, the south slope of Beacon Hill was Boston's most sought-after neighborhood – its wealthy elite decamped only when the more exclusive Back Bay *(see pp90–101)* was built. Many of the district's houses were designed by Charles Bulfinch *(see p55)* and his disciples, and the south slope evolved as a textbook example of Federal architecture. Elevation and view were all, and the finest homes are either on Boston Common or perched near the top of the hill. Early developers abided by a gentleman's agreement to set houses back from the street, but the economic depression of 1807–12 resulted in row houses being built right out to the street.

Cobbled street, once typical of Beacon Hill

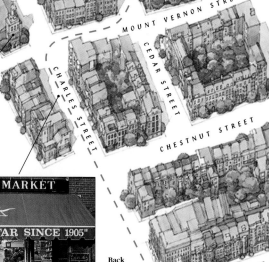

Louisburg Square
The crowning glory of the Beacon Hill district, this square was developed in the 1830s. Today, it is still Boston's most desirable address ❷

Charles Street Meeting House was built in the early 19th century to house a congregation of Baptists.

KEY

– – –   Suggested route

Back Bay and South End

★ Charles Street
This elegant street is the main shopping area for Beacon Hill. Lined with upscale grocers and antique stores, it also has some fine restaurants ❶

STAR SIGHTS

★ Charles Street

★ Nichols House Museum

★ **Nichols House Museum**
This modest museum offers an insight into the life of Beacon Hill resident Rose Nichols, who lived here from 1885 to 1960 ❹

LOCATOR MAP
See Street Finder map 1

0 meters	50
0 yards	50

Mount Vernon Street
Described in the 19th century as the "most civilized street in America," this is where the developers of Beacon Hill (the Mount Vernon Proprietors) chose to build their own homes ❸

→ **Massachusetts State House**

WALNUT STREET

RUCE STREET

BEACON STREET

↘ **Boston Common**

Hepzibah Swan Houses
Elegant in their simplicity, these three Bulfinch-designed houses were wedding gifts for the daughters of a wealthy Beacon Hill proprietress ❺

Beacon Street
The finest houses on Beacon Hill were invariably built on Beacon Street. Elegant, Federal-style mansions, some with ornate reliefs, overlook the city's most beautiful green space, Boston Common ❻

Charles Street, lined with shops catering to the residents of Beacon Hill

Charles Street ❶

Map 1 B4. Ⓣ *Charles/ MGH.*

THIS STREET originally ran
along the bank of the
Charles River, although subsequent landfill has removed it
from the riverbank by several
hundred feet. The main shopping and dining area of the
Beacon Hill neighborhood,
the curving line of Charles
Street hugs the base of Beacon
Hill, giving it a quaint, village-
like air. Many of the houses
remain residential on the upper
stories, while street level and
cellar levels were converted
to commercial uses long ago.
Though most of Charles Street
dates from the 19th century,
widening in the 1920s meant
that some of the houses on
the west side acquired new
façades. The Charles Street
Meeting House, designed by
Asher Benjamin (*see p30*) in
1807, was built for a Baptist
congregation that practiced im-
mersion in the then adjacent
river. It is now a commercial
building. Two groups of striking Greek Revival row houses are situated at the top of
Charles Street, between Revere
and Cambridge Streets. Charles
Street was one of the birth-
places of the antique trade
in the U.S. and now has some
two dozen antique dealers.

Louisburg Square ❷

Map 1 B4. Ⓣ *Charles/ MGH,
Park Street.*

HOME TO millionaire
politicians, best-selling
authors, and corporate
moguls, Louisburg
Square is arguably
Boston's most
prestigious address.
Developed in the
1830s as a shared
private preserve
on Beacon Hill, the
square's tiny patch
of greenery sur-
rounded by a high
iron fence sends a
clear signal of the
square's continued
exclusivity. On the
last private square
in the city, the
narrow Greek

**Columbus Statue,
Louisburg Square**

Revival bow-fronted town
houses sell for a premium
over comparable homes elsewhere on Beacon Hill. Even
the on-street parking spaces
are deeded. The traditions of
Christmas Eve carol singing
and candlelit windows are said
to have begun on Louisburg
Square. A statue of Christopher
Columbus, presented by a
wealthy Greek merchant in
1850, stands at its center.

Mount Vernon Street ❸

Map 1 B4. Ⓣ *Charles/ MGH,
Park Street.*

IN THE 1890s the novelist
Henry James (*see p29*)
called Mount Vernon Street
"the most civilized street in
America," and it still retains
that air of urbane culture.
Most of the developers of
Beacon Hill, who called
themselves the Mount Vernon
Proprietors, chose to build
their private homes along
this street. Architect Charles
Bulfinch (*see p55*) envisioned
Beacon Hill as a district of
large freestanding mansions
on spacious landscaped
grounds, but building costs
ultimately dictated much
denser development. The
sole remaining example
of Bulfinch's vision is the
Second Harrison Gray Otis
House, built in 1800 at No.
85. The current Greek Revival
row houses next door (Nos.
59–83), graciously set back
from the street by 30 ft (9 m),
were built to replace the
single mansion belonging to
Otis's chief devel-
opment partner,
Jonathan Mason.
The original man-
sion was torn
down after Mason's
death in 1836. The
three Bulfinch-
designed houses
at Nos. 55, 57, and
59 Mount Vernon
Street were built
by Mason for his
daughters. No. 55
was ultimately
passed on to the
Nichols family
(*see p47*) in 1883.

OLIVER WENDELL HOLMES AND THE BOSTON BRAHMINS

In 1860, Oliver Wendell Holmes *(see p28)* wrote that Boston's wealthy merchant class of the time constituted a Brahmin caste, a "harmless, inoffensive, untitled aristocracy" with "their houses by Bulfinch, their monopoly on Beacon Street, their ancestral portraits and Chinese porcelains, humanitarianism, Unitarian faith in the march of the mind, Yankee shrewdness, and New England exclusiveness." So keenly did he skewer the social class that the term has persisted. In casual usage today, a Brahmin is someone with an old family name, whose finances derive largely from trust funds, and whose politics blend conservatism with *noblesse oblige* toward those less fortunate. Boston's Brahmins founded most of the hospitals, performing arts bodies and museums of the greater metropolitan area.

Oliver Wendell Holmes (1809–94)

Drawing room of the Bulfinch-designed Nichols House Museum

Nichols House Museum ➍

55 Mount Vernon St. **Map** 1 B4.
 (617) 227-6993. Ⓣ *Park Street.*
 May–Oct: noon–4pm Tue–Sat;
Nov–Apr: noon–4pm Thu–Sat.
 Jan.

THE NICHOLS HOUSE MUSEUM was designed by Charles Bulfinch in 1805 and offers a rare glimpse into the tradition-bound lifestyle of Beacon Hill. Modernized in 1830 by the addition of a Greek Revival portico, the house is nevertheless a superb example of Bulfinch's domestic architecture. It also offers an insight into the life of a true Beacon Hill character. Rose Standish Nichols moved into the house aged 13 when her father purchased it in 1883. She left it as a museum in her will in 1960. A woman ahead of her time,

strong-willed and famously hospitable, Nichols was, among other things, a self-styled landscape designer who traveled extensively around the world to write about gardens.

Hepzibah Swan Houses ➎

13, 15 & 17 Chestnut St. **Map** 1 B4.
Ⓣ *Park Street.* to the public.

THE ONLY WOMAN who was ever a member of the Mount Vernon Proprietors *(see p46)*, Mrs. Swan had these houses built by Bulfinch as wedding presents for her daughters in 1806, 1807 and 1814. Some of the most elegant and distinguished houses on Chestnut Street, they are backed by Bulfinch-designed stables that face onto Mount Vernon Street. The deeds restrict the height of the stables to 13 ft (4 m) so that her daughters would still have a view over Mount Vernon Street. In 1863–65, No. 13 was home to Dr. Samuel Gridley Howe, abolitionist and educational pioneer who, in 1833, founded the first school for the blind in the U.S.

Beacon Street ➏

Map 1 B4. Ⓣ *Park Street.*

BEACON STREET IS LINED with urban mansions facing Boston Common. The American Meteorological Society occupies No. 45, which was built as Harrison Gray Otis's last and finest house, with 11 bedrooms and an elliptical room behind the front parlor where the walls and even the doors are curved. The elite Somerset Club stands at Nos. 42–43 Beacon Street. In the 1920s to 1940s, Irish Catholic mayor James Michael Curley would lead election night victory marches to the State House, pausing at the Somerset to taunt the Boston Brahmins within. The Parkman House at No. 33 Beacon Street is now a city-owned meeting center. It was the home of Dr. George Parkman, who was murdered by Harvard professor and fellow socialite Dr. John Webster in 1849. Boston society was torn apart when the presiding judge, a relative of Parkman, sent Webster to be hanged. The family lived as recluses here from 1859 to 1908 before giving the house to the city. The headquarters of the Unitarian Universalist Association, an international church, and its publishing arm, Beacon Press, occupy premises at No. 25.

Elegant Federal-style houses on Beacon Street, overlooking Boston Common

Boston Common and Public Garden 7

Acquired by Boston in 1634 from first settler William Blackstone, the 48-acre (19-ha) Boston Common served for two centuries as common pasture, military drill ground, and gallows site. British troops camped here during the 1775–76 military occupation. As Boston grew in the 19th century, the Boston Common became a center for open-air civic activity and remains so to this day. By contrast, the 24-acre (10-ha) Public Garden is more formal. When the Charles River mudflats were first filled in the 1830s, a succession of landscape plans were plotted for the Public Garden before the city chose the English-style garden scheme of George F. Meacham in 1869. The lagoon was added to the garden two years later.

The Public Garden, a popular green space in the heart of the city

Make Way for Ducklings
Based on the classic children's story by Robert McCloskey, this sculpture is of a duck and her brood of ducklings.

The Ether Monument memorializes the first use of anaesthesia in 1846.

★ George Washington Statue
Cast by Thomas Ball from bronze, with a solid granite base, this is one the finest memorial statues in Boston. It was dedicated in 1869.

CHARLES STREET

Lagoon Bridge
This miniature, ornamental bridge over the Public Garden lagoon was designed by William G. Preston in 1869 in a moment of whimsy. The lagoon it "spans" was constructed in 1861.

Statue of Reverend William Ellery Channing

Statue of Edward Everett Hale

The Swan Boats, originally inspired by Wagner's *Löhengrin,* have been a feature of the Public Garden lake since 1877.

★ Shaw Memorial
This relief immortalizes the Civil War's 54th regiment of Massachusetts Infantry, the first free black regiment in the Union Army, and their white colonel Robert Shaw.

The Soldiers and Sailors Monument, erected in 1877, features prominent Bostonians from the time of the Civil War.

Blackstone Memorial Tablet recalls the purchase of the common in 1634 and is cited as proof that it belongs to the people.

Park Street subway

Brewer Fountain was purchased at the Paris expo of 1867.

Visitors' Center

Parkman Bandstand
This bandstand was built in 1912 to memorialize George F. Parkman, who bequeathed $5 million for the care of Boston Common and other parks in the city.

The Flagstaff

0 meters	100
0 yards	100

Central Burying Ground
This graveyard, which dates from 1756, holds the remains of many British and American casualties from the Battle of Bunker Hill (see p18). The portraitist Gilbert Stuart is also buried here.

STAR FEATURES

★ Shaw Memorial

★ George Washington Statue

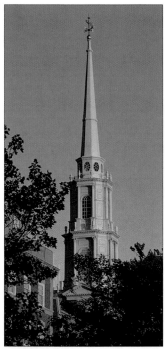

Park Street Church at the corner of Tremont and Park Streets, near Boston Common

Park Street Church ❽

1 Park St. **Map** 1 C4. 📞 *(617) 523-3383.* Ⓣ *Park Street.* ⬜ *Jul–Aug: 9am–3pm Tue–Sat; Sep–Jun: by appointment.* ✝ *Jul–Aug: 8:30am, 11am, 5:30pm Sun; Sep–Jun: 8:30am, 11am, 4:30pm, 6:30pm Sun.* 🚫 ♿ W *www.parkstreet.org*

Park street church's 217-ft (65-m) steeple has punctuated the intersection of Park and Tremont Streets since its dedication in 1810. Designed by English architect Peter Banner, who adapted a design by the earlier English architect Christopher Wren, the church was commissioned by parishioners wanting to establish a Congregational church in the heart of Boston. The church was, and still remains, one of the city's most influential pulpits.

Contrary to popular belief, the sermons of Park Street ministers did not earn the intersection the nickname of "Brimstone Corner." Rather, the name came about during the War of 1812 when the U.S. and Britain were engaged in conflict over British restrictions on trade and freedom of the seas, as well as the U.S.'s ties with Napoleonic France. The U.S. militia, based in Boston, stored its gunpowder in the church basement as safekeeping against bombardment from the British navy, hence the nickname.

Park Street Church later became famous throughout the islands of the Pacific, when in 1819 the church sent a number of Congregational missionaries to carry the Gospel to Pacific islanders from a base in the Hawaiian Islands. In 1829, William Lloyd Garrison (1805–79), fervently outspoken firebrand of the movement to abolish slavery, gave his first abolition speech from the Park Street pulpit. Much later, in 1893, the anthem *America the Beautiful* by Katharine Lee Bates debuted at a Sunday service, while in 1849 a speech entitled *The War System of Nations* was addressed to the American Peace Society by Senator Charles Sumner. Today the church continues, as always, to be involved in religious, political, cultural, and humanitarian activities.

Old Granary Burying Ground ❾

Tremont Street. **Map** 1 C4. Ⓣ *Park Street.* ⬜ *8am–4:30pm daily.*

Named after the early colonial grain storage facility that once stood on the adjacent site of Park Street Church, the Granary Burying Ground dates from 1660. Buried here were three important signatories to the Declaration of Independence *(see p19)* – John Hancock, Samuel Adams, and Robert Treat Paine, along with Benjamin Franklin's parents, merchant-philanthropist Peter Faneuil, and some victims of the Boston Massacre.

The orderly array of gravestones, often featured in films and television shows set in Boston, is the result of modern groundskeeping. Few stones, if any, mark the actual burial site of the person memorialized. In fact, John Hancock may not be here at all. On the night he was buried in 1793, grave robbers cut off the hand with which he had signed his name to the Declaration of Independence, and some scholars believe that the rest of the body was later spirited away during 19th-century construction work. Although many heroes of the Revolution are still known to be buried here, Paul Revere, one of Boston's most famous sons, was nearly denied the honor because the cemetery was technically full when he died in 1818. The city made an exception, and he was able to join his comrades in perpetuity.

Old Granary Burying Ground, final resting place for Revolutionary heroes

Stone frieze decoration on the 19th-century, Renaissance Revival-style Athenaeum

Boston Athenaeum ⑩

10 Beacon St. **Map** 1 C4.
📞 *(617) 227-0270.* Ⓣ *Park Street.*
🕐 *Jun–Aug: 9am–8pm Mon, 9am–5:30pm Tue–Fri; Sep–May: 9am–4pm Sat.* Ⓦ *www.bostonathenaeum.org*

ORGANIZED IN 1807, the collection of the Boston Athenaeum quickly became one of the country's leading private libraries. Sheep farmer Edward Clarke Cabot won the 1846 design competition to house the library, with plans for a gray sandstone building based on Palladio's Palazzo da Porta Festa in Vicenza, a building Cabot knew from a book in the Athenaeum's collection. The building reopened in fall 2002 after extensive renovations. Among the Athenaeum's major holdings are the personal library that once belonged to George Washington and the theological library supplied by King William III of England to the King's Chapel (*see p60*). In its early years the Athenaeum was Boston's chief art museum; when the Museum of Fine Arts was proposed, the Athenaeum graciously donated much of its art, including unfinished portraits of George and Martha Washington purchased in 1831 from the widow of the painter Gilbert Stuart. Non-members of the Athenaeum may visit only the first and second floors of the building, an area that includes the art gallery (with changing exhibitions) and several reading rooms.

Massachusetts State House ⑪

See pp52–3.

African Meeting House ⑫

8 Smith Court. **Map** 1 C3.
📞 *(617) 725-0022.* Ⓣ *Park Street.*
🕐 *10am– 4pm Mon–Sat; Jun–Aug: also 10am–4pm Sun.* ⬤ *public hols.*
📷 📹 Ⓦ *www.afroammuseum.org*

BUILT FROM TOWN HOUSE plans by Asher Benjamin *(see p30)* with materials salvaged from the reconstruction of the Old West Church, the African Meeting House was dedicated in 1806. The oldest black church building in the U.S., it was the political and religious center of Boston's African American society. Cato Gardner, a native African, raised $1,500 toward the eventual $7,700 to build the church and is honored with an inscription above the entrance. The interior is plain and simple but rang with the oratory of some of the 19th century's most fiery abolitionists: from Sojourner Truth and Frederick Douglass to William Lloyd Garrison *(see p28)*, who founded the New England Anti-Slavery Society in 1832. The meeting house basement was Boston's first school for African American children until the adjacent Abiel Smith School was built in 1831. When segregated education was barred in 1855, however, the Smith School closed. The meeting house became an Hasidic synagogue in the 1890s, as most of Boston's African American community moved to Roxbury and Dorchester. The synagogue closed in the 1960s, and in 1987 the African Meeting House reopened as the linchpin site on the Black Heritage Trail.

Holmes Alley, once an escape route for slaves on the run

BLACK HERITAGE TRAIL

In the first U.S. census in 1790, Massachusetts was the only state to record no slaves. During the 19th century, Boston's substantial free African American community lived principally on the north slope of Beacon Hill and in the adjacent West End. The Black Heritage Trail links several key sites, ranging from the African Meeting House to several private homes that are not open to visitors. Among them are the 1797 George Middleton House (Nos. 5–7 Pinckney Street), the oldest standing house built by African Americans on Beacon Hill, and the Lewis and Harriet Hayden House (No. 66 Phillips Street). Escaped slaves, the Haydens made their home a haven for runaways in the "Underground Railroad" of safe houses between the South and Canada. The walking tour also leads through mews and alleys, like Holmes Alley at the end of Smith Court, once used by fugitives to flee professional slave catchers.

Free tours of the Black Heritage Trail are led by National Park Service rangers – (617) 742-5415 – and are offered from Memorial Day weekend to Labor Day 10am, noon, and 2pm daily, departing from the Robert Gould Shaw Memorial.

Abiel Smith School, where Boston's free blacks received an education

Massachusetts State House ⑪

T HE CORNERSTONE OF the Massachusetts State
House was laid on July 4, 1795, by Samuel
Adams and Paul Revere. Completed on January
11, 1798, the Charles Bulfinch-designed center
of state government served as a model for the
U.S. Capitol Building in Washington and as
an inspiration for many of the state capitols
around the country. Later additions were made,
but the original building remains the archetype
of American government buildings. Its dome,
sheathed in copper and gold, serves as the
zero mile marker for Massachusetts, making
it, as Oliver Wendell Holmes (see p47)
remarked, "the hub of the universe."

The State House, from Boston Common

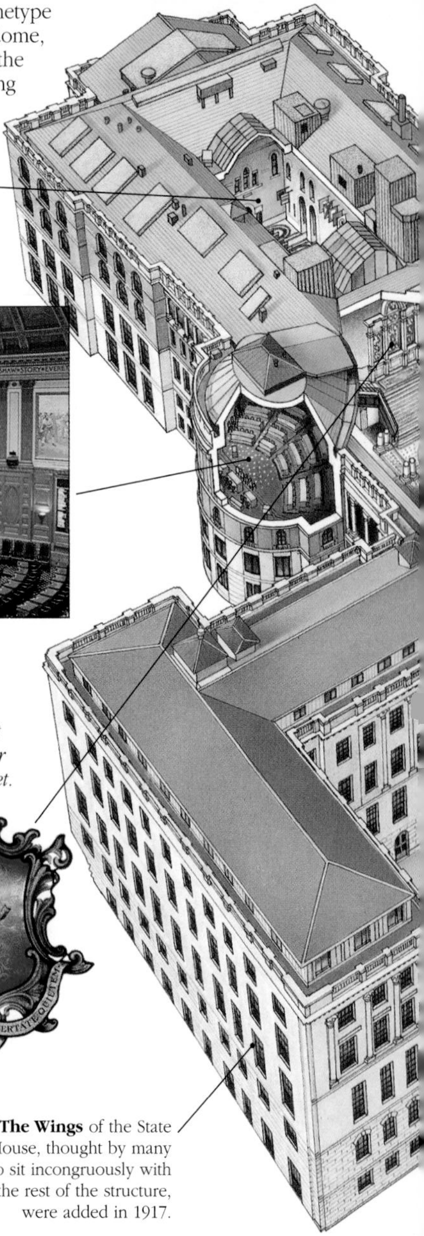

The Great Hall
is the latest addition to the State
House. Built in 1990, it is lined with
marble and topped by a glass dome,
and is used for state functions.

★ House of Representatives
*This elegant oval chamber was built for
the House of Representatives in 1895. The
Sacred Cod, which now hangs over the
gallery, came to the State House when it first
opened in 1798, and it has since hung over
any place where the representatives have met.*

Main Staircase
*Beautiful stained-glass
windows decorate the
main staircase. The win-
dows illustrate the many
varied state seals of
Massachusetts: from its
time as a colony through
to modern statehood.*

STAR SIGHTS

★ **Nurses Hall**

★ **House of
Representatives**

The Wings of the State
House, thought by many
to sit incongruously with
the rest of the structure,
were added in 1917.

Hall of Flags
Flags carried into battle by regiments from the state of Massachusetts are housed here. They are displayed beneath a stained-glass skylight depicting seals of the original 13 colonies.

★ Nurses Hall
This marble hall is lined with murals depicting critical events leading up to the American Revolution. The name derives from the statue of an army nurse here, erected to honor all the nurses who took part in the Civil War.

Administrative offices can be found on the upper floors of the building.

The dome was sheathed in copper in 1802 to prevent water leakage, and, in 1872, gilded in 23-carat gold.

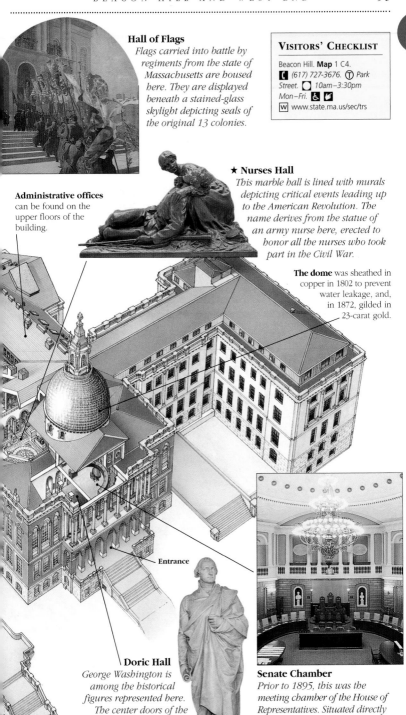

Entrance

Doric Hall
George Washington is among the historical figures represented here. The center doors of the hall are only ever opened for a state governor at the end of his term or for a visiting head of state.

Senate Chamber
Prior to 1895, this was the meeting chamber of the House of Representatives. Situated directly beneath the State House's magnificent dome, the chamber features a beautiful sunburst ceiling, also designed by Charles Bulfinch.

Flamboyantly decorated dining room of the Harrison Gray Otis House

Harrison Gray Otis House **⓭**

141 Cambridge St. **Map** 1 C3.
📞 *(617) 227-3956.* Ⓣ *Charles/ MGH, Government Center.*
🕐 *11am–5pm Wed–Sun.* 📷 Ⓝ
♿ Ⓦ *www.spnea.org*

DESIGNED BY Charles Bulfinch for Harrison Gray Otis, co-developer of Beacon Hill *(see pp44–5)* and Boston's third mayor, this 1796 town mansion was built to serve the needs of a young man on the way up in Federal Boston. Descended from both British colonial administrators and Boston revolutionary patriots, Otis took a practical view of local government that paved the way for Boston's development as a power-house of international trade and finance. Having already made a fortune in the land development of Beacon Hill, Otis commissioned this home as a showpiece, where he could entertain. It was the first of three homes Bulfinch designed for him.

After Otis moved out, the house fell on hard times as the West End neighborhood around it absorbed successive waves of immigration, and tenements replaced single family homes. By the 1830s the Otis house was serving as a ladies' Turkish bath and later became a patent med-icine shop before ending up

as a boarding house. The Society for the Preservation of New England Antiquities (SPNEA) saved the building in 1916 and established its headquarters here. A new gallery in the house depicts the time when the building was a boarding house during the 1950s.

Visitors who tour the Otis house, now restored to the way it looked in around 1800, are often surprised by the bright, even gaudy, style of decoration. Although SPNEA

initially decorated the rooms in the muted Williamsburg Colonial style, subsequent art history detective work revealed that Bostonians had much more flamboyant taste than, for example, the wealthy Virginians. Thus, the house has been restored with touches typical of such upper-class aspirations. The wallpaper in the main entrance has a border of scenes from Pompeii and scores of lithographs showing views of European cities. The colors throughout the rest of the house are bright, and gilt detail flashes from moldings and furniture.

SPNEA also operates an architectural walking tour of Beacon Hill that begins at the Otis House. It runs from May until the end of October.

Old West Church **⓮**

131 Cambridge St. **Map** 1 C3.
📞 *(617) 227-5088.* Ⓣ *Charles/ MGH, Bowdoin.* 🕐 *for Sunday worship.* ✝ *11am Sun.* 📷 ♿

A WOOD-FRAME church built on this site in 1737 was used as a barracks for British soldiers during the occupa-tion of Boston *(see pp18–19)* in the period just prior to the American Revolution. The British later razed the original church in 1775, since they suspected revolutionary sym-pathizers of using the steeple to signal Continental Army troops across the Charles River. Many of the church's timbers were used to con-struct the African Meeting House *(see p51)*. Asher Benjamin *(see p30)*, a protégé of Charles Bulfinch, designed the current red-brick struc-ture, erected in 1806. The swag-ornamented clocks on the sides of the tower are distinctive landmarks, while inside is a superb Fisk tracker-action pipe organ, which is often played in classical organ recordings.

Red-brick façade of Asher Benjamin's Old West Church

Massachusetts General Hospital ⑮

Cambridge & Fruit Sts. **Map** 1 B2.
☎ (617) 726-2000. Ⓣ Charles/ MGH.
◯ 24 hrs daily. **Bulfinch Pavilion and Ether Dome** ◯ 1–3pm Tue–Fri. ♿
ⓦ www.mgh.harvard.edu

THE SPRAWLING complex of Massachusetts General Hospital covers the original site of Harvard Medical School, with which it remains affiliated as one of the world's leading teaching and research hospitals. The main hospital building, the George R. White Memorial Building, is a massive Art Deco structure from 1939, largely hidden from Cambridge Street by many other buildings. The most interesting structure on the campus is the Bulfinch Pavilion and Ether Dome, which was Charles Bulfinch's last Boston commission (1818). Alexander Parris, who would succeed Bulfinch as the city's leading architect, was involved in preparing the drawings for this innovative "modern" hospital built of local Chelmsford granite. The operating theater, with seating for observers, is set beneath a skylit dome. In 1846, the use of ether as a surgical general anesthetic was first demonstrated here. The building has been altered substantially over the years to meet changing hospital needs, but the central columned portico retains its original Neo-Classical grandeur.

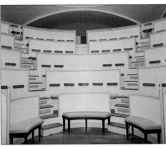

Charles Bulfinch's Ether Dome, part of the Massachusetts General Hospital

Museum of Science and Science Park ⑯

Science Park. **Map** 1 B2.
☎ (617) 723-2500. Ⓣ Science Park. ◯ Labor Day–July 3: 9am–5pm Sat–Thu, 9am–9pm Fri; July 4–Labor Day 9am–7pm Sat–Thu, 9am–9pm Fri. ● Thanksgiving, Dec 25. ♿ 🎥 ⓦ www.mos.org

THE MUSEUM OF SCIENCE straddles the Charles River atop the inactive flood control dam that sits at the mouth of the Charles River. The museum itself was built in 1951, but Science Park has taken shape around it since, virtually obscuring the dam structure with theater and planetarium buildings and a massive parking garage.

With more than 1,000 interactive exhibits covering natural history, medicine, astronomy, and the wonders of the physical sciences, the Science Museum is oriented to families with children. In 1999 the museum absorbed the holdings of Boston's Computer Museum, one of the first of its kind in the world.

The Mugar Omni Theater contains a five-story domed screen with multi-dimensional sound system with wraparound sound, and shows mostly educational films, usually with a natural science theme. The Charles Hayden Planetarium offers daily shows about stars, planets, and other celestial phenomena.

An extensive array of educational toys can be bought from the museum's shop, while the food court has a number of concessions catering to children's tastes.

CHARLES BULFINCH

Born in 1763 in Boston, Charles Bulfinch *(see p30)* was among America's first professional architects and one of the most influential. He rose to prominence with his 1795 plan for the Massachusetts State House *(see pp52–3)*, and went on to design many of the neighboring mansions on Beacon Hill. His own forays into real estate development cast him into bankruptcy, but he continued to enjoy the steady patronage of Boston's wealthiest citizens for his elegant yet boldly confident house designs. These patrons also helped him secure many public commissions, including the renovation of St. Stephen's Church in the North End *(see p74)* and the enlargement of Faneuil Hall *(see p65)*. His application of local granite building stone to the Massachusetts General Hospital surgical pavilion laid out principles later followed by Alexander Parris and others as they forged the Boston Granite style of architecture, exemplified by Quincy Market *(see p66)* and Charlestown Navy Yard *(see p119)*. Bulfinch left Boston in 1818 to assume direction of the construction of the U.S. Capitol Building in Washington, DC.

19th-century view of Massachusetts State House from Boston Common

OLD BOSTON AND THE FINANCIAL DISTRICT

THIS IS AN AREA OF BOSTON where old and new sit one on top of the other. Some of its sights, situated in the older part of the district closest to Boston Common, predate the American Revolution *(see pp18–19)*. Much of what can be seen today, though, was built more recently. The north of the district is home to Boston's late 20th-

British Lion, Old State House

century, modernist-style City Hall and Government Center, while to the east is the city's bustling Financial District. This once formed part of Boston's harbor waterfront, a district built on mercantile wealth. Today, the wharves and warehouses have been replaced by skyscrapers belonging to banks, insurance companies, and high-tech industries.

SIGHTS AT A GLANCE

Historic Streets and Squares
Blackstone Block ⑩
Post Office Square ⑭

Historic Buildings and Churches
Boston Globe Store ④
Center Plaza ⑦
Custom House ⑬
Faneuil Hall ⑪
Government Center ⑨
King's Chapel and Burying Ground ②
New City Hall ⑧
Old City Hall ③
Old South Meeting House ⑤
Old State House pp62–3 ⑥
Omni Parker House ①
Quincy Market ⑫
Verizon Building ⑮

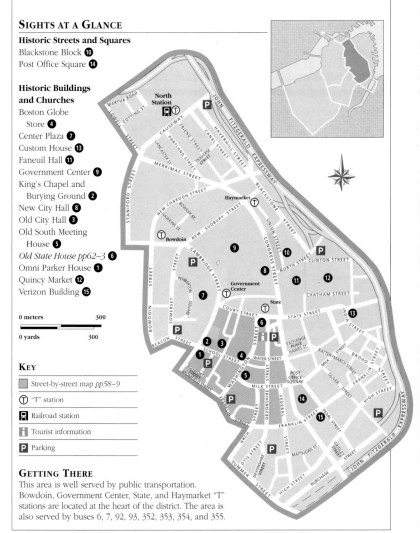

0 meters 300
0 yards 300

KEY

▢ Street-by-street map *pp58–9*

Ⓣ "T" station

🚉 Railroad station

ℹ Tourist information

🅿 Parking

GETTING THERE

This area is well served by public transportation. Bowdoin, Government Center, State, and Haymarket "T" stations are located at the heart of the district. The area is also served by buses 6, 7, 92, 93, 352, 353, 354, and 355.

◁ **Custom House, Boston's original skyscraper and one of the most distinctive buildings on the city skyline**

Street-by-Street: Colonial Boston

AN IMPORTANT PART of Boston's Freedom Trail *(see pp32–5)* runs through this historic core of the city, the site of which predates American Independence. Naturally, the area is now dominated by more recent 19th- and 20th-century development, but glimpses of a colonial past are prevalent here and there in the Old State House, King's Chapel and its adjacent burying ground, and the Old South Meeting House. Newer buildings of interest include the Omni Parker House, as well as the towering skyscrapers of Boston's financial district, located on the northwest edges of this area.

Irish Famine memorial, Washington Street

Government Center

★ King's Chapel and Burying Ground
A church has stood here since 1688, though the current building dates from 1749. The adjacent cemetery is the resting place of some of the most important figures in U.S. history ❷

SCHOOL STREET

PROVINCE STREET

Omni Parker House
This hotel (see p124) first opened its doors in 1855, then underwent many renovations. Famed for its opulence, in the 19th century the hotel also gained a reputation as a meeting place for Boston intellectuals. The current building was erected in 1927 ❶

| 0 meters | | 50 |
| 0 yards | | 50 |

Old City Hall
This building served as Boston's City Hall from 1865 to 1969. Today it houses a number of offices and a trendy French restaurant ❸

STAR SIGHTS

★ **Old South Meeting House**

★ **Old State House**

★ **King's Chapel and Burying Ground**

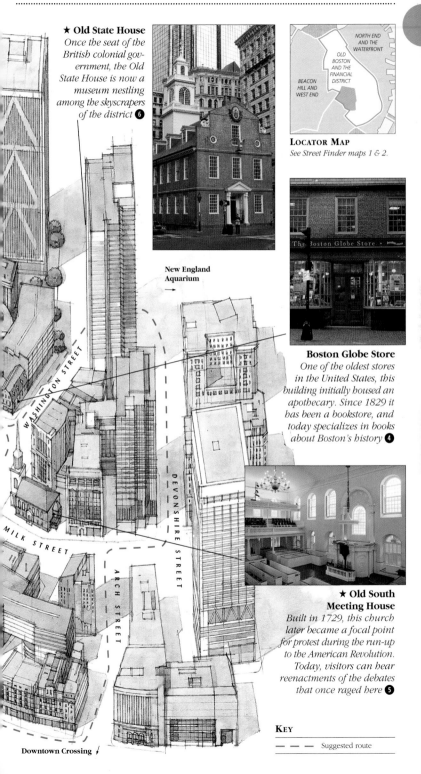

★ **Old State House**
*Once the seat of the
British colonial gov-
ernment, the Old
State House is now a
museum nestling
among the skyscrapers
of the district* ⑥

LOCATOR MAP
See Street Finder maps 1 & 2.

**North End
and the
Waterfront**

**Old
Boston
and the
Financial
District**

**Beacon
Hill and
West End**

**New England
Aquarium**

Boston Globe Store
*One of the oldest stores
in the United States, this
building initially housed an
apothecary. Since 1829 it
has been a bookstore, and
today specializes in books
about Boston's history* ④

The Boston Globe Store

WASHINGTON STREET

DEVONSHIRE STREET

MILK STREET

ARCH STREET

★ **Old South
Meeting House**
*Built in 1729, this church
later became a focal point
for protest during the run-up
to the American Revolution.
Today, visitors can hear
reenactments of the debates
that once raged here* ⑤

Downtown Crossing ↙

KEY

- - - - Suggested route

Omni Parker House ❶

60 School St. **Map** 1 C4.
📞 *(617) 227-8600.* Ⓣ *Park Street, State, Government Center.*
🌐 *www.omnihotels.com*

HARVEY D. PARKER, raised on a farm in Maine, became so successful as the proprietor of his Boston restaurant that he achieved his ambition of expanding the property into a first-class, grand hotel. His Parker House opened in 1855, with a façade clad in white marble, standing five stories high, and featuring the first passenger elevator ever seen in Boston. It underwent several, rapid transformations during its early years, with additions made to the main structure in the 1860s and a 10-story, French chateau-style annex completed later that century. The building saw many successive transformations, and its latest 14-story incarnation has stood across from King's Chapel on School Street since 1927.

This hotel attained an instant reputation for luxurious accommodations and fine, even lavish, dining, typified by 11-course menus prepared by a French chef.

Simply decorated, pure white interior of King's Chapel on Tremont Street

Among Parker House's many claims to fame are its Boston Cream Pie, which was first created here, and the word "scrod," a uniquely Bostonian term for the day's freshest seafood, still in common usage. Two former Parker House employees later became recognized for quite different careers. Vietnamese revolutionary leader Ho Chi Minh worked in the hotel's kitchens around 1915, while black activist Malcolm X was a busboy in Parker's Restaurant in the 1940s.

PARKER HOUSE GUESTS

Boston's reputation as the "Athens of America" was widely acknowledged when members of a distinguished social club began meeting for lengthy dinners and lively intellectual exchanges in 1857. Their get-togethers took place on the last Saturday of every month at Harvey Parker's fancy new hotel. Regular participants included New England's literary elite *(see pp28–9)*: Henry Wadsworth Longfellow, Ralph Waldo Emerson, Nathaniel Hawthorne, and Henry David Thoreau, to name a few. Charles

John Wilkes Booth, infamous Parker House guest

Dickens participated while staying at the Parker House during his American speaking tours, and used his sitting-room mirror to rehearse the public readings he gave at Tremont Temple next door. The mirror now hangs on a mezzanine wall. In 1865, actor John Wilkes Booth, in town to see his brother, a fellow thespian, stayed at the hotel and took target practice at a nearby shooting gallery. Ten days later, at Ford's Theatre in Washington, he pulled a pistol and shot Abraham Lincoln.

King's Chapel and Burying Ground ❷

58 Tremont St. **Map** 1 C4.
📞 *(617) 523-1749.* Ⓣ *Park Street, State, Government Center.* ⬜ *Jul–Aug: 9am–4pm Mon & Thu–Sat, 1–3pm Sun; Apr–Jun & Sep–Oct: 10am–3pm Mon, Fri & Sat; Nov–Mar: 10am–3pm Sat.* ✝ *11am Sun, 12:15pm Wed.* 🌐 *www.kings-chapel.org*

BRITISH CROWN officials were among those who attended Anglican services at the first chapel on this site, which was built in 1688. When New England's governor decided a larger church was needed, the present granite edifice – begun in 1749 – was constructed around the original wooden chapel, which was dismantled and heaved out the windows of its replacement. After the Revolution, the congregation's religious allegiance switched from Anglican to Unitarian. The sanctuary's raised pulpit – dating from 1717 and shaped like a wine glass – is one of the oldest in the U.S. High ceilings, open arches, and clear glass windows enhance the sense of spaciousness and light. The bell inside the King's Chapel is the largest ever cast by Paul Revere *(see p19)*.

Among those interred in the adjacent cemetery, Boston's oldest, are John Winthrop and Elizabeth Pain, the inspiration for adultress Hester Prynne in Nathaniel Hawthorne's moralistic novel *The Scarlet Letter.*

Old City Hall ❸

45 School St. **Map** 2 D4.
Maison Robert 🅒 *(617) 227-3370.*
🅣 *Park Street, State, Government Center.* ⬜ *Only restaurant and café open to public.*

AFINE EXAMPLE of French Second Empire architectural gaudiness, this was Boston's City Hall from 1865 to 1969 – it was superseded by the rakishly modern New City Hall structure at nearby Government Center *(see p64)*. The renovated 19th-century building now accommodates offices and an elegant French restaurant, Maison Robert *(see p135)*.

Previous occupants have included such flamboyant mayors as Honey "Fitz" Fitzgerald *(see p23)* and James Michael Curley. Statues here memorialize Josiah Quincy, Boston's second mayor, and Benjamin Franklin, born around the corner on nearby Milk Street.

19th-century French-style façade of Boston's Old City Hall

Boston Globe Store ❹

1 School St. **Map** 2 D4.
🅒 *(617) 367-4000.* 🅣 *Park Street, State, Government Center.* ⬜ *9am–6pm Mon–Fri, 9:30am–5pm Sat, 11am–4pm Sun.*
🆆 *www.globestore@globe.com*

ADORMERED GAMBREL roof crowns this brick landmark, which opened as Thomas Crease's apothecary shop in 1718 and was reestablished as the Old Corner Bookstore in 1829.

Moving in 16 years later, the Ticknor & Fields publishing company became a gathering place for a notable roster of authors: Emerson, Hawthorne, Longfellow, Thoreau, early feminist writer Margaret Fuller, and *Uncle Tom's Cabin* novelist Harriet Beecher Stowe. The earliest editions of William Dean Howells' erudite *Atlantic Monthly* periodical were printed here – with Julia Ward Howe's rousing tribute to American Civil War bravado, *The Battle Hymn of the Republic*, first appearing in the February 1862 issue. Now owned and managed by the city's leading newspaper, the *Boston Globe*, the corner store specializes in books about Boston past and present.

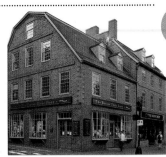

The Boston Globe Store, specializing in books about the history of Boston

Old South Meeting House ❺

310 Washington St. **Map** 2 D4.
🅒 *(617) 482-6439.* 🅣 *Park Street, State, Government Center.* ⬜ *Apr–Oct: 9:30am–5pm daily; Nov–Mar: 10am–4pm daily.* 📷 ∅ 🚫 ♿
🆆 *www.oldsouthmeetinghouse.org*

BUILT IN 1729 for Puritan religious services, this edifice, with a tall octagonal steeple, had colonial Boston's biggest capacity for town meetings – a fact capitalized upon by a group of rebellious rabble-rousers calling themselves the Sons of Liberty *(see p18)*. Their outbursts against British taxation and other royal annoyances drew increasingly large and vociferous crowds to the pews and upstairs galleries.

During a candlelit protest rally on December 16 1773, fiery speechmaker Samuel Adams flashed the signal that led to the Boston Tea Party *(see p77)* down at Griffin's Wharf several hours later. The British retaliated by turning Old South into an officers' tavern and stable for General John Burgoyne's 17th Lighthorse Regiment of Dragoons. Displays, exhibits, and a multimedia

presentation entitled *Voices of Protest* relive those raucous days as well as more recent occurrences well into the 20th century. The Meeting House offers a series of lectures covering a wide range of New England topics and also holds occasional chamber music concerts and organ recitals. The downstairs shop has a selection of merchandise, including books, craft and scrimshaw reproductions, board games with historical themes, pottery, glassware, cards, jewelry and the ubiquitous tins of "Boston Tea Party" tea.

Directly across Washington Street, sculptor Robert Shure's memorial to the 1845–49 Irish Potato Famine was added to the small plaza here in 1998.

Old South Meeting House, in stark contrast to the modern city

Old State House 6

DWARFED BY THE TOWERS of the Financial
District, this was the seat of British
colonial government between 1713 and
1776. The royal lion and unicorn still decorate each corner of the eastern façade.
After independence, the Massachusetts
legislature took possession of the building, and it has had many uses since,
including produce market, merchants'
exchange, Masonic lodge, and Boston
City Hall. Its wine cellars now function
as a downtown subway station. The
Old State House houses two floors of
Bostonian Society memorabilia and a
video presentation documenting the
change from colony to republic.

**Old State House amid the sky-
scrapers of the Financial District**

A gold sculpture of an eagle,
symbol of America, can be
seen on the west façade.

West Façade
*A Latin inscription, relating
to the first Massachusetts
Bay colony, runs around
the outside of this crest. The
relief in the center depicts
a local Native American.*

Entrance

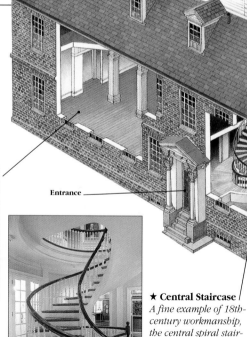

Keayne Hall
*This is named after Robert
Keayne who, in 1658, gave
£300 to the city so that the
Town House, predating the
Old State House, could be built.
Exhibits in the room depict
events from the Revolution.*

★ Central Staircase
*A fine example of 18th-
century workmanship,
the central spiral stair-
case has two beautifully
crafted wooden hand-
rails. It is one of the few
such staircases still in
existence in the U.S.*

SITE OF THE BOSTON MASSACRE

A circle of cobblestones below the balcony on the eastern façade of the Old State House marks the site of the Boston Massacre *(see pp18–19)*. After the Boston Tea Party *(see p77)*, this was one of the most inflammatory events leading up to the American Revolution.

Cobbled circle: site of the Boston Massacre

On March 5, 1770, an unruly mob of colonists taunted British guardsmen with insults, rocks, and snowballs. The soldiers opened fire, killing five colonists. A number of articles relating to the Boston Massacre are exhibited inside the Old State House, including a musket found near the site and a coroner's report detailing the incident.

VISITORS' CHECKLIST

Washington and State Sts.
Map 2 D4. ▐ *(617) 720-3290*
Ⓣ *State.* ☐ *9am–5pm daily.*
▨ ⊘ ♿ ▯
Ⓦ www.bostonhistory.org

The tower is a classic example of Colonial style. In 18th-century paintings and engravings it can be seen clearly above the Boston skyline.

British Unicorn and Lion
A royal symbol of Britain, the original lion and unicorn were pulled down when news of the Declaration of Independence reached Boston in 1776.

★ **East Façade**
This façade has seen many changes. An earlier clock from the 1820s was removed in 1957 and replaced with an 18th-century replica of the sundial that once hung here. The clock has now been reinstated.

Council Chamber
Once the chambers for the royal governors, and from 1780 chambers for the first governor of Massachusetts (John Hancock), this room has seen many key events. Among them were numerous impassioned speeches made by Boston patriots.

The Declaration of Independence was read from this balcony in 1776. In the 1830s, when the building was City Hall, the balcony was enlarged to two tiers.

STAR SIGHTS

★ **East Façade**

★ **Central Staircase**

Center Plaza ❼

Cambridge St. **Map** 1 C3.
Ⓣ *Government Center.*

DOWNTOWN'S OLD, irregular street pattern has given rise to some unusual buildings, including the Center Plaza, which was designed in the mid-1960s by Welton Beckett & Associates. It was designed specifically to follow the long curve of the existing Cambridge Street, and the low-slung office complex is often referred to as a "skyscraper laid sideways." Shops and restaurants run at street level along Center Plaza's sidewalk arcade, on the Government Center side, while the plaza behind incorporates some much older city center buildings.

Curved, Modernist structure of Center Plaza, on Cambridge Street

New City Hall ❽

City Hall Plaza. **Map** 2 D3.
Ⓒ (617) 635-4000. Ⓣ *Government Center.* ⓞ *9am–5pm daily.* Ⓖ
Ⓦ *www.cityofboston.com*

THE FIRM OF ARCHITECTS Kallmann, McKinnell & Knowles won a nationwide design competition for their striking city hall, a seemingly top-heavy, cantilevered, Modernist building. Completed in 1968, the concrete-and-brick City Hall combines the offices and services of municipal government, with ample space for holiday-season concerts, school band and glee-club performances, and community art exhibits. An outdoor stage on City Hall's north side is often the venue for evening rock and pop concerts during the summer months.

Old-fashioned flower stall on the sidewalk outside Center Plaza

Government Center ❾

Cambridge, Court, New Sudbury & Congress Sts. **Map** 2 D3.
Ⓣ *Government Center.*

THIS CITY CENTER development was built on the site of what was once Scollay Square, demolished as part of the fad for local urban-renewal that began in the early 1960s. Some viewed the development as controversial; others did not lament what was essentially a disreputable cluster of saloons, burlesque theaters, tattoo parlors, and scruffy hotels. The overall master plan for Government Center was inspired by the alfresco vitality and spaciousness of Italian piazzas. Architects I.M. Pei & Partners re-created some of this feeling by surrounding Boston's new City Hall with a vast terraced plaza covering 56 acres (23 ha), paved with 1,800,000 bricks. Its spaciousness makes it an ideal venue for events such as skateboard contests, political and sports rallies, food fairs, patriotic military marches, and concerts. The Cambridge Street side accommodates a farmers' market on Mondays and Wednesdays from around the middle of May to the middle of November.

A remnant of old Boston hangs from the Sears Block at City Hall Plaza's Court Street perimeter. This gilded, 227-gallon *Steaming Tea Kettle* was made for the Oriental Tea Company by a firm of coppersmiths in 1873. Near New Sudbury Street, the John F. Kennedy Federal Office Building features two pieces of abstract art: Dmitry Hadzi's 15-ft (4.5-m) high *Thermopylae* sculpture, and Robert Motherwell's *New England Elegy*, a mural recalling the tragic assassination of President Kennedy in Dallas in 1963. A memorial standing in front of the building marks the site of Alexander Graham Bell's first significant breakthrough toward his invention of the "electrical speech machine" in 1876 *(see p67.)*

New City Hall and Government Center, one of Boston's main focal points

Blackstone Block ⑩

Union, Hanover, North & Blackstone Sts. **Map** 2 D3. Ⓣ *Government Center, Haymarket.*

COBBLESTONES PAVE Boston's only surviving web of 17th-century lanes and alleyways, a remnant of what was once the oldest neighborhood in Boston, with historical associations dating back to the colonial period. The district's most famous son, Benjamin Franklin, grew up near Union and Hanover Streets, where his father owned a candleworks. Prior to the landfill programs that expanded the city, the block was close to the water's edge, a fact suggested by the names of the streets in this small district: Marsh Lane, Creek Square, and Salt Lane.

The oldest surviving building in the Blackstone Block dates from 1714 – the Duke of Chartres, later to be crowned France's King Louis Philippe, was a guest here in 1798 and gave French lessons to support himself while waiting for funds. Since 1826 the building has housed the Union Oyster House (*see p134*), renowned for its original mahogany raw oyster bar, its political clientele, including Congressman John F. Kennedy, and of course its oysters.

The Millennium Bostonian Hotel can also be found here, wedged among the Blackstone Block's twisting street pattern, while from early morning to dusk on Fridays and Saturdays vendors sell fruit, vegetables, and fish from stands along Blackstone, Hanover, and North Streets. Across Union Street is the New England Holocaust Memorial, dedicated in 1995 to the Jewish victims of World War II. Designed as a sculpture that the public can walk through, to do so is a surreal, justly disquieting experience.

Liberty and Union, Now and Forever by George Healy, Faneuil Hall

Faneuil Hall ⑪

Dock Sq. **Map** 2 D3. Ⓚ *No phone.* Ⓣ *Government Center, Haymarket, State.* **Great Hall** ⭘ *9am–5pm daily.* ♿ ▣ ⌂

A GIFT TO BOSTON from the wealthy merchant Peter Faneuil in 1742, this Georgian, brick landmark has always functioned simultaneously as a public market and town meeting place. Master tinsmith Shem Drowne modeled the building's grasshopper weathervane after the one on top of the Royal Exchange in the City of London, England. Revolutionary gatherings packed the hall, and as early as 1763 Samuel Adams used the hall as a platform to suggest that the American colonies should unite against British oppression and fight to establish their independence (*see pp18–19*); hence the building's nickname "Cradle of Liberty" and the bold posture of the statue of Sam Adams at the front of the building.

Toward the end of the 18th century it became apparent that the existing Faneuil Hall could no longer house the capacity crowds that it regularly attracted. The commission to expand the building was undertaken by Charles Bulfinch (*see p55*), who completed the work from 1805 to 1806. The building then remained unchanged until 1898, when it was expanded still farther according to long-standing Bulfinch stipulations. Faneuil Hall was restored in the 1970s as part of the wider redevelopment of Quincy Market (*see p66*).

Sam Adams statue, in front of Faneuil Hall

Among the paintings upstairs in the Neoclassical Great Hall is George Healy's enormous canvas, *Liberty and Union, Now and Forever*, showing Massachusetts Senator Daniel Webster in full oratorical passion. The uppermost floor contains the headquarters and armory of the Ancient and Honorable Artillery Company, chartered in 1638 for defense of the Massachusetts Bay Colony and an occupant of Faneuil Hall since 1746. Displays include weapons, commendations, medals, documents, flags, battle drums, paintings, and portraits.

The Union Oyster House, one of Boston's most famous restaurants, Blackstone Block

Gallery of the Greek Revival main dome in Quincy Market's central hall

Quincy Market ⑫

Between Chatham & Clinton Sts.
Map 2 D3. ☎ *(617) 338-2323.* Ⓣ
Government Center, State. ◯ *10am–9pm Mon–Sat, noon–6pm Sun.* ♿
Ⓦ *www.faneuilhallmarketplace.com*

THIS IMMENSELY popular shopping and dining complex attracts in the region of 14 million people every year, and was developed from the buildings of the former Faneuil Hall produce and meat market, or Quincy Market. These buildings had fallen into disrepair before they underwent a widely acclaimed restoration by the architects Benjamin Thompson & Associates in the 1970s. The imposing centerpiece, a granite Greek Revival structure *(see p30)* dating from 1825, was planned as an extension to the first Faneuil Hall Markets, which had become overstretched by Boston's rapid development. Originally called the New Faneuil Hall Market, the building came to be known as Quincy Market after the mayor, Josiah Quincy, whose original vision was responsible for the new market's creation. The façade's four Doric columns were, at the time of construction, the largest single pieces of granite ever to be quarried in the U.S. The 535-ft (163-m) long colonnaded hall is now filled with fast food stalls and a comedy nightclub, located in the spectacular Rotunda. Completing the ensemble are twin North and South Market buildings – these individual warehouses have been refurbished to accommodate boutiques, restaurants, pubs, stores, and upstairs offices.

Custom House ⑬

3 McKinley Square. **Map** 2 E3.
☎ *(617) 310-6300.* Ⓣ *Aquarium.*
Museum ◯ *8am–11pm daily.*
Ⓦ *www.marriott.com/vacationclub*

BEFORE LANDFILL altered downtown topography, early Boston's Custom House perched at the water's edge. A temple-like Greek Revival structure with fluted Doric columns, the granite building had a skylit dome upon completion in 1847. Since 1915, however, it has supported an anachronistic tower rising 495 ft (150 m), which means that for the best part of the 20th century, the Custom House was Boston's only bona fide skyscraper. Four sculpted eagles and a four-sided illuminated clock add decorative flourishes. The public has free access to a small museum of maritime history in the 19th-century rotunda. It displays objects on loan from the Peabody Museum in Salem, including maritime paintings, nautical instruments, items that depict Boston's trade with China, and several pieces of decorative art. The observatory, which offers panoramic views, is also open to the public. The rest of the building is occupied by a Marriott hotel and timeshare apartments, not open to the public.

Glass fountain on the Pearl Street side of Post Office Square

Post Office Square ⑭

Between Congress & Pearl Sts.
Map 2 D4. Ⓣ *State, Aquarium.*

THIS BEAUTIFULLY landscaped park, a small island of green situated amid the soaring skyscrapers of the financial district, replaced an ugly concrete garage that once stood here – it was demolished and rebuilt as an underground parking facility in 1990. Vines climb a 143-ft (44-m) long trellis along one side of the park, and a fountain made of green glass cascades on the square's Pearl Street side. On Angell Memorial Plaza across the road, a fountain dating from 1912 commemorates George Thorndike Angell, founder of the Massachusetts' Society

Greek Revival Custom House tower, one of Boston's most striking sights

ALEXANDER GRAHAM BELL (1847–1922)

A native of Edinburgh, Scotland, and son of a deaf mother, Bell moved to Boston in 1871 to embark on a career of teaching speech to the deaf. It led to his appointment, two years later, as professor of vocal physiology at Boston University. In a rented fifth-floor garret assisted by young repair mechanic and model maker Thomas Watson, Bell worked in his spare time on an apparatus for transmitting sound by electrical current. Initial success came on June 3, 1875, when the barely intelligible utterings of a human voice (his own) traveled over a laboratory wire. History was made on March 17, 1876, when Bell, while experimenting on voice transmission, upset a battery, spilling acid on his clothing. He called to another room: "Mr. Watson, come here. I want you." With each of those seven words reaching Watson clearly and distinctly, the "electrical speech machine" was invented. In August that year, Bell proved its practical value by sending messages over Canadian telegraph wires. By 1878, he had set up the first public telephone exchange in New Haven, Connecticut. Six years later, long-distance calls were being made between Boston and New York City.

Distinctive, Art Deco-style Verizon Building, built in the 1940s

Verizon Building ⑮

185 Franklin St. **Map** 2 D4.
🔴 *(617) 743-4747.* ⓣ *State, Aquarium.* **Museum** ⬜ *24 hours daily.* ♿

DATING FROM 1947 and overlooking the south side of Post Office Square, this Art Deco building is still in use today. Dean Cornwell's monumental 160-ft (49-m) long *Telephone Men and Women at Work* mural – populated by 197 life-size figures – has encircled the lobby since 1951 and is a truly remarkable work of art. The small museum at street level features an accurate restoration of Alexander Graham Bell's Court Street laboratory *(see p29)*, complete with his tools, books, actual workbench, and one of his garret window-frames overlooking a diorama of Scollay Square. The exhibit was constructed from parts of Bell's original workshop, put to one side and lovingly preserved when the house where he lived was demolished in the 1920s. It was opened on June 3, 1959, coincidentally the 84th anniversary of the invention of the telephone. The world's first commercial telephone and first telephone switchboard, both dating from May 1877, are also displayed in the museum.

for the Prevention of Cruelty to Animals. The most important buildings overlooking the square and plaza include the Verizon Telephone Building and downtown's main post office, housed in the John W. McCormack courthouse building, and which has a special department catering to stamp collectors. There is also Le Meridien Hotel *(see p125)*, a classic Renaissance Revival showpiece completed in 1922 that was originally the Federal Reserve Bank, and One Post Office Square, which offers great views

over Boston Harbor and Downtown – these can be seen from the atrium at the top of the building, which, not strictly open to the public, may be accessible through polite inquiry. A focal point for the whole district, the grassy space of the square comes into its own during the warmer months of the year, when office workers can be seen sprawling across its well-kept lawns – a great place for visitors to rest their weary feet and watch Bostonians take a few minutes out.

Telephone Men and Women at Work, **Verizon Building**

GRIFFIN'S WHARF

NORTH END AND THE WATERFRONT

THIS WAS BOSTON'S first neighborhood, and one that has been key to the city's fortunes. Fringed by numerous wharves, the area prospered initially through shipping and shipbuilding, with much of America's early trade passing through its warehouses. The more recent importance of finance and high-tech industries, however, has seen the waterfront evolve; its

Statue in Old North Church garden

old warehouses transformed into luxury apartment blocks and offices. Away from the waterfront, the narrow streets of the North End have historically been home to European immigrants, drawn by the availability of work. The area today is populated largely by those of Italian descent, whose many cafés, delis, and restaurants make it one of the city's most distinct communities.

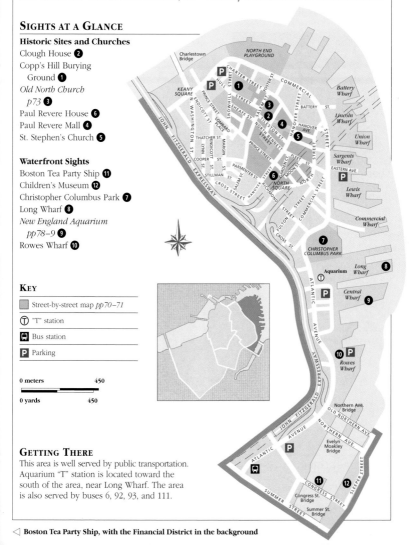

SIGHTS AT A GLANCE

Historic Sites and Churches
Clough House ❷
Copp's Hill Burying Ground ❶
Old North Church p73 ❸
Paul Revere House ❻
Paul Revere Mall ❹
St. Stephen's Church ❺

Waterfront Sights
Boston Tea Party Ship ⓫
Children's Museum ⓬
Christopher Columbus Park ❼
Long Wharf ❽
New England Aquarium pp78–9 ❾
Rowes Wharf ❿

KEY

▨	Street-by-street map *pp70–71*
Ⓣ	"T" station
🚌	Bus station
P	Parking

0 meters   450
0 yards   450

GETTING THERE
This area is well served by public transportation. Aquarium "T" station is located toward the south of the area, near Long Wharf. The area is also served by buses 6, 92, 93, and 111.

◁ **Boston Tea Party Ship, with the Financial District in the background**

Street-by-Street: North End

Old North Church clock

T HE MAIN ARTERIES of this area are Hanover and Salem Streets. Topped by the Old North Church, Salem Street is indicative of this area's historical connections – indeed the Old North Church is one of Boston's premier Revolutionary sights. In general the area consists of narrow streets and alleys, with four- and five-story tenements, many of which are now expensive condominiums. Hanover Street, like much of the area, has a distinctly Italian feel, while just south of here is North Square, site of the famous Paul Revere House *(see p75).*

Clough House
Period furnishings can be seen in this house by Ebenezer Clough, who also helped build the Old North Church ❷

Copp's Hill Burying Ground
During the American Revolution, the British used this low hilltop to fire cannon at American positions across Boston Harbor. Created in 1659 it is the city's second oldest graveyard ❶

Charlestown

HULL STREET

SHEAFE STREET

SALEM STREET

NORTH BENN

PRINCE STREET

★ Old North Church
Built in 1723 and famous for the part it played in Paul Revere's midnight ride (see p19), this is Boston's oldest religious building. On festive occasions, the North End still rings with the sound of its bells ❸

KEY

– – – Suggested route

↓
Government Center

STAR SIGHTS
★ Old North Church
★ Paul Revere House
★ Paul Revere Mall

0 meters   50

0 yards   50

★ Paul Revere Mall

Linking the Old North Church to Hanover Street, this tree-lined mall dates only from 1933. Its antique feel is enhanced by a statue of Paul Revere, which was sculpted in 1885 ❹

LOCATOR MAP
See Street Finder map 2

St. Stephen's Church

North End's Italian theme continues in this church, though only by chance. Long before the first Italians arrived, Charles Bulfinch (see p55) incorporated Italian Renaissance features and a bell tower into his refit of an earlier church building ❺

Hanover Street is the most Italian of all Boston's streets, brought to life by Italian restaurants and cafés, as well as the day-to-day activities of its ethnic community.

➘ **The waterfront**

★ Paul Revere House

This is the house where Paul Revere began his midnight ride (see p19). Revere's home from 1770 to 1800, it is now a museum ❻

Slate tombstones of Boston's early settlers, Copp's Hill Burying Ground

Copp's Hill Burying Ground ❶

Entrances at Charter & Hull Sts.
Map 2 D2. Ⓣ *Government Center, North Station.* ⬜ *8am–5pm daily.*

EXISTING SINCE 1659, this is Boston's second-oldest cemetery after the one by King's Chapel *(see p60)*. Nicknamed "Corpse Hill," the real name of the hill occupied by the cemetery derives from a local man by the name of William Copp. He owned a farm on its southeastern slope from 1643, and much of the cemetery's land was purchased from him. His children can be found buried here. Other more famous

Quiet, leafy street, typical of the area around Copp's Hill

people interred here include Robert Newman, the sexton who hung Paul Revere's signal lanterns in the belfry of Old North Church *(see p73)*, and Edmund Hartt, builder of the *U.S.S. Constitution (see p119)*. Increase, Cotton, and Samuel Mather, three generations of a family of highly influential colonial period Puritan ministers, are also buried here. Hundreds of Boston's Colonial-era black slaves and freedmen are also buried here, including Prince Hall, a free black man who founded the African Freemasonry Order in Massachusetts.

During the British occupation of Boston, the site was used by British commanders who had an artillery position here. They would later exploit the prominent hilltop location during the Revolution, when they directed cannon fire from here across Boston harbor toward American positions in Charlestown. King George III's troops were said to have used the slate headstones for target practice, and pockmarks from their musket balls are still visible on some of them.

Copp's Hill Terrace, directly across Charter Street, is a prime observation point for

Decorative column, Copp's Hill

views over to Charlestown and Bunker Hill. It is also the site where, in 1919, a 2.3-million-gallon molasses tank exploded, creating a huge, syrupy tidal wave that killed 21 people.

Clough House ❷

21 Unity St. **Map** 2 E2.
Ⓣ *Haymarket, Aquarium.* ⬜ *Jun–Sep: 10am–2pm Wed.*

EBENEZER CLOUGH was a master mason and one of the Sons of Liberty who participated in the Boston Tea Party *(see p77)*. One of two masons who helped to build the neighboring Old North Church *(see p73)*, he was also the head of a syndicate that laid out Unity Street in 1710 and built a series of six town houses here. The only building to survive is the one at No. 21 Unity Street, which was built in 1712, and was the house in which Ebenezer Clough himself lived. In a bad state of decay for many years, and in danger of demolition, the house was only saved when the Reverend P. Kellet, vicar of Christ Church, launched a fund-raising campaign in 1962. A rather austere three-story building, it is typical of much of Boston's colonial architecture. Now fully restored to its former condition, the house has finely executed window and door lintels, decorated with raised brick panels over the first-floor windows and simple, carved-brick detailing over the door. The Heritage Room on the second floor features typical period furnishings and household accessories.

Clough House once stood alongside an identical brick residence, which was acquired by Benjamin Franklin in 1748. He bought the house for his two widowed sisters but never lived here himself. It was demolished in the 1930s to make way for the Paul Revere Mall *(see p74)*.

Old North Church™ ❸

CHRIST EPISCOPAL CHURCH is the official name of this, Boston's oldest surviving religious edifice, which dates from 1723. It was built of brick in the Georgian style similar to that of St. Andrew's-by-the-Wardrobe in Blackfriars, London, designed by Sir Christopher Wren. The church was made famous on April 18, 1775, when sexton Robert Newman, aiding Paul Revere *(see p19)*, hung a pair of signal lanterns in the belfry. These were to warn the patriots in Charlestown of the westward departure of British troops, on their way to engage the revolutionaries.

(see p19)

VISITORS' CHECKLIST

193 Salem St. **Map** 2 E2. ☐
(617) 523-6676. ⓉHaymarket,
Aquarium, North Station. ☐
*9am–6pm daily (Nov–May until
5pm).* ☐ *9am, 11am & 4pm
Sun (also 5pm Jul–Aug).* ☐ &
☐ ☐ *www.oldnorth.com*

★ **Box Pews**
*The unusual, high-sided box
pews in the church were designed
to enclose footwarmers, which were
filled with hot coals or bricks
during wintry weather.*

★ **Bell Tower
and Steeple**
*Views from the top of the
bell tower, such as this
one toward the Finan-
cial District, are well
worth the climb. Famous
as the place where
Robert Newman hung
his lanterns, the tower
contains the first set of
church bells in North
America, cast in 1745.*

Entrance —

STAR SIGHTS

★ **Bell Tower
and Steeple**

★ **Box Pews**

Bust of George Washington
*This marble bust of the first U.S.
president, modeled on an earlier
one by Christian Gullager, was
presented to the church in 1815.*

Paul Revere Mall ❹

Tileston St. **Map** 2 E2.
Ⓣ *Haymarket, Aquarium.* ♿

THIS BRICK-PAVED plaza gives the crowded neighborhood of the North End a precious stretch of open space between Hanover and Unity Streets. A well-utilized municipal resource, the Mall is always full of local people: children, teenagers, young mothers, and older residents chatting in Italian and playing cards or checkers. Laid out in 1933, and originally called the Prado, its focal point is Cyrus Dallin's equestrian statue of local hero Paul Revere, which was originally modeled in 1885. However, it was only sculpted and placed here in 1940. Bronze bas-relief plaques on the mall's side walls commemorate a number of North End residents who have played an important

Equestrian statue by Cyrus Dallin, Paul Revere Mall

role in the history of Boston. Benches, a fountain, and twin rows of linden trees complete the space, which has a distinctly European feel.

St. Stephen's Church ❺

401 Hanover St. **Map** 2 E2.
📞 *(617) 523-1230.* Ⓣ *Haymarket, Aquarium.* ◯ *7am–dusk daily.*
✝ *8:30am & 11am Sun, 5:15pm Mon & Sat, 7:30am Tue–Fri.*

OPENED IN 1714 as a humble Congregationalist meeting house, St. Stephen's Church was extensively enlarged and embellished by the architect Charles Bulfinch *(see p55)* in 1802–04. Bulfinch incorporated a range of harmonious Italian Renaissance motifs in his re-design, adding a number of decorative pediments and pedestals, tall arched windows, as well as

St. Stephen's Church, with its Renaissance-style bell tower

an ornate bell tower that is topped by a gilded cap. One year after that project's completion, the first-ever bell cast by the famous revolutionary and master metalworker, Paul Revere *(see p19)*, was hung in the belfry.

The church's present name dates from 1862, when it became Roman Catholic to accommodate the North End's increasing numbers of Irish immigrants. When Hanover Street was widened in 1869, the entire structure was moved back 16 ft (5 m) and, a year later, it was raised 6 ft (2 m) to accommodate a basement chapel. Damaged by fires in 1897 and 1929, and redecorated each time, the church was restored to its Bulfinch design in 1965.

The church's interior features include a gracefully curved ceiling, original white-painted pine columns, and a pair of pewter chandeliers, which are copies of those hanging in the Doric Hall of the Massachusetts State House. The church's pews were donated in honor of the numerous Irish, Italian, and Portuguese parishioners who live in the neighborhood, while the Italian mahogany Stations of the Cross are part of the 1965 refit. St. Stephen's is listed on the National Register of Historic Places.

THE GREAT BRINKS ROBBERY

Masterminded by Tony Pino, this infamous event took place on the night of January 17, 1950 on North End's Commercial Street. Disguised as Brinks guards, seven of Pino's men made off with $2,775,395.12 in payroll money – including cash totaling $1,218,211.29 – from the head-quarters of the Brinks Armored Car Company. Nationwide headlines trumpeted the robbery as the biggest heist in U.S. history. Even though all members of the Brinks gang were eventually caught and imprisoned, only $60,000 of the loot has been recovered more than half a century after the event.

Members of the infamous Brinks gang, in police custody

Paul Revere House ❻

19 North Sq. **Map** 2 E2.
📞 (617) 523-2338. Ⓣ *Haymarket, Aquarium.* ◻ *mid-Apr–Oct: 9:30am–5:15pm daily; Nov–mid-Apr: 9:30am–4:15pm daily.* ◑ *Jan–Mar: Mon.* 🏛 ♿ ⊘ 🔔
Ⓦ www.paulreverehouse.org

Tᴴᴱ ᴄɪᴛʏ's oldest surviving clapboard frame house is historically significant, for it was here in 1775 that Paul Revere began his legendary horseback ride to warn his compatriots in Lexington of the impending arrival of British troops *(see p19)*. This historic event was later immortalized in a boldly patriotic, epic poem by Henry Wadsworth Longfellow *(see p110)*. It begins "Listen, my children, and you shall hear of the midnight ride of Paul Revere."

Colonial banknotes, exhibited in the Paul Revere House

Revere, a Huguenot descendent, was by trade a versatile gold- and silversmith, copper engraver, and maker of church bells, cannons, and false teeth. He and his second wife Rachel, mother of eight of his 16 children, owned the house from 1770 to 1800. Small leaded casement windows, an overhanging upper story, and nail-studded front door all contribute to make it a fine example of 17th-century Early American architecture. In the courtyard along one side of the house is a large bronze bell, cast by Paul Revere for a church in 1804 – Revere made nearly 200 church bells. Three rooms in the house contain period artifacts, including original pieces of family furniture, items made in Revere's workshop, and colonial banknotes. The house, which by the mid-19th century had become a decrepit tenement fronted by stores, was saved from demolition by preservationists' efforts led by a great-grandson of Revere.

Next door, the early 18th-century Pierce-Hichborn House is the earliest brick town house remaining in New England. It features Georgian English motifs such as shallow arches over the doors and windows, and twin chimneys. Admission is via the Paul Revere House.

Paul Revere House kitchen, as it was in the 17th century

Christopher Columbus Park ❼

Atlantic Avenue, between Long & Commercial Wharves. **Map** 2 E3.
📞 *No phone.* Ⓣ *Aquarium.*

Eᴬᴛᴱɴsɪᴠᴇ ᴜʀʙᴀɴ renewal along the Inner Harbor resulted in the completion of this handsome park in 1976. It covers 4.5 acres (2 ha) with wisteria clinging to a 340-ft (104-m) long arched trellis, and is a superlative spot for views of the waterfront and the Financial District. The commemorative Rose Fitzgerald Kennedy Garden was added to the park's layout in 1987.

View toward the Custom House and the Financial District, across Christopher Columbus Park

Rowes Wharf development, typical of Boston's waterfront regeneration

Long Wharf **8**

Atlantic Avenue. **Map** 2 E3.
Ⓣ *Aquarium.*

THE NATION's oldest continuously operated wharf was built in 1710 to accommodate the boom in early maritime commerce. The following century was to be Boston's international maritime heyday; it was the busiest port in North America and one of the most important in the colonies, surpassed only by London and Bristol in the amount of cargo that it handled. Once extending 2000 ft (610 m) into Boston harbor, and lined with shops and warehouses, Long Wharf provided secure mooring for the largest ships of the time.

Today, Long Wharf is used by boat services to Provincetown, Charlestown Navy Yard, and the Harbor Islands. The attractive esplanade at the end also offers good views across the city's waterfront.

Running along the waterfront, Harbor Walk connects Long Wharf with other adjacent wharves, such as Union, Lewis, and Commercial wharves. Dating from the early 1800s, most are now converted to fashionable harborside apartments and condominiums.

New England Aquarium **9**

See pp78–9.

Rowes Wharf **10**

Atlantic Avenue. **Map** 2 E4.
Ⓣ *Aquarium.*

COMPLETED IN 1987, this fine example of waterfront revitalization replaced the two-part India wharf dating from the 1760s. Built of Bostonian red brick, this modern development features a large archway that links the city to the harbor. Skidmore, Owings & Merrill designed the sprawling complex, which comprises the luxury Boston Harbor Hotel, opulent condominiums, offices, and a marina from which a water shuttle runs to the airport.

Boston Tea Party Ship **11**

Congress St. Bridge. **Map** 2 E5.
🄲 *(617) 338-1773.* Ⓣ *South Station.* ◯ *Jun–Sep: 9am–6pm daily; Oct–May: 9am–5pm daily.* 🄳
🅆 *www.historictours.com/boston*

GRIFFIN's WHARF, where the Boston Tea Party took place on December 16, 1773 (*see p77*), was buried beneath landfill many years ago. Since 1973, the Danish-built sailing brig *Beaver II* has been anchored on Fort Point Channel a short distance south of the old Griffin's Wharf site. The vessel resembles one of the three original British East India Company ships involved in the Tea Party protest. Today, modern-day patriots toss imitation bales of tea overboard, recreating one of the acts of American defiance that prompted Britain to close

View down Long Wharf toward the waterfront and Custom House

Boston Harbor in 1773 and put the Massachusetts Bay Colony under martial law.

On an adjacent pier, ship models, Tea Party memorabilia, and other educational exhibits are displayed in a museum.

Playing on the mini-construction site at Boston's Children's Museum

Children's Museum ⑫

300 Congress St. **Map** 2 E5.
C (617) 426-8855. **T** South Station. **O** mid-Jun–Aug: 10am–5pm Sat–Thu, 10am–9pm Fri; Sep–mid-Jun: 10am–5pm Tue–Sun.
& **W** www.bostonkids.org

OVERLOOKING Fort Point Channel, a rejuvenated 19th-century wool warehouse contains one of the country's best children's museums. There are many interesting exhibits, and youngsters are able to participate in games and learning activities, and climb through a two-story maze.

A hands-on recycling area provides barrels of materials of various kinds for children to use in self-instructive creative projects. In addition, careers can be sampled as children work on a mini-construction site, weave fabrics on looms, or act in kidstage plays.

An international flavor is added to the proceedings by a visit to the silk merchant's house transplanted from Kyoto in Japan (Boston's sister city), while Teen Tokyo introduces children to Japanese youth culture in an area featuring a Tokyo subway car, a karaoke booth, and an animation computer.

A towering milk bottle from a local dairy stands outside in front of the museum building and is used as an ice-cream stand in summer.

THE BOSTON TEA PARTY

In 1767, when Britain decided to tax its American colonies, there was outrage. Boycotts were placed on British goods, and protesters took to the streets. One such protest in 1773 culminated in the Boston Massacre (see p18).

Despite a subsequent reduction in taxation, tax on tea remained. Parliament then granted the British East India Company sole rights to sell tea in the colonies, which caused prices to rise further. In November 1773, ships arrived in Boston Harbor loaded with tea, and merchants, who refused to buy the tea, came under pressure from Thomas Hutchinson, the Monarchist governor. On the night of December 16, however, around 7,000 rebels, gathered by Samuel Adams, marched to the wharf declaring "Tonight Boston Harbor is a teapot!" Fifty men, dressed as Mohawks, boarded the ships and dumped their cargoes into the water.

Britain reacted strongly, closing the port and putting Massachusetts under martial law. This retribution unified patriots across America, and the "Boston Tea Party," as the protest was soon known, became the spark that ignited the Revolutionary War.

Thomas Hutchinson
Governor of Boston and staunch monarchist, Thomas Hutchinson tried to force the rebels to comply with British colonial law.

Many of the rebels were dressed as Mohawks.

342 bales of tea were thrown into the sea.

A crowd of about 7,000 watched the events from the quayside.

The Boston Tea Party, depicted in a 19th-century engraving

New England Aquarium **9**

The waterfront's prime attraction dominates Central Wharf. Designed by a consortium of architects in 1969, the aquarium's core encloses a vast four-story ocean tank, which contains an innumerable array of marine animals. A curving walkway runs around the outside of the tank from top to bottom and provides viewpoints of the interior of the tank from different levels. Also resident at the aquarium are colonies of penguins, while the west wing contains an outdoor tank with harbor seals. Opened on the wharf in 2001, the Simons IMAX Theater presents changing programs of 3-D films on a giant screen.

Edge of the Sea Tidepool
A fiberglass shore recreates a world where the land meets the sea. It is home to animals such as horseshoe crabs and sea urchins.

Penguin Pool
One of the main attractions of the aquarium, the penguin pool runs around the base of the giant tank. It contains African, rockhopper, and blue penguins.

★ Whale Watch
Trips leave Boston Harbor for whale feeding grounds far offshore. Tours also explore aspects of oceanography, such as studying the harbor's ecosystem.

Main entrance

Harbor Seals
The west wing, an outdoor tank covered by a steel canopy, is home to a lively colony of harbor seals.

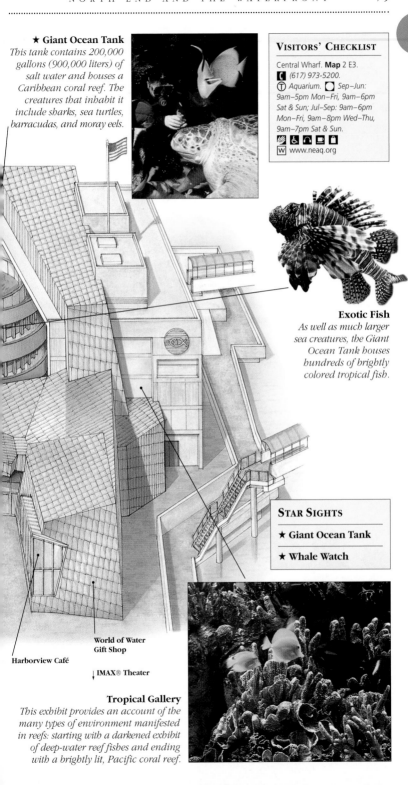

★ Giant Ocean Tank
This tank contains 200,000 gallons (900,000 liters) of salt water and houses a Caribbean coral reef. The creatures that inhabit it include sharks, sea turtles, barracudas, and moray eels.

VISITORS' CHECKLIST

Central Wharf. **Map** 2 E3.
(617) 973-5200.
Aquarium. Sep–Jun: 9am–5pm Mon–Fri, 9am–6pm Sat & Sun; Jul–Sep: 9am–6pm Mon–Fri, 9am–8pm Wed–Thu, 9am–7pm Sat & Sun.
w www.neaq.org

Exotic Fish
As well as much larger sea creatures, the Giant Ocean Tank houses hundreds of brightly colored tropical fish.

STAR SIGHTS

★ Giant Ocean Tank

★ Whale Watch

World of Water Gift Shop

Harborview Café

IMAX® Theater

Tropical Gallery
This exhibit provides an account of the many types of environment manifested in reefs: starting with a darkened exhibit of deep-water reef fishes and ending with a brightly lit, Pacific coral reef.

CHINATOWN AND THE THEATER DISTRICT

LOCATED south of Boston Common *(see pp48–9)* and west of the Financial District, this part of town has a noticeably gritty, more down-to-earth ambience. The area around Washington Street, with Downtown Crossing at its center *(see pp82–3)*, is the city's main shopping district. South of here is Chinatown, one of the most populous in the United States – only the Chinatowns in San Francisco

Gilt cherub, the Colonial Theater

and New York are larger. West of Chinatown is the city's Theater District, where pre- or post Broadway shows feature regularly. A long-time red-light district, the "Combat Zone" grew up at the lower end of Washington Street, between Chinatown and the Theater District. Today, it is being gentrified and, though an area where caution should be exercised, is moving increasingly upscale.

SIGHTS AT A GLANCE

Historic Streets, Buildings, and Churches
Bay Village ⑩
Brattle Book Shop ④
Chinatown ⑧
Downtown Crossing ②
Filene's Department Store ③
Jacob Wirth ⑨
Massachusetts State Transportation Building ⑥
St. Paul's Cathedral ①

Theaters
Colonial Theater ⑦
Opera House ⑤
Shubert Theater ⑪
Wang Center for the Performing Arts ⑫

KEY
▨ Street-by-street map *pp82–3*
Ⓣ "T" station
Ⓟ Parking

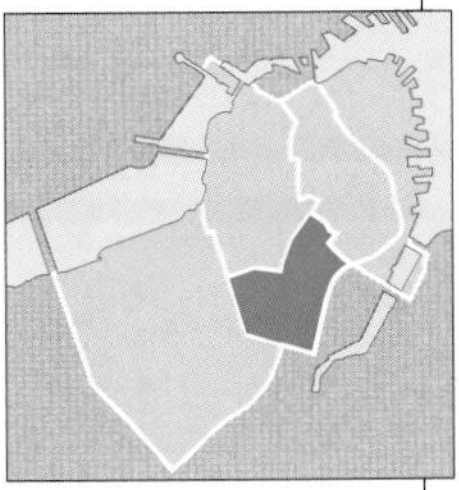

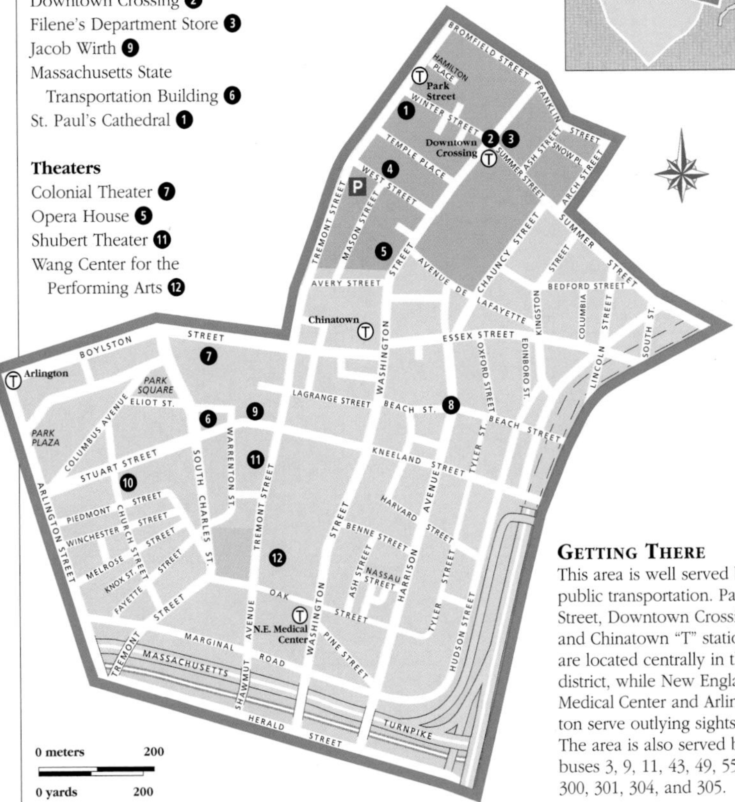

GETTING THERE

This area is well served by public transportation. Park Street, Downtown Crossing, and Chinatown "T" stations are located centrally in the district, while New England Medical Center and Arlington serve outlying sights. The area is also served by buses 3, 9, 11, 43, 49, 55, 300, 301, 304, and 305.

0 meters 200
0 yards 200

◁ **Colorful August Moon Festival, held in Boston's Chinatown**

Street-by-Street: Around Washington Street

Exterior decoration, Filene's

RUNNING NORTHEAST from the Theater District, Washington Street lies at the heart of Boston's main shopping area. Its main focal point, Downtown Crossing, lies at its intersection with Winter and Summer Streets. Saturday afternoons here, in particular, offer visitors a glimpse of Boston's sophisticated, and often multi-ethnic population, as they go about their shopping. Filene's and Macy's are the two main stores, though Washington Street and the streets off it offer a range of outlets such as bookstores, camera stores, and jewelers. Just to the south, the Theater District and Chinatown are only a few minutes away on foot. Visitors should note that incidences of petty crime sometimes occur in this crowded area.

Sidewalk café on Summer Street

Boston Common

St. Paul's Cathedral
Dating from around 1820, this was one of the first Greek Revival granite buildings to go up in Boston. Today it is still used to broadcast Sunday morning religious programs **1**

★ Brattle Book Shop
At first glance, there is not a lot to recommend a second look at this Boston literary landmark. Inside, however, are more than 250,000 rare books and magazines, a treat for any lover of the printed word **4**

Theater District and Chinatown

Opera House
This building was opened as a theater in 1928. Today it is closed and, like the surrounding district, a little shabby. Nevertheless the elegant Spanish Baroque-style façade recalls the theater's heyday **5**

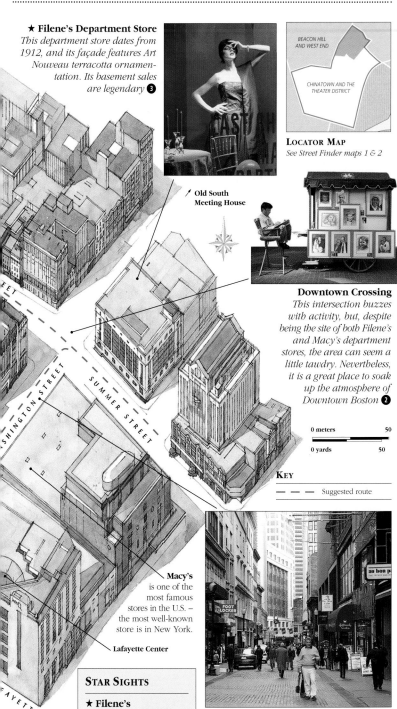

★ Filene's Department Store
This department store dates from 1912, and its façade features Art Nouveau terracotta ornamentation. Its basement sales are legendary ❸

LOCATOR MAP
See Street Finder maps 1 & 2

BEACON HILL AND WEST END

CHINATOWN AND THE THEATER DISTRICT

Old South Meeting House

Downtown Crossing
This intersection buzzes with activity, but, despite being the site of both Filene's and Macy's department stores, the area can seem a little tawdry. Nevertheless, it is a great place to soak up the atmosphere of Downtown Boston ❷

0 meters   50
0 yards   50

KEY
- - - - Suggested route

Macy's
is one of the most famous stores in the U.S. – the most well-known store is in New York.

Lafayette Center

STAR SIGHTS

★ **Filene's Department Store**

★ **Brattle Bookshop**

Boston Tea Party Ship

Washington Street
The main street of this district, Washington Street has many stores. New developments, such as the Lafayette Center, make it increasingly upscale.

Classical chancel and box pews of the interior of St. Paul's Cathedral, typically austere in style

St. Paul's Cathedral ❶

138 Tremont St. **Map** 4 E1.
📞 *(617) 482-5800.* Ⓣ *Park Street.*
🕐 *8am, 10am & 12:30pm daily; also 12:10pm & 1pm Mon & Tue–Fri.* ♿
Ⓦ *www.diomass.org*

CONSECRATED in 1820, Boston's second example of Greek Revival architecture was designed by Alexander Parris, five years before the completion of his Quincy Market hall *(see p66)*, which also has the outward appearance of a Greek temple. The first Greek Revival Church in Boston came about with Charles Bulfinch's design for the façade of the original New South Church, which was subsequently demolished.

The stone work on St. Paul's Cathedral is by Solomon Willard, who gave the church a portico of six unfluted stone columns with Ionic capitals. The building's pediment was initially intended to feature a frieze depicting St. Paul preaching before King Agrippa, but this was never constructed due to considerations of the cost involved.

The interior of the church, dominated by a classical chancel, curved apse, and box pews, is spacious and austere, typical of a style found in New England churches.

In 1908 the church became the cathedral of Massachusetts' Episcopal diocese, the largest in the U.S. The United States' longest-running religious radio program has been broadcast from the cathedral each Sunday since the 1920s.

Downtown Crossing ❷

Washington, Winter & Summer Sts.
Map 4 F1. Ⓣ *Downtown Crossing.*

As AN ANTIDOTE to heavy traffic congestion, this shopping-district crossroads was laid out as a pedestrian zone between 1975 and 1978. Downtown's department stores with their contrasting architectural styles – Beaux Arts Filene's and Modernist Macy's (previously Jordan Marsh until 1996) – are the main focal points of the area. Smaller retail outlets, some in restored buildings with terracotta and cast-iron façades, are plentiful in some of the streets radiating from Downtown Crossing and Washington Street. South of Downtown Crossing, the area retains an atmosphere of an earlier era when this inner city district went by the name of the Combat Zone.

Filene's Department Store ❸

Washington & Summer Sts.
Map 4 F1. 📞 *(617) 357-2100.*
Filene's Basement 📞 *(617) 542-2011.* Ⓣ *Downtown Crossing.*
🕐 *9:30am–7:30pm Mon–Sat, 11am–7pm Sun.*
Ⓦ *www.filenes.com*

THIS SPECIALITY shop, founded by William Filene in 1881, has grown into New England's biggest and best-known department store. This flagship of Filene's branches, which are scattered throughout the region, covers one city block. Completed in 1912, the eight-story building was designed by Chicago architect Daniel Burham, who gave the Beaux Arts façade green terracotta ornamentation, and a tower that features a pair of clocks and a four-bell carillon.

In 1908 Filene's son, Edward, introduced a cut-price department called Filene's Automatic Bargain Basement, which became a trademark for the stores across the Filene's empire.

Beaux Arts façade of Filene's department store, Downtown Crossing

According to Edward's strategy, quality merchandise that had not sold within a pre-determined period in upstairs departments was moved to the basement, where it was marked down in progressive stages: 25% after two weeks, 50% after three weeks, 75% after one month. Items left unsold after another week traditionally went to charity. Filene's Basement at the Downtown Crossing store still operates, but it is no longer part of the Filene's company. Nevertheless, it is still a Boston institution, with remarkable bargains, and a great leveler, where Boston Brahmins can still be seen shopping alongside those of more modest means.

Vintage magazines displayed at the Brattle Book Shop

Brattle Book Shop ❹

9 West St. **Map** 4 E1.
📞 (617) 542-0210. Ⓣ Park Street, Downtown Crossing. ◷ 9am–5:30pm Mon–Sat. ♿
🅦 www.brattlebookshop.com

Founded in 1825 and located at various sites around Boston since, this bibliophiles' treasure house is packed with more than 250,000 used, rare, and out-of-print books. Proprietor Kenneth Gloss also stocks back issues of periodicals, *Life*, *Look*, and *Collier's* magazines among them, along with antiquarian ephemera such as maps, prints, post-cards, greeting cards, and autographed manuscripts. In front of and alongside the three-story building, passers-by browse through bins and carts full of discounted bargain books priced in the range of $1 to $5.

Spanish Baroque, terracotta ornamentation on the façade of the Opera House

Opera House ❺

539 Washington St. **Map** 4 E1.
Ⓣ Downtown Crossing, Chinatown, Boylston. ● for refurbishment. ♿

The building that is now the Opera House has been known by many names. Built on the site of the original Boston Theater, and designed by Thomas Lamb, it opened in 1928 as the B. F. Keith Memorial Theater, named after the late 19th-century showman who added the term "vaudeville" to show business vocabulary. It was renamed the Savoy Theater in the 1940s. As home of the Opera Company of Boston from the late 1950s onward, the venue became internationally recognized for Sarah Caldwell's daringly innovative productions. After financial misfortunes befell her company, however, the Opera House closed in 1991. There are currently vague plans for the future of the Opera House, with increasingly hopeful speculation about its refurbishment.

With its white Spanish Baroque, terracotta façade, high ceilings, chandeliered lobby, and three-tier horse-shoe balconies, the theater has become one of the landmarks of Washington Street, and still retains an air of its past glory.

LIBERTY TREE

At the corner of Washington Street and Boylston Street, a low relief of a tree marks the exact site of the famous Liberty Tree, where the Sons of Liberty would meet during the prelude to the American Revolution. The tree's fame first became widespread when it became a focal point for opposition to the Stamp Act *(see p18)*. The British stamp master, Andrew Oliver, was hung in effigy from its branches, an incident that caused people from all over the region to gather around it. The tree was also a meeting place in the days running up to the Boston Tea Party *(see p77)*. In August 1775, during the early part of the Revolution when Boston was still occupied by the British, a mob of Redcoats vented their anger on the tree and chopped it down.

Bostonians protest the Stamp Act of 1765, around the Liberty Tree

Massachusetts State Transportation Building **⑥**

8–10 Park Plaza, Stuart & Charles Sts.
Map 4 E2. ⓣ *Boylston.* **Atrium restaurants** ⬚ *11am–8pm Mon–Fri, noon–6pm Sat.* ♿

THE MAIN FEATURE of the Massachusetts State Transportation Building, constructed in 1983, is its seven-story-high, skylit City Place atrium, which is directly accessible to the public. Covering most of a sizeable city block, this red-brick and glass cantilevered building has won several prestigious design awards. It incorporates offices and public-service facilities, maintained by the state's transportation administrators, around a central mall of wide-ranging shops and restaurants.

Lunchtime concerts, pop or light-classical music, are frequently scheduled in the central mall, while gallery showings are often held on the upper levels overlooking the atrium. Other facilities in the building include a bank, newsstand, and several fast-food eateries.

The City Place atrium in the Massachusetts State Transportation Building

Gilt ornamentation from the lavishly decorated interior of the Colonial Theater

Colonial Theater **⑦**

106 Boylston St. **Map** 4 E2.
🄲 *(617) 426-9366.* ⓣ *Boylston.* ⬚ *phone to check.* ♿

CLARENCE H. BLACKALL designed 14 Boston theaters during his architectural career, among them the Colonial, which is the city's oldest theater to have been in continuous operation under the same name. A two-story loggia sits atop Blackall's structure, which is otherwise quite plain. The interior, on the other hand, is an impressively opulent showpiece by H.B. Pennell: his Rococo lobby boasts chandeliers, gilded trim, and lofty arched ceilings. The 1,658-seat auditorium is decorated with allegorical figures, frescoes, and friezes.

The theater opened on December 20, 1900 with a suitably extravagant performance of the melodrama *Ben Hur,* featuring a cast of 350 and an on-stage chariot race involving a dozen horses pulling Roman chariots on treadmills. Today the theater is best remembered for premiering lavish musical productions. In particular it was the venue for productions by musical directors such as Irving Berlin, Sigmund Romberg, and Rodgers and Hammerstein, and is where Ziegfeld premiered his Follies *(see p89).*

Chinatown **⑧**

Bounded by Kingston, Kneeland, Washington & Essex Sts. **Map** 4 E2.
ⓣ *Chinatown.*

THIS AREA IS THE third largest Chinatown in the U.S. after those in San Francisco and New York. It covers blocks of filled land that had been the South Cove tidal backwater until the early 19th century. Pagoda-topped telephone booths, as well as a three-story gateway guarded by four marble lions, set the neighborhood's Oriental tone.

The first 200 Chinese to settle in New England came by ship from San Francisco in 1870. Mostly unskilled, they were recruited to break a labor strike at a shoe factory in Massachusetts, but were jobless by 1874. At this time, some drifted to Boston, at first pitching their tents on Oliver Place, which they renamed

Colorful, contemporary city mural in Chinatown

Ping On Alley – "the Street of Peace and Security." In the 1880s another wave of Chinese immigration from California was prompted by an economic boom that led to job openings in construction, on the railroad, and the laying of telephone lines. Boston's Chinese colony was fully established by the turn of the 19th century, and with it came ubiquitous new garment and textile industries.

Political turmoil in China immediately following World War II, and more recent arrivals from Vietnam, Laos, Korea, Thailand, and Cambodia, have swelled Chinatown's population, which now stands at around 8,000. Restaurants, bakeries, food markets, curio shops, and dispensers of Chinese medicine are especially numerous along the main thoroughfare of Beach Street, as well as on Tyler, Oxford, and Harrison Streets.

Typical store and restaurant façades in Boston's Chinatown

Jacob Wirth **9**

31–37 Stuart St. **Map** 4 E2. **(** (617) 338-8586. **T** Boylston, Chinatown. **◻** 11:30am–8pm Sun & Mon, 11:30am–10pm Tue–Thu & Sat, 11:30am–midnight Fri. **&**

OCCUPYING A 19th-century row house, Jacob Wirth has been in business since 1868. It is Boston's second oldest restaurant after the Union Oyster House (see p134). When Rhineland-born restaurateur Jacob Wirth opened his restaurant, he had the majestic mahogany restaurant bar shipped in small pieces from Russia. Overall, the old-fashioned beer-hall, with its globe lighting, ceiling fans, dark paneling, bare wood floors, and brass railings, has barely changed since the time that it opened. Sausage-and-sauerkraut menu staples, combined with draft beers and Rhine wines, make this the only authentic German restaurant in a city that is far more famous for its Irish and Italian heritage.

Bay Village **10**

Bounded by Tremont, Arlington & South Charles Sts. **Map** 4 D2. **T** New England Medical Center, Boylston.

ORIGINALLY AN expanse of mud flats, the Bay Village area was drained in the early 1800s and initially became habitable with the construction of a dam in 1825. Many carpenters, cabinetmakers, artisans, and house painters involved in the construction of Beacon Hill's pricier town houses built their own modest but well-crafted residences here. As a result there are many similarities between the two neighborhoods, including plenty of red brick, arched doorways, window boxes and shutters, courtyards, tidy gardens, and antique gas lamps. Fayette Street was laid out in 1824 to coincide with the triumphant U.S. visit of the Marquis de Lafayette, the French general who allied himself with George Washington for some of the campaigns of the Revolutionary War.

Bay Street, located just off Fayette Street, features a single dwelling and is generally regarded as the city's

Bay Village doorway, similar to those of Beacon Hill

shortest street. In 1809, poet and short-story writer Edgar Allen Poe was born in a boarding house on Carver Street, where his thespian parents were staying while in Boston on tour with a traveling theatrical company.

In the 1920s, at the height of the Prohibition era, clandestine speakeasies gave Bay Village its still-prevalent bohemian ambience. More recently, the neighborhood has become a center for Boston's gay community.

Bay Village's Piedmont Street is noteworthy for two very different reasons. The W. S. Haynes Company at No. 12 has been hand-crafting flutes and piccolos since 1888, and has acquired a worldwide reputation for its instruments among soloists and symphony orchestra performers alike.

The street's other claim to faim is less auspicious. The Cocoanut Grove nightclub fire of 1942, when 491 of the club's patrons died, remains one of the United States' highest fire death tolls. This devastating occurrence resulted in infamy for the area but, ultimately, to more stringent fire-safety codes throughout the United States.

The vast Grand Lobby of the Wang Center for the Performing Arts

Shubert Theater ⓫

265 Tremont St. **Map** 4 E2.
📞 *(617) 482-9393.* Ⓣ *Boylston,
New England Medical Center.*
⭕ *phone to check.* ♿
ⓦ *www.boston.com/wangcenter*

THE 1,650-SEAT Shubert
Theater rivals the Colonial
Theater *(see p86)* for its long
history of staging major
pre-Broadway musical pro-
ductions. Designed by the
architects Charles Bond and

**Palladian-style window over the
entrance to the Shubert Theater**

Thomas James, the theater
first opened its doors in 1910,
and during its heyday many
famous stars walked the boards
here. Among them were
Sarah Bernhardt, W.C. Fields,
Cary Grant, Mae West,
Humphrey Bogart,
Ingrid Bergman,
Henry Ford, and
Rex Harrison.
The Shubert
Theater is listed on
the National Register
of Historic Places,
and features a white,
Neoclassical façade with
a pair of Ionic columns
flanking a monumental,
Palladian-style window that
sits over the entrance. The
entrance also boasts an ornate, wrought-iron canopy.
The theater closed for a
number of years but reopened in 1997 to premiere the
pre-Broadway hit *Rent*. The
Boston Ballet *(see p150)*
is now in residence for
repertory performances.
A plaque to the side of
the main entrance recounts
the history of the theater.

**Ornate, gilt
decoration at
the Wang**

Wang Center for the Performing Arts ⓬

270 Tremont St. **Map** 4 E2.
📞 *(617) 482-9393.* Ⓣ *Boylston,
New England Medical Center.*
⭕ *phone to check.* ♿
ⓦ *www.boston.com/wangcenter*

OPENED IN 1925 as the
Metropolitan Theater and
later named the Music Hall,
New England's most ornate
variety theater was inspired
by the Paris Opera House,
and was originally intended
to be a movie theater. Like
the nearby Colonial Theater,
the Metropolitan was de-
signed by Clarence Blackall,
working with a team of
associate architects. When it
was first built the auditorium
had over 4,000 seats, which
made it one of the largest
in the world. It was so big
that at its opening, which
over 20,000 people attended,
one Hollywood magnate
described it as a theater
of "mountainous splendour,
a movie palace of fabulous
grandeur and stupendous
stage presentations." Another
observer described it as a
"cathedral of the movies."
The theater was restored,
transformed and renamed as
the Wang Center for the Performing Arts in 1983.
The five-story Grand
Lobby and seven-
story auditorium
are designed in
Renaissance Re-
vival style: gold-plated
chandeliers, bronze
detailing, stained glass,
florid ceiling murals,
rose jasper pillars,
and marble-framed doorways.
There are also three lobbies,
which visitors must pass
through before finally
arriving at the Grand Lobby.
Today, the theater is used
primarily as a venue for
Broadway road shows,
Metropolitan Opera pro-
ductions visiting from New
York, celebrity concert
appearances, and motion-
picture revivals. It is also
the main performance venue
for the prestigious Boston
Ballet Company *(see p150)*.

The History of Boston's Theater District

BOSTON'S FIRST THEATER opened in 1793 on Federal Street. Fifty years later Boston had become a major tryout town and boasted a number of lavish theaters. The U.S. premiere of Handel's *Messiah* opened in 1839, the U.S. premiere of Gilbert and Sullivan's *H.M.S. Pinafore* in 1877, and the premiere of Tchaikovsky's *First Piano Concerto* in 1875. In the late 19th century theaters came under fire from the censorious Watch and Ward Society. Later, in the 20th century, dramas such as Tennessee Williams' *A Streetcar Named Desire* and Eugene O'Neill's *Long Day's Journey into Night* debuted here. Musicals included *Ziegfeld Follies*, Gershwin's *Porgy and Bess*, and works by Rodgers and Hammerstein.

South Pacific, Rodgers and Hammerstein

Theatergoers in 19th-century Boston came primarily from the city's social elite, who were often patrons of the arts. In this way Boston's theaters flourished.

The planned new theater remained in use until 1835. It became the Academy of Music from 1835 to 1846.

Old theater

Athena

Cupids

The Federal Street Theater, designed by Charles Bulfinch, burned down in 1798. The old and new theaters are depicted in this allegorical painting, possibly a set design, which also shows characters from Greek mythology. Other Bulfinch buildings are also shown.

Tennessee Williams' A Streetcar Named Desire *premiered at Boston's Wilbur Theater. It starred a young Marlon Brando and Jessica Tandy.*

Tell Me Little Gypsy

Ziegfeld Follies, *produced in the 1920s, had eight pre-Broadway "tryouts" at the Colonial Theater (see p86).*

The Rodgers and Hammerstein *musical* Oklahoma! *premiered in Boston as a production entitled* Away We Go! *It was refined in Boston before hitting Broadway.*

BACK BAY AND SOUTH END

UNTIL THE 19th century Boston was situated on a narrow peninsula surrounded by tidal marshes. Projects to fill Back Bay began in the 1850s and were made possible by new inventions such as the steam shovel. The Back Bay was filled by 1880 and developers soon moved in. Planned along French lines, with elegant boulevards, Back Bay is now one of Boston's most exclusive neighborhoods. The more bohemian South End, laid out on an English model of town houses clustered around squares, is home to many artists and Boston's gay community.

Sargent mural, Boston Public Library

SIGHTS AT A GLANCE

Historic Streets and Squares
Boylston Street **8**
Commonwealth Avenue **4**
Copley Place **14**
Copley Square **7**
The Esplanade **1**
Newbury Street **5**
Union Park **16**

Christian Science Center **13**
First Baptist Church **3**
Gibson House Museum **2**
Institute of Contemporary Art **11**
John Hancock Tower **10**
Prudential Center **12**
Trinity Church pp96–7 **6**

Historic Buildings, Churches, and Museums
Boston Center for the Arts **15**
Boston Public Library **9**

KEY

▧	Street-by-street map *pp92–3*
Ⓣ	"T" station
🚆	Railroad station
🚌	Bus station
ℹ	Tourist information
🅿	Parking

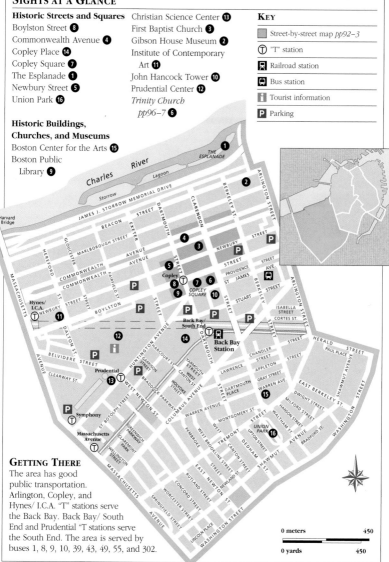

GETTING THERE
The area has good public transportation. Arlington, Copley, and Hynes/ I.C.A. "T" stations serve the Back Bay. Back Bay/ South End and Prudential "T stations serve the South End. The area is served by buses 1, 8, 9, 10, 39, 43, 49, 55, and 302.

| 0 meters | 450 |
| 0 yards | 450 |

◁ **View of Back Bay's characteristic row houses, from the top of the Prudential Center Skywalk observatory**

Street-by-Street: Back Bay

T HIS FASHIONABLE DISTRICT unfolds westward from the Public Garden *(see pp48–9)* in a grid that departs radically from the twisting streets found elsewhere in Boston. Commonwealth Avenue, with its grand 19th-century mansions and parkland, and Newbury and Boylston Streets are its main arteries. Newbury Street is a magnet for all of Boston wanting to indulge in some upscale shopping, whereas the more somber Boylston Street bustles with office workers. Copley Square anchors the entire area and is the site of Henry Hobson Richardson's magnificent Trinity Church *(see pp96–7)* and the 60-story John Hancock Tower *(see p99),* the tallest building in New England.

Weekly summer and fall farmers' market, Copley Square

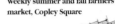

Copley Square
This square was a marsh until 1870. It took on its present form only in the late 20th century as buildings around its edges were completed. A farmers' market, concerts, and folk-dancing feature regularly ❼

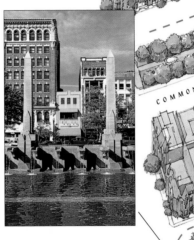

COMMONWEALTH AVEN

NEWB

Fenway Park

DARTMOUTH STREET

Boylston Street
The site of the Prudential Center (see p100) and the Institute of Contemporary Art (see p99), Boylston Street is also the location of the fabulous New Old South Church (see p98) ❽

★ **Boston Public Library**
One of the first free public libraries in the world, this building was designed by Charles McKim. Inside are murals by John Singer Sargent ❾

BOYLSTON STREET

South End

First Baptist Church
By Henry Hobson Richardson (see p94), this church is a fine example of his Romanesque Revival style ❸

Beacon Hill

LOCATOR MAP
See Street Finder map 3

BEACON HILL AND WEST END

BACK BAY AND SOUTH END

COMMONWEALTH AVENUE

CLARENDON STREET

TREET

Public Garden

Commonwealth Avenue
Envisioned as Boston's Champs-Elysées, this avenue boasts beautiful town houses and a tree-lined central mall ❹

★ Newbury Street
High fashion outlets, galleries, and restaurants characterize this street – Boston's most fashionable, and a great place for people-watching ❺

KEY

— — — Suggested route

STAR SIGHTS

★ Newbury Street

★ Trinity Church

★ Boston Public Library

★ Trinity Church
Acknowledged as Henry Hobson Richardson's Romanesque Revival masterpiece, this is one of the most important churches in the U.S. ❻

0 meters 50
0 yards 50

The Esplanade ❶

Map 1 A4. Ⓣ *Charles/ MGH.*
🅞 *24 hrs daily.* 🅖 🅦 www.ci.boston.
ma.us/parks/openspaces

RUNNING ALONG the Boston side of the Charles River, between Longfellow Bridge and Dartmouth Street, are the parkland, lagoons, and islands known collectively as the Esplanade. While the park is used most extensively for in-line skating, cycling, and strolling, it is also the main access point for boating on the river, and is the site of the city's leading outdoor concert venue.

In 1929, Arthur Fiedler, then the young conductor of the Boston Pops Orchestra, chose the Esplanade for a summer concert series that became a tradition. The Hatch Memorial Shell was constructed in 1939, and its stage is widely used by musical ensembles and other groups throughout the summer. Fourth of July concerts by the Boston Pops, which are followed by fireworks, can attract upward of 500,000 spectators *(see p37)*.

Fountains at the Esplanade, next to the Charles River

Gibson House Museum ❷

137 Beacon St. **Map** 1 A4.
📞 *(617) 267-6338.* Ⓣ *Arlington.*
🅞 *obligatory tours at 1pm, 2pm, 3pm Wed–Sun.* 🗺 🚫 🎥
🅦 www.gibsonhouse.org

AMONG THE FIRST houses built in the Back Bay, the Gibson House preserves its original Victorian decor and furnishings throughout all six stories. The 1860 brownstone and red-brick structure was

The original Victorian-style library of the Gibson House Museum

designed in the popular Italian Renaissance Revival style for the widow Catherine Hammond Gibson, who was one of the few women to own property in this part of the city. Her grandson Charles Hammond Gibson, Jr., a noted eccentric, poet, travel writer, horticulturalist, and bon vivant, arranged for the house to become a museum after his death in 1954. As a prelude to this, Gibson began to rope off the furniture in the 1930s, instead inviting his guests to sit on the stairs to drink martinis made with his own bathtub gin.

One of the most modern houses of its day, the Gibson House boasted such technical advancements as gas lighting, indoor plumbing in the basement, and coal-fired central heating. Visitors can see a full dinner setting in the dining room or admire the whimsical Turkish pet pavilion. But it is Gibson's preservation of the 1860s decor (with some modifications in 1888) that makes the museum a true time capsule of Victorian life in Boston.

Detail of Bartholdi's frieze atop the distinctive square tower of the First Baptist Church

First Baptist Church ❸

110 Commonwealth Ave. **Map** 3 C2.
📞 *(617) 267-3148.* Ⓣ *Arlington.*
🅞 *for Sunday worship.* ✝ *11am Sun.* 🚫 🅖

THE ROMANESQUE-STYLE First Baptist Church on the corner of Commonwealth Avenue and Clarendon Street was Henry Hobson Richardson's *(see p30)* first major architectural commission and became an instant landmark when it was finished in 1872. Viewed from Commonwealth Avenue, it is one of the most distinctive buildings of the city skyline.

Richardson considered the nearly freestanding bell tower, which he modeled roughly on Italian campaniles, to be the church's most innovative structure. The square tower is topped with a decorative frieze and arches protected by an overhanging roof. The frieze was modeled in Paris by Bartholdi, the sculptor who created the Statue of Liberty, and was carved in place by Italian artisans after the stones were set. The faces in the frieze, which depict the sacraments, are likenesses of prominent Bostonians of that time, among them Henry Wadsworth Longfellow and Ralph Waldo Emerson *(see p29)*. The trumpeting angels at the corners of the tower gave the building its nickname, "Church of the Holy Bean Blowers."

Four years after the church was completed, the Unitarian congregation dissolved because it was unable to bear the expense of the building. The church stood vacant until 1881, when the First Baptist congregation from the South End took it over.

Commonwealth Avenue ❹

Map 3 B2. ⓣ *Arlington, Copley, Hynes Convention Center/ ICA.*

BACK BAY was Boston's first fully planned neighborhood, and architect Arthur Gilman made Commonwealth Avenue, modeled on the elegant boulevards of Paris, the centerpiece of the design. At 200 ft (61 m) wide, with a 10ft (3 m) setback from the sidewalks to encourage small gardens in front of the buildings, Commonwealth became an arena for America's leading domestic architects in the second half of the 19th century. A walk from the Public Garden to Massachusetts Avenue is like flicking through a catalog of architectural styles.

Few of the grand buildings on either side of the avenue are open to the public, although the Boston Center

for Adult Education at No. 5 can be toured by appointment. The mansion, built in 1912 in Italianate style, was a late addition to Back Bay. Textile industrialist owner Walter C. Baylies later added a ballroom modeled on the Petit Trianon in Versailles, just outside Paris.

A statue of the fervent abolitionist William Garrison (1805– 79) stands on Commonwealth Avenue's central mall.

William Garrison statue on Commonwealth Avenue

🏛 Center for Adult Education
5 Commonwealth Ave.
📞 *(617) 267-4430.* 🕐 *9am–7pm Mon–Thu, 9am–5pm Fri.*
● *May 11.* 🚫 ♿ 🛒
Ⓦ *www.bcae.org*

Newbury Street ❺

Map 3 C2. ⓣ *Arlington, Copley, Hynes Convention Center/ ICA.*

NEWBURY STREET is a Boston synonym for "stylish." The elegant Ritz-Carlton Hotel on the corner with Arlington Street sets an elegant tone for the street that continues with a mix of prestigious and often

well-hidden art galleries, stylish boutiques, and some of the city's most *au courant* restaurants.

Churches provide vestiges of a more decorous era. The Church of the Covenant at No. 67 Newbury contains the world's largest collection of Louis Comfort Tiffany stained-glass windows and an elaborate Tiffany lantern. A chorus and orchestra perform a Bach cantata each Sunday at Emmanuel Church on the corner of Newbury and Berkeley Streets.

The Newbury Street Mural at the corner of Newbury and Dartmouth highlights the street's role as a place to be seen. It depicts 72 of the famous and not so famous, from Sam Adams to Tom Yawkey, who owned the Boston Red Sox for 44 years. Modern-day aspiring celebrities may be spotted at the sidewalk tables of Newbury's "hottest" restaurants, such as Sonsie *(see p137).*

⛪ Church of the Covenant
67 Newbury St. 📞 *(617) 266-7480.* 🕐 *10am daily for church service.*
🚫 ♿ 🛒 🛍
Ⓦ *www.churchofthecovenant.org*

Stylish Newbury Street, with its elegant shops, galleries, and restaurants, the epitome of Boston style

Trinity Church ❻

Routinely voted one of America's 10 finest buildings, this masterpiece by Henry Hobson Richardson dates from 1877. Trinity Church was founded in 1733 near Downtown Crossing, but the congregation moved the church to this site in 1871. The church is a granite and sandstone Romanesque structure standing on wooden piles driven through mud into bedrock, surmounted with granite pyramids. John LaFarge designed the interior, while some of the windows are designed by Edward Burne-Jones and executed by William Morris.

The Bell Tower
was inspired by the Renaissance cathedral at Salamanca, central Spain.

Bas-relief in Chancel
On the wall of the chancel, behind the altar, are a series of gold bas-reliefs. This one shows St. Paul before King Agrippa.

★ **North Transept Windows**
Designed by Edward Burne-Jones and executed by William Morris, the three stained-glass windows above the choir relate the story of Christmas.

Parish House

The Pulpit is covered with carved scenes from the life of Christ, as well as portraits of great preachers through the ages.

Chancel
Designed by Charles Maginnis, the present-day chancel was not dedicated until 1938. The seven windows by Clayton & Bell, of London, show the life of Christ.

David's Charge to Solomon
Located in the baptistry, to the right of the chancel, this beautiful window is also the result of a partnership between Edward Burne-Jones and William Morris. The story shown is one of the few in the church from the Old Testament.

John LaFarge's lancet windows show Christ in the act of blessing. They were designed at the request of Phillips Brooks – he wanted LaFarge to create an inspirational design for the west nave, which he could look at while preaching.

★ **West Portico**
Richardson disliked the original flat façade of Trinity Church, and so modeled the deeply sculpted west portico after St. Trophime in Arles, France. It was added after his death.

Carving of Phillips Brooks and Christ

PHILLIPS BROOKS

Born in Boston in 1835 and educated at Harvard, Brooks was a towering charismatic figure. Rector of Trinity Church from 1869, he gained a reputation for powerful sermons. From 1872 Brooks worked closely with Henry Hobson Richardson on the design of the new Trinity Church – at least five sculpted likenesses of him can be seen in and around the building.

STAR SIGHTS

★ **West Portico**

★ **North Transept Windows**

Main Entrance

**The New Old South Church,
which looks across Copley Square**

Copley Square ❼

Map 3 C2. ⓣ *Copley.*

N AMED AFTER John Singleton Copley, the great Boston painter born nearby in 1737, Copley Square is a hive of civic activity surrounded by some of Boston's most striking architecture. Summer activities include weekly farmers' markets, concerts, and even folk-dancing.

The inviting green plaza took years to develop; when Copley was born it was just a marshy riverbank, which remained unfilled until 1870. Construction of the John Hancock Tower in 1975 anchored the southeastern side of Copley Square, and Copley Place *(see p101)* completed the square on the southwestern corner in 1984. Today's Copley Square, a wide open space of trees, grass, and fountains, took shape in the heart of the city in the 1990s, after various plans to utilize this hitherto wasted space were tendered.

A large plaque honoring the Boston Marathon, which ends at the Boston Public Library, was set in the sidewalk in 1996 to coincide with the 100th race. As well as pushcart vendors, the plaza has a booth for discounted theater, music, and dance tickets.

Boylston Street ❽

Map 3 C2. ⓣ *Boylston, Arlington, Copley, Hynes Convention Center/ ICA.*

A BRASS TEDDY BEAR sculpture, outside F.A.O. Schwarz, is one of Boylston Street's principal landmarks. It is a reproduction of the toy company's famous New York Fifth Avenue symbol. The French Academic-style building at the corner of Boylston and Berkeley Streets was originally built for the Museum of Natural History, which was the forerunner of the Museum of Science *(see p55)*. Its present occupant is the upscale clothier Louis. The Art Deco building at the corner of Arlington and Boylston Streets houses Shreve, Crump & Low, Inc., well known as Boston's finest jewelers.

Some notable office buildings stand on Boylston Street. The lobby of the New England building at No. 501 features large historical murals and dioramas depicting the process of filling Back Bay during the late 19th century. The towers of the Prudential Center *(see p100)* dominate the skyline on upper Boylston Street. Adjoining

the Prudential is the Hynes Convention Center. It was enlarged in 1988 to accommodate the city's burgeoning convention business.

The Italian Gothic-style **New Old South Church**, at the corner of Dartmouth and Boylston Streets, was built in 1874–5 by the congregation that had met previously at the Old South Meeting House *(see p61)*.

🔼 **New Old South Church**
645 Boylston St. **Map** 3 C2.
📞 *(617) 536-1970.*
⏲ *8am–7pm daily* 🔼 *11am Sun.*
🚫 ♿ 🔽 🔂
🅦 www.oldsouth.org

Boston Public Library ❾

Copley Square. **Map** 3 C2.
📞 *(617) 536-5400.* ⓣ *Copley.*
⏲ *Apr–Sep: 9am–9pm Mon–Thu, 9am–5pm Fri–Sat; Oct–May: 9am–9pm Mon–Thu, 9am–5pm Fri–Sat, 1pm–5pm Sun.* ● *public hols.* ♿
🔂 🔂 🅦 www.bpl.org

F OUNDED IN 1848, the Boston Public Library was America's first metropolitan library for the public. It quickly outgrew its original building, hence the construction of the Italian *palazzo*-style Copley Square building in 1887–95, with "Free to All" emblazoned above the entrance. The architect Charles McKim drew on the highly skilled force of mostly Italian construction workers and artisans who had come to Boston to build mansions in the Back Bay and South End. Sculptor Daniel Chester French, best known for the Lincoln Memorial in Washington DC, fashioned the huge bronze doors that represent Music and Poetry, Knowledge and Wisdom, and Truth and Romance. French painter Puvis de Chavannes executed the murals that wind up the staircase and along the second-floor

**The vast Bates Hall in the Boston Public Library,
noted for its high barrel-vaulted ceiling**

corridor. Edward Abbey's Pre-Raphaelite murals of the Quest for the Holy Grail line the book request room, and John Singer Sargent's murals of Judaism and Christianity cover a third-floor gallery.

The McKim building, largely restored for its 1995 centennial, is a marvel of fine wood and marble detail. Bates Hall, on the second floor, is particularly noted for the soaring barrel-vaulted ceiling that terminates in coffered apses.

The library's circulating collection is housed in the 1971 Boylston Street addition, a modernist structure by architect Philip Johnson.

John Hancock Tower ⑩

200 Clarendon St. **Map** 3 C2.
Ⓣ *Copley.* ● *to the public.*

THE TALLEST BUILDING in New England, the 740-ft (226-m) rhomboid that is the John Hancock Tower cuts into Copley Square with its slimmest edge, its mirrored façade reflecting the surroundings and sky. The innovative design has created a 60-story office building that shares the square with its neighbors, the Romanesque Trinity Church and the Italian Renaissance Revival Copley Plaza Hotel, without dwarfing them. When the tower was under construction, 65 windows, each weighing 500lb (1,100 kg), came crashing to the ground. All 10,344 panes were replaced at a cost of almost $7 million before the building could be occupied in 1975.

Designed by Henry Cobb of I.M. Pei & Partners, the magnificent building inspired Massachusetts author John Updike to observe: "All art, all beauty, is reflection". From one angle viewers can see the reflections of Trinity Church and the original (1947) Hancock Building, topped by a weather beacon.

The observatory on the 60th floor of the tower closed for safety reasons following the tragic events in September 2001 at the World Trade Center in New York.

View over Back Bay and the Charles River

Institute of Contemporary Art ⑪

955 Boylston St. **Map** 3 A3.
Ⓒ *(617) 266-5152.* Ⓣ *Hynes Convention Center/ ICA.* ● *noon–5pm Wed & Fri, noon–9pm Thu, 11am–5pm Sat & Sun.* ● *public hols.* 🏛 🚻 📷
Ⓦ www.icaboston.org

THIS RICHARDSONIAN Romanesque brick-and-stone building, with its next-door twin still serving as a fire station, was renovated in 1975 under the direction of leading Boston architect Graham Gund. Its new function was to house the Institute of Contemporary Art, which, initially founded in 1936, is one of the oldest non-collecting art organizations in the U.S. The result is an extremely nontraditional institution juxtaposed against a traditional shell. Although the I.C.A. is not strictly a museum – it does not have a permanent collection – the interior is renowned in its own right for its open design with multilevel gallery spaces. And, because there is no formal collection, the I.C.A. is able to mount cutting-edge art exhibitions that reflect the latest innovations of the contemporary art world.

Apart from paintings and sculpture, the institute is notably sympathetic to video and multimedia art. One of the I.C.A.'s curatorial strengths has been its broadly international vision as it has forged an identity apart from the New York art scene. Frequent gallery talks and videotaped interviews with artists help to explain the exhibits.

Richardsonian Romanesque-style façade of the Institute of Contemporary Art

Prudential Center

800 Boylston St. **Map** 3 B3.
▐ *(617) 859-0648.* **Ⓣ** *Prudential,*
Hynes Convention Center/ ICA.
Skywalk ◻ *10am–10pm daily.* ●
Thanksgiving, Dec 25. 🎨 ⬤ ♩

WHEN IT WAS erected in
1965, the Prudential
Tower was the first skyscraper
in the Back Bay, rising 52
floors. Office buildings and a
shopping center now girdle
its base, and the "Pru" is
linked through indoor
walkways with the Hynes
Convention Center and the
Sheraton Back Bay Hotel
in one unified complex.
An enclosed walkway even
links its shops to the more

**Prudential Tower viewed across the
Christian Science reflecting pool**

Inside the beautiful, stained-glass Mapparium, Christian Science Center

glamorous Copley Place
across busy Huntington
Avenue. Apart from the shops
and food courts, the principal
attraction of the "Pru" is the
Skywalk on the 50th floor.
The Skywalk is the only 360-
degree aerial observatory in
Boston, and its location near
the top of Boylston Street hill
provides striking views of the
Emerald Necklace *(see p105)*
as well as downtown and the
waterfront. Signs on the
windows assist in identifying
the landmarks below. A
similar view, which visitors
do not need to pay for, is
available at the Top of the
Hub restaurant on the 52nd
floor. Some of the bar windows here face west, so
those having a drink can
enjoy spectacular sunset
views over Boston.

Christian Science Center ⓭

175 Huntington Ave. **Map** 3 B3.
▐ *(617) 450-3790.* **Ⓣ** *Symphony.*
Mother Church ◻ *10am–4pm*
Mon–Sat, 11:30am–1pm Sun.
Mapparium ◻ *10am–4pm Mon–*
Sat. 🔼 *Jul–Aug: 10am Sun, 12pm*
Wed; Sep–Jun: 10am Sun, 12pm
Wed, 7pm Wed. ⬤ 🖋
W *www.marybakereddylibrary.org*

THE WORLD HEADQUARTERS of
the First Church of Christ,
Scientist, occupies 14 acres on
the corner of Huntington and
Massachusetts Avenues. Known
also as the Christian Science
Church, this religious body
was formed in 1879 by Mary
Baker Eddy. The granite,
Romanesque-style Mother
Church dates from 1894, but
it serves only as a chapel at
the rear of a grander basilica,
which was built in 1906 to
seat 5,000 worshipers. The
basilica houses the western
hemisphere's largest pipe organ, manufactured in Boston
by the Aeolian-Skinner Company. From 1968 to 1973 the
Christian Science complex
expanded to its present
design, with an elegant office
tower, reflecting pool, and
monumental plaza. The New
Library for the Betterment of
Humanity on the Massa-
chusetts Avenue side of the
complex is home to one of
Boston's most unusual
attractions, the Mapparium.
This huge stained-glass
globe, constructed from 1932
to 1934, represents the worldwide activities of Christian
Science. Visitors literally

MARY BAKER EDDY

Born in Concord, New Hampshire in 1821, Mary Baker
was plagued with poor health for much of her early life.
Fearing death after a severe fall in 1866, she sought
comfort in her Bible, where she found an account of
how Jesus had healed a palsied man. Her own miraculous
recovery led her to the principle of Christian Science, a
doctrine which emphasizes spiritual regeneration and
healing through prayer alone. In 1875 she published her
ideas in *Science and Health with Key to the Scriptures*,
the textbook of Christian Science, and
gathered students around her, including Asa Gilbert Eddy, whom she
married in 1877. Two years later
she organized the First Church of
Christ, Scientist, in Boston, from
which Christian Science churches
spread across the world. Mrs. Eddy
remained the active leader of the
Christian Science movement until
her death in 1910. She is buried at
Mount Auburn Cemetery in Cambridge.

walk through the center of the globe viewing the planet from the inside. The colored land areas represent the world political boundaries as they were in the early 1930s.

Copley Place

Huntington Ave & Dartmouth St.
Map 3 C3. Ⓣ *Back Bay/ South End, Copley.* ☐ *8am–11pm daily.* &

COPLEY PLACE is a creature of late 20th-century urban development, with hotels and an upscale shopping center with a nine-screen cinema. Offices and luxury apartments are also part of the development, which rises on land created above the Massachusetts Turnpike. Copley Place bears little relation to Copley Square, but the shopping mall was a success from the day it opened in 1984 and still ranks as Boston's most luxurious indoor shopping mall. Its stores include the jeweler Tiffany's and the status-conscious department store Nieman-Marcus *(see p143)*.

Boston Center for the Arts ⑮

539 Tremont St. **Map** 4 D3.
Ⓒ *(617) 426-5000.* Ⓣ *Back Bay/ South End.* **Cyclorama** ☐ *9am–5pm Mon–Fri.* **Mills Gallery**
☐ *1–4pm Sun–Wed, 7–10pm Thu–Sat.* ● *public hols.* ☒ *for performances.* ∅ &
Ⓦ *www.bcaonline.org*

THE CENTERPIECE of a resurgent South End, the BCA complex includes three theaters, an art gallery, and artists' studios as well as the Boston Ballet Building, home to the company's educational programs, rehearsal space, and administrative offices.

The Tremont Estates Building at the corner of Tremont Street, an organ factory in the years after the Civil War, now houses artists' studios, rehearsal space, and an art gallery.

The largest of the BCA buildings is the circular, domed Cyclorama, which opened in

Bow-fronted, red-brick houses, typical of South End's Union Park

1884 to exhibit the 50-ft (15-m) by 400-ft (121-m) painting *The Battle of Gettysburg* by the French artist Paul Philippoteaux. The painting was removed in 1889 and is now displayed at Gettysburg National Historic Park. For many years, the Cyclorama was Boston's leading venue for indoor spectacles, especially prize fights, and was also the city's wholesale flower market. Today it is a challenging performance and exhibition space.

The Mills Gallery houses exhibitions focusing on emerging contemporary artists, with the emphasis on multimedia installations and shows with confrontational, often provocative, themes.

Union Park ⑯

Tremont & Shawmut Sts. **Map** 4 D4.
Ⓣ *Back Bay/ South End.* &

UNION PARK is the green gem of the South End, built from 1857 to 1859 when the neighborhood was still fashionable. South End property values crashed in the Panic of 1873, and the entire district, Union Park included, became tenement housing for immigrants arriving from eastern Europe and the Middle East. The South End remains broadly mixed by ethnicity, race, and sexual orientation. The handsome town houses along Union Park led the South End's economic resurgence in the 1970s, and it has become, once again, a coveted address. A pair of fountains, an iron fence, and large shade trees present a truly parklike setting for the beautifully restored brick row houses. The 19th-century ornamental ironwork on and around these houses is particularly prized by architecture buffs. Union Park is strictly residential, although there are a few small shops, and restaurants which have become very popular for Saturday and Sunday brunch.

Red-brick façade of the Boston Center for the Arts, site of theaters and exhibition spaces

Farther Afield

The late 19th and 20th centuries saw Boston expand out of the central colonial and Victorian city into the surrounding area. The old marshlands of the Fenway now house two of Boston's most important art museums, the Museum of Fine Arts and the Isabella Stewart Gardner Museum. Southeast of the city center, Columbia point was developed in the mid-20th century and is home to the John F. Kennedy Library and Museum. West of central Boston, across the Charles River, lies Cambridge, sometimes referred to as the "Socialist Democratic Republic of Cambridge," a reference to the politics of Harvard and the Massachusetts Institute of Technology, its two major colleges. Harvard Square is a lively area of bookstores, cafés, and street entertainers. Charlestown is the site of the Bunker Hill Monument and the Charlestown Navy Yard, where the U.S.'s most famous warship, the *U.S.S. Constitution*, is moored. Farther northwest lie historic Concord and Lexington, where the first major battle of the Revolutionary War took place in 1775.

Statue of William Prescott, Bunker Hill Monument

Sights at a Glance

Towns
Cambridge **7**
Charlestown **8**
Concord and
   Lexington **9**

Museums and Historic Sites
Isabella Stewart Gardner
   Museum **5**

John F. Kennedy Library
   and Museum **1**
John F. Kennedy National
   Historic Site **4**
*Museum of Fine Arts
   pp106–9* **6**

Gardens and Zoos
Arnold Arboretum **3**
Franklin Park Zoo **2**

Key

	Main sightseeing area
	Urban area
✈	Airport
🚊	Railroad station
▬	Highway
▬	Major road
=	Minor road
—	Railroad

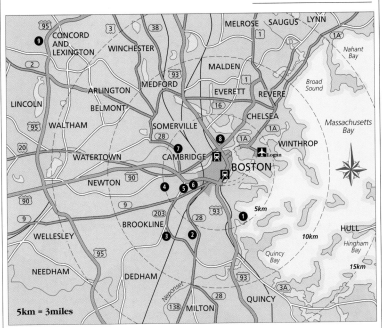

5km = 3miles

◁ **Central courtyard of the *palazzo*-style Isabella Stewart Gardner Museum**

John F. Kennedy Library and Museum ❶

Columbia Point, Dorchester.
📞 (617) 929-4523. Ⓣ JFK/ U Mass.
🕐 9–5 daily. ⬤ Jan 1, Thanksgiving,
Dec 25. 📷 ♿ ✓ 🎧
🌐 www.jfklibrary.org

THE SOARING WHITE concrete and glass building housing the John F. Kennedy Library stands sentinel on Columbia Point near the mouth of the Boston Harbor. This striking white and black modern building by the architect I. M. Pei is equally dramatic from the interior, with a 50-ft (15-m) wall of glass looking out over the sea. Exhibitions extensively chronicle the 1,000 days of the Kennedy presidency with an immediacy uncommon in many other historical museums. Kennedy was among the first politicians to grasp the power of media. The museum takes full advantage of film and video footage to use the president's own words and image to tell his story: his campaign for the Democratic Party nomination, landmark television debates with Republican opponent Richard M. Nixon (who later became infamous for the Watergate Scandal), and his many addresses to the nation.

Several rooms re-create key chambers of the White House during the Kennedy administration, including the Oval Office, and gripping film clips capture the anxiety of nuclear brinksmanship during the Cuban missile crisis as well as the inspirational spirit of the space program and the founding of the Peace Corps. Recently expanded exhibits on Robert F. Kennedy's role as Attorney General touch on both his deft handling of race relations and his key advisory role to his brother. The combination of artifacts, displays, and television footage evoke both the euphoria of "Camelot" and the numb horror of the assassination.

Lowland gorilla with her baby in the simulated natural environment of Franklin Park Zoo

Franklin Park Zoo ❷

1 Franklin Park Rd. 📞 (617) 541-5466. Ⓣ Forest Hills. 🚌 16 from Forest Hills subway. 🕐 Apr–Sep: 10am–5pm Mon–Fri, 10am–6pm Sat–Sun; Oct–Mar: 10am–4pm daily. ⬤ Jan 1, Thanksgiving, Dec 25. 📷 ♿ 🌐 www.zoonewengland.com

THE ZOO, originally planned as a small menagerie, has expanded dramatically over the past century and long ago discarded caged enclosures in favor of simulated natural environments. Lowland gorillas roam a forest edge with caves for privacy, lions lounge around a rocky kingdom while zebras, ostriches, and giraffes are free to graze on open grassland. The Butterfly Landing is a dense garden within a large hooped enclosure where as many as 1,000 butterflies flit from flower to flower, especially on a warm afternoon. New Age and light classical music augment the sense of fantasy. In the small petting zoo youngsters can meet farm animals.

Arnold Arboretum ❸

125 Arborway, Jamaica Plain.
📞 (617) 524-1718. Ⓣ Forest Hills.
🚌 39. 🕐 sunrise–sunset daily.
Visitors Center 🕐 10am–4pm
Mon–Fri, noon–4pm Sat–Sun. ⬤
public hols. ♿ 🌐 www.arboretum.
harvard.edu

FOUNDED BY Harvard University in 1872 as a living catalog of all the indigenous and exotic trees and shrubs adaptable to New England's climate, the

Dramatic, modern structure of the John F. Kennedy Library and Museum

Arboretum is planted with more than 15,000 labeled specimens. It is the oldest arboretum in the U.S. and a key resource for botanical and horticultural research. The Arboretum also serves as a park where people jog, stroll, picnic, and paint.

The park's busiest time is on the third Sunday in May – Lilac Sunday – when tens of thousands come to revel in the sight and fragrance of the lilac collection, one of the largest in the world. The range of the Arboretum's collections guarantees flowers from late March into November, beginning with cornelian cherry and forsythia. Blooms shift in late May to azalea, magnolia, and wisteria, then to mountain laurel and roses in June. Sweet autumn clematis bursts forth in September, and native witch hazel blooms in October and November. The Arboretum also has fine fall foliage in September and October.

A large scale model of the Arboretum can be seen in the Visitors' Information Center just inside the main gate.

John F. Kennedy National Historic Site ❹

83 Beal St, Brookline. 【 (617) 566-7937. ⓣ Coolidge Corner.
◯ Apr–mid-Nov: 10am–4:30pm Wed–Sun. ● Thanksgiving. 🎫 Ⓕ
🅱 🅲 🆆 www.nps.gov/jofi

The FIRST HOME of the late president's parents, this Brookline house saw the birth of four of nine Kennedy children, including J.F.K. on May 29, 1917. Although the Kennedys moved to a larger house in 1921, the Beal Street residence held special memories for the family, who repurchased the house in 1966 and furnished it with their belongings circa 1917 as a memorial to John F. Kennedy. The guided tour includes a taped interview of J.F.K.'s mother Rose. A walking tour takes in other neighborhood sites relevant to the Kennedy family's early years.

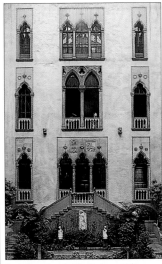
Central courtyard of the *palazzo*-style Isabella Stewart Gardner Museum

Isabella Stewart Gardner Museum ❺

280 The Fenway. 【 (617) 566-1401.
ⓣ MFA. ◯ 11am–5pm Tue–Sun.
● Jan 1, Thanksgiving, Dec 25.
🎫 Ⓕ 🅲
🆆 www.gardnermuseum.org

The ONLY THING more surprising than a Venetian *palazzo* on The Fenway is the collection of more than 2,500 works of art inside. Advised by scholar Bernard Berenson,

the strong-willed Isabella Stewart Gardner turned her wealth to collecting art in the late 19th century, acquiring a notable collection of Old Masters and Italian Renaissance pieces. Titian's *Rape of Europa*, for example, is considered his best painting in a U.S. museum. The eccentric "Mrs. Jack" had an eye for her contemporaries as well. She purchased the first Matisse to enter an American collection and was an ardent patron of James McNeill Whistler and John Singer Sargent. The paintings, sculptures, and tapestries are displayed on three levels around a stunning skylit courtyard. Mrs. Gardner's will, which was instrumental in the setting up of the museum, stipulates the collection should remain assembled in the manner that she originally intended. Unfortunately, her intentions could not be upheld; in 1990 thieves made off with 13 of these priceless works, including a rare Rembrandt seascape, *Storm on the Sea of Galilee*, then conservatively valued in the region of $200 million.

THE EMERALD NECKLACE

Best known as designer of New York's Central Park, Frederick Law Olmsted based himself in Boston, where he created parks to solve environmental problems and provide a green refuge for inhabitants of the 19th-century industrial city. The Emerald Necklace includes the green spaces of Boston Common and the Public Garden *(see pp48–9)* and Commonwealth Avenue *(see p95)*. To create a ring of parks, Olmsted added the Back Bay Fens

Jamaica Pond, part of Boston's fine parklands

(site of beautiful rose gardens and gateway to the Museum of Fine Arts and the Isabella Stewart Gardner Museum), the rustic Riverway, Jamaica Pond (sailing and picnicking), Arnold Arboretum, and Franklin Park (a golf course, zoo, and cross-country ski trails). The 5-mile (8-km) swath of parkland makes an excellent bicycle tour or ambitious walk.

The Museum of Fine Arts ❻

THIS MUSEUM OPENED IN 1876 on Copley Square and moved to its present location in the Fenway in 1909. It is the largest art museum in New England and one of the five largest in the United States, with a permanent collection of approximately 500,000 objects, ranging from Egyptian artifacts to paintings by John Singer Sargent. The original Classical-style building was augmented in 1981 by the addition of the West Wing, designed by I. M. Pei.

★ **Japanese Temple Room**
This room was created in 1909 to provide a space in which to contemplate Buddhist art. The M.F.A. has one of the finest Japanese collections outside Japan.

American Silver
The revolutionary Paul Revere (see p19) was also a noted silversmith and produced many beautiful objects, such as this ornate teapot.

First floor

Entrance

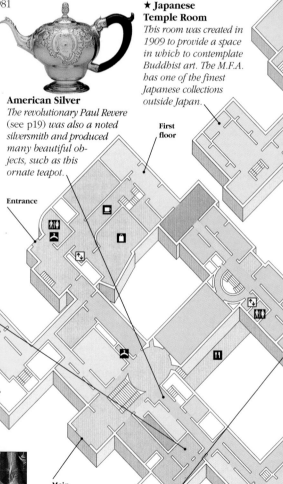

★Egyptian Mummies
Among the museum's Egyptian and Nubian art are these coffins of Nesmut-aat-neru (700–675 BC) of Thebes.

Main Entrance

★ **Copley Portraits**
John Singleton Copley (1738–1815) painted the celebrities of his day, hence this portrait of a dandyish John Hancock (see p19).

A two-headed amphora from Athens (530–520 BC) is among the Classical Greek artifacts.

★ Impressionist Paintings
Boston collectors were among the first to appreciate French Impressionism. La Japonaise (1876) by Monet is typical of the M.F.A. collection.

VISITORS' CHECKLIST

Avenue of the Arts, 465 Huntington Ave. 🄲 *(617) 267-9300.* Ⓣ *MFA.* ◯ *10am–4:45pm Mon–Tue, 10am–9:45pm Wed–Fri (West Wing: only Thu & Fri), 10am–5:45pm Sat–Sun.* ◯ *Thanksgiving, Dec 25.* 📷 ♿ 📷 🄰 ***Lectures, concerts, and films.*** 🍴 🔲 🄰 ⓦ *www.mfa.org*

KEY

▢ Art of Africa, Oceania, and the Ancient Americas

▢ American paintings, decorative arts, and sculpture

▢ Ancient Egyptian, Nubian, and Near Eastern art

▢ Asian art

▢ Classical art

▢ Contemporary art

▢ European paintings, decorative arts, and sculpture

▢ Musical instruments

▢ Works on paper

▢ Special/temporary exhibitions

▢ Nonexhibition space

Second floor

Medieval frescoes and French silverware feature among the exhibits of European decorative art.

Sargent Murals
John Singer Sargent spent the last years of his life creating these murals for the M.F.A.'s domed rotunda.

Court level

GALLERY GUIDE
Classical, Far Eastern, and Egyptian artifacts can be seen on both floors of the museum. American decorative arts and painting are on the first floor, while European decorative arts and paintings are on the second.

Ram's Head
Once part of a much larger statue, this marble Greek ram's head dates from the 4th century BC.

STAR EXHIBITS

★ Copley Portraits

★ Impressionist Paintings

★ Egyptian Mummies

★ Japanese Temple Room

Exploring the Museum of Fine Arts

IN ADDITION TO THE major collections noted below, the Museum of Fine Arts has important holdings in the arts of Africa, Oceania, and the ancient Americas. The museum also houses collections of works on paper, contemporary art, and musical instruments. Several galleries, large and small, are devoted to temporary thematic exhibitions. The modern West Wing of the museum houses a seminar room, lecture hall, and well-stocked bookstore. An important research center, the museum has played a major role in the excavation of artifacts around the world.

11th-century, silver Korean ewer

Boston Harbor by the Luminist painter Fitz Hugh Lane (1804–65)

AMERICAN PAINTINGS, DECORATIVE ARTS, AND SCULPTURE

THE AMERICAN PAINTING galleries on the first floor begin with the Colonial portrait gallery. The M.F.A. owns more than 60 portraits by John Singleton Copley, perhaps America's most talented 18th-century painter, as well as works by Gilbert Stuart and Charles Willson Peale. The next gallery houses 19th-century landscapes, including harbor scenes by Fitz Hugh Lane, an early Luminist painter. Farther on are the lush society portraits of John Singer Sargent, and those of other late 19th-century artists who constituted the "Boston School." There are also notable seascapes by Winslow Homer, who often painted on the Massachusetts coast, as well as the muscular figure portraiture of Thomas Eakins. The large and airy Lane Gallery of Modern Painting

and Sculpture presents a sampling of works by 20th-century masters including Stuart Davis, Jackson Pollock, Georgia O'Keeffe, and Arthur Dove.

A corridor gallery of American silver leads from the first-floor rotunda eastward to the American decorative arts galleries. Two cases contain tea services and other pieces by Paul Revere (see p75). The next gallery traces the development of the Boston style of 18th-century furniture through a definitive collection of desks, high chests, and tall clocks. The reconstructed Oak Hill dining room, parlor, and bedroom from an early 19th-century mansion evoke the well-to-do lifestyle of the Federal era. Earlier period rooms are found on the Court Level, along with a gallery of ship models and an outstanding collection of contemporary crafts.

EUROPEAN PAINTINGS, DECORATIVE ARTS, AND SCULPTURE

EUROPEAN PAINTINGS and sculpture from the 16th to the 20th centuries are on the second floor of the museum. They begin with 17th-century Dutch paintings, including a number of portraits by Rembrandt. The Koch Gallery of European Paintings from 1550 to 1700 is impressive both for the drama of the space – a great hall with travertine marble walls and high, wooden coffered ceiling – and for the range of art works, which ranges from Francisco de Zurbarán and El Greco to Paolo Veronese, Titian, and Peter Paul Rubens.

Boston's 19th-century collectors enriched the M.F.A. with wonderful French painting: the museum features several paintings by Pierre François Millet (the M.F.A. has, in fact, the largest collection of his work in the world) as well as by other well-known 19th-century French artists, such as Edouard Manet, Pierre-Auguste Renoir, and Edgar Degas. One of the museum's most popular galleries displays *La Japonaise* (1876) by Claude Monet and *Dance at Bougival* (1883) by Renoir. The M.F.A.'s Monet holdings are unsurpassed outside of Paris, and there is also a good collection of paintings by the

La Berceuse by the Dutch painter Vincent van Gogh (1853–90)

Part of the Processional Way of Ancient Babylonia (6th century BC)

Dutch artist Vincent van Gogh. Early 20th-century European art is also exhibited.

The M.F.A. is also well known for its extensive collection of European decorative arts. A series of galleries displays tableware, ceramics, and glass clustered by period from the early 17th to early 20th centuries. An impressive array of 18th-century French silver is displayed in a gallery where the walls are painted with Neoclassical, Louis XVI-style motifs – these were originally installed in the town house of a New York banker. There is also a striking display of 18th-century Chinese export porcelain, which is set against the imported backdrop of a Parisian hotel's Louis XV-style interior.

ANCIENT EGYPTIAN, NUBIAN, AND NEAR EASTERN ART

THE M.F.A.'S COLLECTION of Egyptian and Nubian materials is unparalleled outside of Africa, and derives primarily from M.F.A.-Harvard University excavations along the Nile, which began in 1905. The first floor houses a 1998 installation showing Egyptian Funerary Arts, which uses the M.F.A.'s superb collection of mummies from nearly three millennia to illustrate the technical and art historical aspects of Egyptian burial practices. The adjacent gallery of Ancient Near East artifacts displays Babylonian, Assyrian, and Sumerian reliefs. Another gallery is devoted to ancient Nubia, the

cultural region around the Nile stretching roughly between the modern African cities of Aswan and Khartoum.

The Egyptian and Nubian collections continue on the second floor. Highlights include two monumental sculptures of Nubian kings from the Great Temple of Amen at Napata (620–586 BC and 600–580 BC). A few of the galleries are set up to re-create Nubian burial chambers, which allows cuneiform wall carvings to be displayed in something akin to an original setting; a superb example is the offering chapel of Sekhem-ankh-Ptah from Sakkara (2450–2350 BC).

CLASSICAL ART

THE M.F.A. BOASTS one of America's top collections of Greek ceramics, particularly red- and black-figured vases, which are displayed in a large gallery on the first floor, as well as in smaller

Roman fresco, excavated from a Pompeian villa (1st century AD)

galleries on the second floor. In general, the Classical galleries of the museum are arranged thematically to highlight the influence of Greek arts on both Etruscan and Roman art. The Etruscan gallery on the first floor has several carved sarcophagi, while the Roman collection on the second floor features grave markers, portrait busts, and a series of wall panel paintings unearthed in Pompeii in an M.F.A. expedition of 1900–01.

ASIAN ART

THE ASIAN COLLECTIONS, occupying some of the most elegant galleries in the M.F.A., are said to be the most extensive under one roof in the world. The first-floor galleries are primarily devoted to Indian, Near Eastern, and Central Asian art. Among the highlights are Indian sculpture and changing exhibitions of Islamic miniature paintings and Indian narrative paintings.

Tang Dynasty Chinese Horse (8th century)

A beautiful stairway adorned with carved lions and a portal of a dragon in the clouds announces the entrance to the main Chinese and Japanese galleries on the second floor. Extensive holdings and limited display space mean that specific exhibitions change often, but the M.F.A.'s exhibitions of Japanese and Chinese scroll and screen paintings is, nevertheless, unmatched in the West. The strength of the M.F.A.'s Japanese art collection is largely due to the efforts of collectors such as Ernest Fenollosa and William Bigelow Sturgis. In the 19th century they encouraged the Japanese to maintain their traditions, and salvaged Buddhist temple art when the Japanese imperial government had withdrawn subsidies from these institutions. The Buddhist Temple Room is considered to contain some of the finest examples of Asian temple art in the world.

Cambridge ❼

P ART OF THE GREATER BOSTON metropolitan area, Cambridge is, nonetheless, a town in its own right, and has the mood and feel of such. Principally a college town, it is dominated by Harvard University and other college campuses. It also boasts a number of important historic sights, such as Christ Church and Cambridge Common, which have associations back to the American Revolution. Harvard Square is the area's main entertainment and shopping district.

Site of the Washington Elm, on Cambridge Common

🏛 Longfellow National Historic Site

105 Brattle St. 📞 *(617) 876-4491.*
⏲ *May–Oct: 10:30am–4pm Wed–Sun.* 📷 🚫 ♿ 🎁
Ⓦ *www.nps.gov/long*

This house on Brattle Street, like many around it, was built by Colonial-era merchants loyal to the British Crown during the Revolution. It was seized by American revolutionaries and served as George Washington's headquarters during the Siege of Boston.

The poet Henry Wadsworth Longfellow boarded here in 1837, was given the house as a wedding present in 1843, and lived here until his death in 1888. He wrote his most famous poems here, including *Tales of a Wayside Inn* and *The Song of Hiawatha*. Longfellow's status as literary dean of Boston meant that Nathaniel Hawthorne and Charles Sumner, among others, were regular visitors.

🏛 Harvard Square

📱 *(617) 497-1630.* ♿
Ⓦ *www.harvardsquare.com*

Even Bostonians think of Harvard Square as a stand-in for Cambridge – the square was the original site of Cambridge from around 1630. Dominating the square is the Harvard Cooperative Society ("the Coop"), a Harvard institution, that sells inexpensive clothes, posters, and books.

Harvard's large student population is very much in evidence here, adding color to the character of the square. Many trendy boutiques, inexpensive restaurants, and numerous cafés cater to their needs. Street performers abound, especially on the weekends, and the square has long been a place where pop trends begin. Club Passim *(see p152)*, for example, has incubated many successful singer-songwriters since Joan Baez first debuted here in 1959.

Street musician, Harvard Square

🏛 Cambridge Common

Set aside as common pasture and military drill ground in 1631, Cambridge Common has served as a center for religious, social, and political activity ever since. George Washington took command of the Continental Army here on July 3, 1775, beneath the Washington Elm, now marked by a stone. The common served as the army's encampment from 1775 to 1776. Today the ball fields and playgrounds are popular with families. In 1997 the first monument in the U.S. to the victims of the Irish Famine was unveiled on the common.

⛪ Christ Church

Garden St. 📱 *(617) 876-0200.*
⏲ *7:30am–6pm Mon–Fri & Sun, 7:30am–3pm Sat.* 🔔 *8am, 10am Sun; also 12:30pm & 5pm in winter.*
🚫 ♿ Ⓦ *www.christchurch.com*

With its square bell tower and plain, gray shingled edifice, Christ Church is a restrained example of an Anglican church. Designed in 1761 by Peter Harrison, the architect of Boston's King's Chapel *(see p60)*, Christ Church came in for rough treatment as a barracks for Continental Army troops in 1775 – British loyalists had almost all fled Cambridge by this time. The army even melted down the organ pipes to cast musket balls. The church was restored on New Year's Eve, 1775, when George Washington and his wife Martha were among the worshipers. Anti-Anglican sentiment remained strong in Cambridge, and Christ Church did not have its own rector again until the 19th century.

Simple interior of Christ Church, designed prior to the Revolution in 1761

Radcliffe Institute for Advanced Studies

Brattle St. *(617) 495-1573.* www.radcliffe.edu

Radcliffe College was founded in 1879 as the Collegiate Institution for Women, when 27 women began to study by private arrangement with Harvard professors. By 1943, members of Harvard's faculty no longer taught separate undergraduate courses to the women of Radcliffe, and in 1999 Radcliffe ceased its official existence as an independent college. It is now an institute for advanced study promoting scholarship of women's culture. The first Radcliffe building was the 1806 Federal-style mansion, Fay House, on the northern corner of what became Radcliffe Yard. Schlesinger Library, on the west side of the yard, is considered a significant example of

Stained glass, Radcliffe Institute

Colonial Revival architecture. The library's most famous holdings are an extensive collection of cookbooks and reference works on gastronomy.

M.I.T.

77 Massachusetts Ave. *(617) 253-4795.* **MIT Museum** 10am–5pm Tue–Fri, noon–5pm Sat–Sun. **Hart Nautical Gallery** 9am–5pm daily. **List Visual Arts Center** Oct–Jun: noon–6pm Tue–Sun, 6–8pm Fri. www.mit.edu

Chartered in 1861 to teach students "exactly and thoroughly the fundamental principles of positive science with application to the industrial arts," the Massachusetts Institute of Technology has evolved into one of the world's leading universities in engineering and the sciences. Several architectural masterpieces dot M.I.T.'s 135-acre (55-ha) campus along the Charles River,

VISITORS' CHECKLIST

Harvard. 1, 69. Harvard Square Information Booth *(617) 497-1630*, Cambridge Office of Tourism *(800) 862-5678, (617) 441-2884.* Wed. June 24. www.harvard.edu/tour or www.cambridge-usa.org

including Eero Saarinen's Kresge Auditorium and Kresge Chapel, built in 1955. The Wiesner Building is a major collaboration between architect I. M. Pei and several artists, including Kenneth Noland, whose relief mural dominates the atrium. The building houses the **List Visual Arts Center**, noted for its avant-garde art.

The **Hart Nautical Gallery** in the Rogers Building focuses on marine engineering, with models of ships and exhibits of the latest advances in underwater research. The **M.I.T. Museum** blends art and science, with exhibits such as Harold Edgerton's groundbreaking stroboscopic flash photographs, and the latest holographic art.

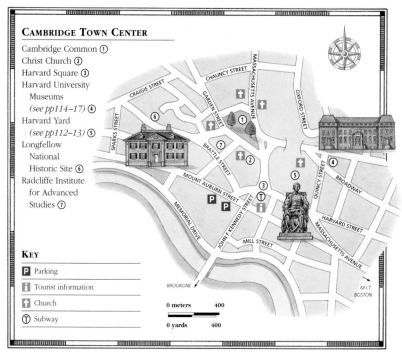

CAMBRIDGE TOWN CENTER

Cambridge Common ①
Christ Church ②
Harvard Square ③
Harvard University Museums *(see pp114–17)* ④
Harvard Yard *(see pp112–13)* ⑤
Longfellow National Historic Site ⑥
Radcliffe Institute for Advanced Studies ⑦

KEY

P Parking
i Tourist information
Church
T Subway

0 meters 400
0 yards 400

Harvard Yard

IN 1636 Boston's well-educated Puritan leaders founded a college in Newtowne. Two years later cleric John Harvard died and bequeathed half his estate and all his books to the fledgling college. The colony's leaders bestowed his name on the school and rechristened the surrounding community Cambridge after the English city where they had been educated. The oldest university in the U.S., Harvard is now one of the world's most prestigious centers of learning. The university has expanded to encompass more than 400 buildings, but Harvard Yard is still at its heart.

Holden Chapel
Built in 1742, the chapel was the scene of revolutionary speeches and was later used as a demonstration hall for human dissections.

Hollis Hall was used as barracks by George Washington's troops during the American Revolution.

Massachusetts Hall, built in 1720, is Harvard's oldest building.

★ **Old Harvard Yard**
This leafy yard dates from the founding of the college in 1636. Freshman dormitories dot the yard, and throughout the year it is a focal point for students.

Harvard University Information Center

★ **John Harvard Statue**
This statue celebrates Harvard's most famous benefactor. Almost a place of pilgrimage, graduates and visitors invariably pose for photographs here.

University Hall, designed by Charles Bulfinch, was built in 1816.

★ **Widener Library**
This library memorializes Harry Elkins Widener who died on the Titanic *in 1912. With more than 3 million volumes, it is the third largest library in the U.S.*

★ **Memorial Church**
This church was built in 1931 and copies earlier styles. For example, the steeple is modeled on that of the Old North Church (see p73) in Boston's North End.

VISITORS' CHECKLIST

Massachusetts Ave. Ⓣ *Harvard.*
◯ *24 hrs.* ● *2nd Thu in Jun (Commencement).* ♿ 📷 🎧
Lectures, concerts and films.
Harvard Information Center
📞 *(617) 495-1573.* **Harvard Box Office** 📞 *(617) 496-2222.*
Harvard Film Archive 📞 *(617) 495 4700. Films shown nightly.*
🌐 *www.harvard.edu*

Memorial Hall, a Ruskin Gothic building, memorializes Harvard's Union casualties from the Civil War.

Sackler and Peabody Museums, and Harvard Museum of Natural History *(see pp116–17)*

Sever Hall
One of the most distinctive of Harvard's Halls, this Romanesque style-building was designed by Henry Hobson Richardson (see p30).

Fogg Art and Busch-Reisinger Museums *(see pp114–15)*

Tercentenary Theater

STAR SIGHTS

★ **Old Harvard Yard**

★ **John Harvard Statue**

★ **Widener Library**

★ **Memorial Church**

0 meters   50

0 yards   50

Carpenter Center for Visual Arts
Opened in 1963, the Carpenter Center is the only building in the U.S. designed by the avant-garde French architect Le Corbusier.

The Harvard University Museums

HARVARD'S MUSEUMS were originally conceived to revolutionize the process of education; students were to be taught by allowing them access to artifacts from around the world. Today, this tradition continues, with the museums housing some of the world's finest university collections: art from Europe and America in the Fogg Art and Busch-Reisinger Museums, archaeological finds in the Peabody Museum, Near and Far Eastern art in the Sackler Museum, and a vast collection of artifacts in the Harvard Museum of Natural History.

Main entrance to the Fogg Art and Busch-Reisinger Museums

Fogg Art and Busch-Reisinger Museums

32 Quincy St. 📞 (617) 495-9400. ⏰ 10am–5pm Mon–Sat, 1–5pm Sun. ● public hols.
🖼 ♿ 📷
🌐 www.art museums.harvard.edu

Until the Fogg Museum was created by a surprise bequest in 1891, Harvard, like most universities, used prints of famous paintings and casts of sculptures to teach art history. Both the Fogg and the Busch-Reisinger, which was grafted onto the Fogg in 1991, have small but select collections of art from Europe and America.

The Fogg building was completed in 1927, and is a red-brick Georgian building similar to other buildings at Harvard. The collections, which focus on Western art from the late Middle Ages to the present, are organized around a central courtyard modeled on a 16th-century church in Montepulciano, Italy. The ground-floor corridors surrounding the courtyard feature 12th-century capitals from Moutiers St-Jean in Burgundy, France.

Two small galleries near the entrance, and the two-story Warburg Hall, display the Fogg's collections that prefigure the Italian Renaissance. The massive altarpieces and suspended crucifix in the Warburg are particularly impressive. The ground-floor galleries on the left side of the entrance are devoted to 17th-century Dutch, Flemish, and English painting, 17th- and 18th-century Neapolitan painting, and European and North American art of the 18th century. Among the English and American 18th-century paintings are a series of unfinished studies made by John Singleton Copley.

The museum's second level is dominated by a collection of Pre-Raphaelite painting and a few select works by John Singer Sargent. The small galleries along the front of the building change exhibitions frequently but tend to focus on drawings and graphic arts, and on 19th-century French and American art. The highlight of the second level is the Maurice Wertheim Collection of Impressionist and Post-Impressionist art,

most of it collected in the late 1930s. With a number of important paintings by Renoir, Manet, and Degas, the Wertheim gallery is the Fogg's most popular. An adjacent gallery displays American art from after 1950, for example by the minimalist painter Frank Stella, one of the more important exponents of color-field painting.

The museum also houses rotating displays from its collection of 19th- and 20th-century American art.

Werner Otto Hall, which contains the Busch-Reisinger Museum, is entered through the second level of the Fogg. The museum's collections focus on Germanic art and

Copley Studies
These unfinished studies by John Singleton Copley were made for his 1787 painting The Siege of Gibraltar.

First floor

Main entrance

GUIDE TO THE FOGG ART AND BUSCH-REISINGER MUSEUMS

Art from the Middle Ages to the 18th century is on the first floor of the Fogg Art Museum. French and American art from the 19th and 20th centuries and 20th-century American art are on the second floor. The Busch-Reisinger Museum focuses on Germanic art.

***Light-Space Modulator** (1923–30) by the Hungarian Moholy-Nagy*

design from after 1880, with an emphasis on German Expressionism. Harvard was a safe haven for many Bauhaus artists, architects, and designers who fled Nazi Germany, and both Walter Gropius and Lyonel Feininger chose the Busch-Reisinger as the depository of their personal papers and drawings. Periodic exhibitions explore aspects of the work and philosophy of the Bauhaus movement. Although small, the museum owns major paintings and sculptures by 20th-century masters such as Max Beckmann, Lyonel Feininger, Wassily Kandinsky, Moholy-Nagy, Paul Klee, Oskar Kokoschka, Emil Nolde, and Franz Marc.

Central Courtyard of the Fogg Art Museum

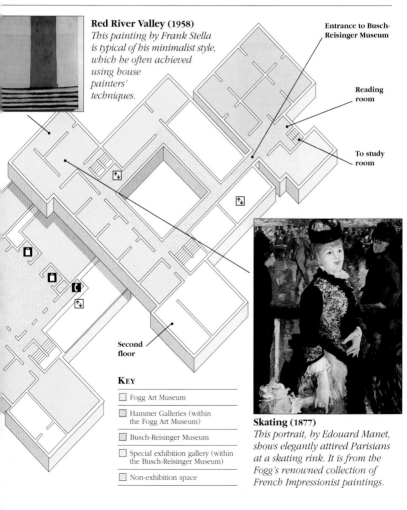

Red River Valley (1958)
This painting by Frank Stella is typical of his minimalist style, which he often achieved using house painters' techniques.

Entrance to Busch-Reisinger Museum

Reading room

To study room

Second floor

KEY
- ☐ Fogg Art Museum
- ☐ Hammer Galleries (within the Fogg Art Museum)
- ☐ Busch-Reisinger Museum
- ☐ Special exhibition gallery (within the Busch-Reisinger Museum)
- ☐ Non-exhibition space

Skating (1877)
This portrait, by Edouard Manet, shows elegantly attired Parisians at a skating rink. It is from the Fogg's renowned collection of French Impressionist paintings.

Peabody Museum of Archaeology and Ethnology

11 Divinity St. 📞 (617) 496-1027.
🕐 9am–5pm daily. ● Jan 1, Jul 4,
Thanksgiving, Dec 25. 📷 ⚐ ✔
🆆 www.peabody.harvard.edu

The Peabody Museum of Archaeology and Ethnology was founded in 1866 as the first museum in the Americas devoted solely to anthropology. The many collections, which include several million artifacts and more than 500,000 photographic images, come from all around the world. The Peabody's pioneering investigations began with excavations of Mayan sites in Central America, research on the precontact Anasazi people of the American Southwest, and on the cultural history of the later Pueblo tribes of the same region. Joint expeditions sponsored by the Peabody Museum and the Museum of Fine Arts (see pp106–9) also uncovered some of the richest finds of dynastic and predynastic Egypt. Later research embraced the cultures of the islands of the South Pacific.

The Native American tribes of the Northern Plains are interpreted largely through an exhibition detailing the 1804–6 expedition, from the east to the west coast, by Lewis and Clark, who collected innumerable artifacts on the way. Other outstanding exhibits include totem carvings by Pacific Northwest tribes and a wide range of historic and contemporary Navajo weavings. The third floor is devoted to Central American anthropology, with casts of some of the ruins uncovered at Copán in Honduras and Chichen Itza in Mexico. The fourth floor concentrates on Polynesia, Micronesia, and other islands of the Pacific.

Native American totem pole, Peabody Museum

Harvard Museum of Natural History

26 Oxford St. 📞 (617) 495-3045.
🕐 9am–5pm daily. ● Jul 4,
Thanksgiving, Dec 25. 📷 ⚐ ✔
🆆 www.hmnh.harvard.edu

The Harvard Museum of Natural History is actually three museums rolled into one, with collections from the Mineralogical and Geological Museum, the Museum of Comparative Zoology, and the Botanical Museum.

The mineralogical galleries include some of Harvard University's oldest specimen collections. Virtually every New England mineral, rock, and gem type is represented, including rough and cut gemstones and one of the world's premier meteorite collections.

The zoological galleries owe their inception to the great 19th-century biologist Louis Agassiz and include his personal arachnid collection. The collection of taxidermied bird, mammal, and reptile specimens is comprehensive, and there is also a collection of dinosaur skeletons.

The collections in the botanical galleries include the Ware Collection of Blaschka Glass Models of Plants, popularly known as the "glass flowers." Between 1887 and 1936, father and son artisans Leopold and Rudolph Blaschka created these 3,000 exacting models of 850 plant species. Each species is illustrated with a scientifically accurate lifesize model and magnified parts.

Sackler Museum

485 Broadway, Cambridge.
📞 (617) 495-9400. 🕐 10am–5pm
Mon–Sat, 1–5pm Sun. ● public
hols. 📷 ⚐ ✔
🆆 www.artmuseums.harvard.edu

Named after a famous philanthropist, physician, and art collector, the Arthur M. Sackler Museum is home to Harvard's

Triceratops skull in the Harvard Museum of Natural History

collection of ancient, Asian, Indian, and Near Eastern art. Opened in 1985, it is housed in a modern building designed by James Stirling and is itself a bold artistic statement, while the starkly modern interior galleries provide optimal display space. The 30-ft (10-m) entrance lobby features a 1997 wall-painting by Conceptual artist Sol Lewitt, whose trademark colorful geometric shapes appear to float in space.

The Sackler is best toured by ascending to the permanent collections on the fourth floor and working back down to the lobby. The head of the stairwell terminates at gallery 10, where changing exhibitions highlight aspects of Harvard's collections of ancient Greek art. A small adjacent gallery displays Egyptian, ancient Near Eastern, Etruscan, and Bronze Age art. The fourth floor galleries continue with rooms devoted to ancient Roman art, and then through Indian, Southeast Asian, and Chinese art.

The second-floor galleries host changing, thematic exhibitions of the Sackler's extensive collections of Islamic art from the Near East and central Asia. The first-floor gallery, behind the ticket booth, hosts ambitious and thought-provoking special exhibitions.

Southeast Asian Buddha head, Sackler Museum

Charlestown ❽

SITUATED ON THE NORTH BANK of the Charles River, directly opposite the North End, Charlestown exudes history. The site of the infamous Battle of Bunker Hill, when American troops suffered huge losses in their fight for independence, today the district forms a major part of Boston's Freedom Trail (see pp32–5).

Granite obelisk of the Bunker Hill Monument, erected in 1843

⚑ Bunker Hill Monument

Monument Square. 【 (617) 242-5641. ◯ daily. ● Jan 1, Thanksgiving, Dec 25.
ⓦ www.charlestown.ma.us

In the Revolution's first pitched battle between British and colonial troops, the British won but failed to escape from Boston. Following the June 17, 1775 battle, American irregulars were joined by other militia to keep British forces penned up until George Washington forced their evacuation by sea the following March. A Tuscan-style pillar was erected in 1794 in honor of Dr. Joseph Warren, a Boston revolutionary leader who died in the battle, but Charlestown citizens felt something grander was in order. Accordingly, they began raising funds for the Bunker Hill Monument in 1823, laid the cornerstone in 1825, and dedicated the 221-ft (67-m) granite obelisk in 1843. It was for many years the tallest monument in the U.S., until the Washington Monument was erected in 1885. The building has no elevator, but 294 steps lead to the top and give spectacular views of Boston harbor.

🏛 Bunker Hill Pavilion

Water St. 【 (617) 241-7575. ◯ daily. ● Thanksgiving. 🎥 ∅ 🔊
Next to Charlestown Navy Yard, Bunker Hill Pavilion shows a multimedia presentation *The Whites of Their Eyes*. The title comes from the purported order that American troops not fire until they could see the whites of the Redcoats' eyes.

⚑ John Harvard Mall

Ten families founded Charlestown in 1629, a year before the rest of Boston was settled. They built their homes and a palisaded fort on Town Hill, a spot now marked by John Harvard Mall. A small monument within the enclosed park pays homage to John Harvard, the young cleric who ministered to the settlers (see p112).

When John Winthrop arrived with three shiploads of Puritan refugees in 1630 (see p16), they settled nearby in the marshes at the base of Town Hill, now City Square.

Municipal art in City Square

⚑ Charlestown Navy Yard

【 (617) 242-5601. ◯ daily. ● Jan 1, Thanksgiving, Dec 25. 🔊 🎥
Established in 1800, for 174 years Charlestown Navy Yard played a key role in supporting the U.S. Atlantic fleet, as the Navy moved from wooden sailing ships to steel giants. The yard was designed by Alexander Parris, architect of Quincy Market (see p66), and was one of the first examples of industrial architecture in Boston.

On decommissioning, the facility was transferred to the National Park Service, and rangers now give tours of the *U.S.S. Constitution* and the World War II destroyer *U.S.S. Cassin Young*.

⚑ U.S.S. Constitution

Charlestown Navy Yard. 【 (617) 242-5670. ◯ daily. 🔊 🎥
ⓦ www.ussconstitution.navy.mil

The oldest commissioned warship afloat, the *U.S.S. Constitution* saw immediate action in the Mediterranean protecting American shipping from the Barbary pirates. In the War of 1812, she won fame and her nickname of "Old Ironsides" when cannonballs bounced off her in a battle with the British ship *Guerriere*. In the course of her active service, she won 42 battles, lost none, captured 20 vessels, and was never boarded by an enemy.

She underwent her most thorough overhaul in time for her 1997 bicentennial, able to carry her own canvas into the wind for the first time in a century. On July 4 each year, she is taken out into the harbor for an annual turnaround that reverses her position at the Navy Yard pier to ensure equal weathering on both sides. A small museum documents her history.

***U.S.S. Constitution*, built in 1797, moored in Charlestown Navy Yard**

Concord and Lexington 9

THE PEACEFUL, PROSPEROUS suburban look of modern-day Concord and neighboring Lexington masks an eventful past. These small towns were at the heart of two important chapters in US history. The first was marked by bloody skirmishes in each town between armed Colonists and British troops on April 19, 1775, which acted as catalysts for the Revolutionary War. The second spanned several generations, as 19th-century Concord blossomed into the literary heart and soul of the US, with many of the nation's great writers establishing homes in the area.

North Bridge in Minute Man National Historical Park

Exploring Concord and Lexington

At Concord's center lies Monument Square. It was also at the center of the battle fought between British troops and Colonists more than 200 years ago. Having seized the gun cache of rebel forces, the British soldiers began burning them. Nearby Colonist forces spotted the smoke and, believing the British were torching the town, rushed to Concord's defense, precipitating the Revolutionary War.

🏛 Minute Man National Historical Park

174 Liberty St, Concord. 📞 (978) 369-6993 ext 22. ⬤ May–Oct: 9am–5pm daily; Nov–Apr: 9am–4pm daily. ⬤ Jan 1, Thanksgiving, & Dec 25. ♿

On April 19, 1775, a group of militia, ordinary citizens, and Colonist farmers known as minutemen confronted British troops who were patrolling the North Bridge. The minutemen fought valiantly, driving three British companies of troops from the bridge and chasing them back to Boston.

This 990-acre (400-ha) park preserves the site and tells the story of the American victory. The Minute Man Visitor Center also features a massive battle mural and a 22-minute multimedia show called "Road to Revolution." The Battle Road Trail traces the five-mile

Minute Man statue in Concord

(8-km) path followed by the British as they advanced from Lexington to Concord – the same route they took in retreat.

The park's North Bridge Unit is the place where the first major engagement was fought. This so-called "shot heard around the world" set off the war. Across the bridge is the famous *Minute Man* statue by Concord native Daniel Chester French (1850–31). A short trail leads from the bridge to the North Bridge Visitor Center. A reenactment of the battle takes place every year in April.

🏛 Historical Society Houses, Lexington

Hancock-Clarke House 36 Hancock St. **Buckman Tavern** 1 Bedford St. **Munroe Tavern** 1332 Massachusetts Ave. 📞 (781) 862-1703. 🌐

While on their way to Concord, British troops clashed with minutemen on **Lexington Battle Green**. Three houses in Lexington now display artifacts from the Revolutionary era. **Buckman Tavern** served as the meeting place for the minutemen before the confrontation and as a makeshift hospital for their wounded. Boston silversmith Paul Revere undertook his "midnight ride" to **Hancock-Clarke House** to warn patriots Samuel Adams and John Hancock, two of the eventual signatories to the Declaration of Independence, of the approaching British troops *(see p19)*. **Munroe Tavern** served as headquarters for British forces.

Along the Battle Road, by John Rush, a representation of what a battle of the time might have been like

Concord's Old Manse: home to 19th-century literary giants

🏛 **The Old Manse**

Monument St, Concord. **(** (978) 369-3909. ◯ mid-April–Oct: daily. 🏷

The parsonage by the North Bridge was built in 1770 by the grandfather of writer Ralph Waldo Emerson (1803–82). Author Nathaniel Hawthorne (1804–64) wrote *Mosses from an Old Manse* (1846) here, giving the house its name. The house contains family possessions and period furniture.

🏛 **Concord Museum**

Jct of Lexington Rd & Cambridge Tpk, Concord. **(** (978) 369-9763. ◯ Jan–Mar: 11am–4pm Mon–Sat, 1pm–4pm Sun; Apr–Dec: 9am–5pm Mon–Sat, 12pm–5pm Sun. 🏷 &

The museum's eclectic holdings include decorative arts from the 17th, 18th, and 19th centuries, and the lantern that Paul Revere ordered hung to warn of the British advance.

🏛 **Emerson House**

Cambridge Tpk, Concord. **(** (978) 369-2236. ◯ mid-Apr–late Oct: Thu–Sun & public hols. 🏷

Ralph Waldo Emerson lived in this house from 1835 until his death in 1882, writing essays, organizing lecture tours, and entertaining friends and admirers. Much of Emerson's furniture, writings, books, and family memorabilia are on display.

🍂 **Walden Pond State Reservation**

915 Walden St, Concord. **(** (978) 369-3254. ◯ call for hours. 🏷 🏷 &

Essayist Henry David Thoreau (1817–62) lived at Walden Pond from 1845 to 1847, compiling the material for his seminal work *Walden; or, Life in the Woods* (1854), which called for a return to simplicity and a respect for nature. The pond and woodlands are popular for walking, fishing, and swimming, though the reservation limits visitors to 1,000 people at one time.

Fisherman on the tranquil waters of Walden Pond

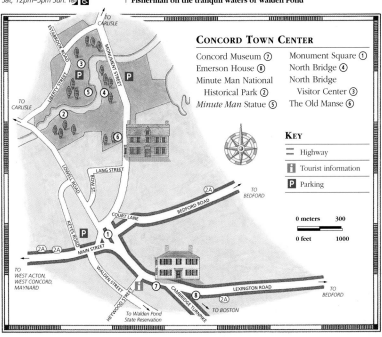

CONCORD TOWN CENTER

Concord Museum ⑦	Monument Square ①
Emerson House ⑧	North Bridge ④
Minute Man National	North Bridge
Historical Park ②	Visitor Center ③
Minute Man Statue ⑤	The Old Manse ⑥

KEY

═ Highway

🛈 Tourist information

🅿 Parking

0 meters   300

0 feet   1000

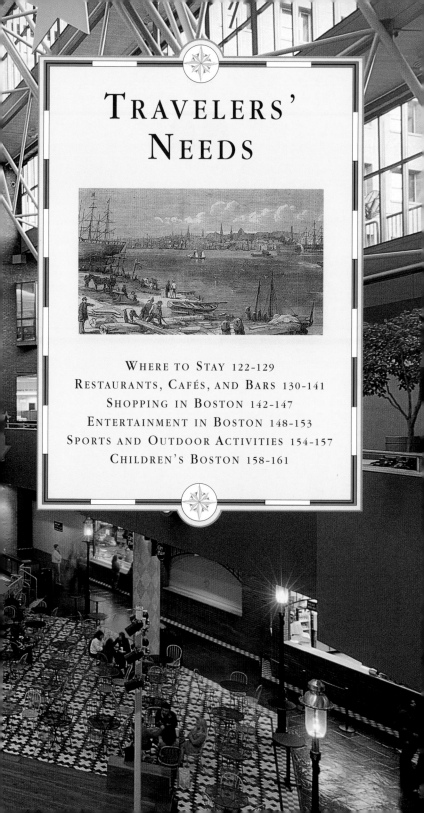

TRAVELERS' NEEDS

WHERE TO STAY

Boston offers the visitor almost every type of accommodation: modest guesthouses, luxury hotels, chain motels, Victorian brownstone bed and breakfasts, and elegant, designer "boutique" hotels. Many older hotels have been renovated to provide traditional charm with modern conveniences, while new hotels and B&Bs open in the

Ritz-Carlton door-man *(see p128)*

city every year. Nevertheless, the city has a perennial hotel shortage, which keeps prices high and makes it difficult to book rooms during peak seasons. Even in winter, it's rare to find rooms under $100 per night; in summer "budget" rates can approach $150 or more. Information is available from Boston's tourist information offices *(see p164)*.

The elegant Omni Parker House *(see p125)*

WHERE TO STAY

The centrally located Back Bay has the greatest concentration of hotels and is convenient for tourists as well as business travelers. In the gentrified South End, nearby, an increasing number of restored Victorian brownstones have been converted to B&Bs. Accommodation in the Financial District, close to the waterfront, caters to business people during the week, but often offers good value to vacationers on the weekends. Across the Charles River, Cambridge has a large number of hotels, particularly around Harvard Square and Kendall Square. In more suburban Brookline, situated a little way west of Back Bay, there are several guesthouses, as well as a selection of more upscale B&Bs.

HOTEL GRADING AND FACILITIES

Boston does not have an official hotel grading system. While higher prices generally indicate more amenities, some lodgings in prime locations, or with unique historic features, may

command prices that exceed what the facilities might otherwise warrant. B&Bs generally do not offer fitness facilities, business services, or restaurants, and may be somewhat less expensive, although some at the high end of the price scale now have amenities – and prices – that rival the best hotels. Most large hotels have at least a basic fitness room, while some have arrangements with nearby clubs for guest use. Swimming pools are less common, except at the big hotels, and outdoor pools generally open only between June and early September. One recent development that travelers may find beneficial is that Boston's hotels now house many of the city's top restaurants; only a few years ago the reputation of Boston's hotel dining rooms had become questionable.

HOW TO BOOK

Most hotels have toll-free reservation numbers, and many now take reservations by fax or via the internet. Room rates are often quoted for two people sharing a room, not including tax or breakfast, although some B&Bs provide a morning meal. You may find last-minute rooms during the winter months, but book in advance during the rest of the year. Boston hotels are very busy in May and June for college graduations, July and August for summer vacations, and September and October for the fall foliage season.

HIDDEN EXTRAS

If you have a car in Boston, you'll pay dearly for parking. Ask your hotel if parking is included; if not, budget at least $20-25 extra per day. Taxes in Boston will also add 12.45 percent to the hotel bill. If breakfast is not included, expect to spend at least $3 for coffee and a pastry in a nearby café or $15 and up for a full hotel breakfast.

Lobby of the Swissôtel *(see p126)*

Glass Atrium of the Inn at Harvard *(see p129)*, **Cambridge**

DISCOUNTS

HOTEL PRICES vary significantly with the seasons, with the lowest rates found in January and February. Through the year, many hotels catering to business travelers, such as in the Financial District, around Hynes Convention Center, and in Cambridge's Kendall Square, offer discount weekend rates. B&Bs may offer better prices mid-week.

BED AND BREAKFAST

BOSTON HAS A good selection of small hotels and B&Bs, offering personal service and charm. If you are looking for a classic B&B – a room or two in the owner's home – contact one of Boston's B&B booking agencies. A recent trend is the "boutique" hotel, a small, elegantly appointed hotel, though prices at these reflect the level of service and luxury.

BUSINESS TRAVELERS

BUSINESS TRAVELERS will find that all major hotels provide fax and internet access. Some new or newly refurbished hotels offer in-room fax machines, multiline phones, and private voice mail. It is wise, though, to check that older hotels have the facilities you require.

DISABLED TRAVELERS

DISABLED TRAVELERS may be most comfortable in the city's newer hotels that have been built to conform to access requirements. Some of the large older hotels have been refitted, but many small B&Bs have steps, narrow hallways, or other architectural features that may make access difficult. For information about hotels, transportation, tour services, and other resources, contact the **Massachusetts Network of Information Providers for People with Disabilities**.

CHILDREN

CHILDREN ARE welcome in most of the larger hotels and often stay free in their parents' rooms. Some deluxe hotels provide child-friendly amenities, ranging from bedtime milk and cookies to the telephone "bedtime story line" at the Charles Hotel *(see p129)*. Suites are available in many big hotels giving families space to spread out. For families on more moderate budgets, some guesthouses, such as the Copley Inn *(see p127)*, and the Shawmut Inn *(see p124)*, offer apartment-style accommodations that are suitable for families. Many B&Bs cannot accommodate young children.

A Cambridge House Bed and Breakfast *(see p129)*, **Cambridge**

BUDGET OPTIONS

IT CAN BE HARD finding budget accommodation in Boston. The **Boston International Youth Hostel** has mostly six-bed dormitories, and there are some inexpensive chain hotels, such as **Days Inn**, in the suburbs, which offer functional lodging. The North Shore towns of Salem and Rockport, just north of Boston, have good selections of mid-priced B&Bs and are accessible from the city by M.B.T.A. commuter rail – contact the **North of Boston Convention and Visitors' Bureau** for more details.

DIRECTORY

BED AND BREAKFAST AGENCIES

Bed and Breakfast Agency of Boston
47 Commercial Wharf. **Map** 2 E3. 🄲 *(617) 720-3540.*
🄲 *(800) 248-9262.*
🅆 www.boston-bnbagency.com

Bed and Breakfast Associates Bay Colony, Ltd.
P.O. Box 57166, Babson Park Branch, Needham, MA 02457.
🄲 *(617) 720-0522.*
🄲 *(888) 384-7203.*
🅆 www.bnbboston.com

Host Homes of Boston
Box 117, Waban Branch, Boston, MA 02468. 🄲 *(617) 244-1308.* 🄲 *(800) 600-1308.*

DISABLED TRAVELERS

Massachusetts Network of Information Providers for People with Disabilities
200 Trapelo Rd, Waltham, MA 02452.
🄲 *(781) 642-0248.* 🄲 *(800) 642-0249.*
TTY (for people who cannot hear) 🄲 *(800) 764-0200.*
🅆 www.disabilityinfo.org

HOSTELS

Boston International Youth Hostel
12 Hemenway St. **Map** 3 A3.
🄲 *(617) 536-9455.*
🅆 www.bostonhostel.org

BUDGET AND CHAIN HOTELS

Day's Inn
Several locations.
🄲 *(800) 329-7466.*
🅆 www.daysinn.com

Best Western
Several locations.
🄲 *(800) 528-1234.*
🅆 www.bestwestern.com

North of Boston Convention and Visitors' Bureau
17 Peabody Sq., Peabody, MA 01960.
🄲 *(978) 977-7760.*
🅆 www.northofboston.org

Choosing a Hotel

THESE HOTELS have been selected across a wide price range for their excellent facilities, good location, character, and value. They are listed by area and then by price category, with symbols highlighting some of the amenities that may influence your choice of where to stay. Map references help you locate the hotels on the Street Finder *(pp176–181)*.

	CREDIT CARDS	NUMBER OF ROOMS	RECOMMENDED RESTAURANT	CHILDREN'S FACILITIES	GARDEN OR TERRACE
BEACON HILL AND WEST END					
JOHN JEFFRIES HOUSE $$ 14 David G. Mugar Way. **Map** 1 B3. (617) 367-1866. FAX (617) 742-0313. Redbrick inn at the foot of Beacon Hill overlooking the Charles River. Rooms are Victorian in style, and while some are tiny, the two-room suites are good value. Most of the rooms have kitchenettes.	AE DC MC V D	46 (23)		●	
BEACON HILL BED & BREAKFAST $$$$ 27 Brimmer Street. **Map** 1 A4. (617) 523-7376. @ bhillbb@aol.com The two large bedrooms in this six-story Victorian townhouse are furnished with a mix of antiques and more contemporary furnishings. The rates are high, but the location near the Public Garden is excellent.		2			
HOLIDAY INN SELECT GOVERNMENT CENTER $$$$ 5 Blossom Street. **Map** 1 B3. (800) 465-4329 or (617) 742-7630. FAX (617) 742-4192. W www.sixcontinentshotel.com A modern, 15-story, business-class chain hotel. On the north side of Beacon Hill near Massachusetts General Hospital, a short walk from Government Center.	AE DC MC V D	303 (2)		●	
BEACON HILL HOTEL & BISTRO $$$$$ 19 Charles Street. **Map** 1 B4. (888) 959 2442 or (617) 723-7575. FAX (617) 723-7525. W www.beaconhillhotel.com A renovated brick townhouse that blends the charm of Beacon Hill with modern amenities such as flat-screen TV and internet access. Rooms over- look bustling Charles Street. The excellent bistro is a bonus.	AE MC V	13	■		●
CHARLES STREET INN $$$$$ 94 Charles Street. **Map** 1 B4. (877) 772-8900 or (617) 314-8900. FAX (617) 371-0009. W www.charlesstreetinn.com Deluxe boutique hotel in an 1860s townhouse. All the sumptuous antiques-filled rooms have working fireplaces, as well as whirlpool tubs, two-line telephones, internet connections, and CD players.	AE DC MC V D	9			
OLD BOSTON AND THE FINANCIAL DISTRICT					
SHAWMUT INN $$ 280 Friend Street. **Map** 1 C2. (800) 350-7784 or (617) 720-5544. FAX (617) 723-7784. W www.shawmutinn.com Simply furnished rooms, all with kitchenettes, in a former state office building one block from North Station. A fine budget choice; suites are good value for families.	AE MC V D	65 (11)		●	
HARBORSIDE INN $$$ 185 State Street. **Map** 2 E3. (888) 723-7565 or (617) 723-7500. FAX (617) 670-6015. W www.hagopianhotels.com The small guest rooms in this old mercantile warehouse have exposed brick walls, Victorian-style furniture, and wooden floors with Oriental rugs. Near Faneuil Hall but surrounded by the "Big Dig."	AE DC MC V D	54 (2)			
FIFTEEN BEACON $$$$$ 15 Beacon Street. **Map** 1 C4. (877) 982-3226 or (617) 670-1500. FAX (617) 670-2525. W www.xvbeacon.com Coolly opulent boutique hotel in a former office building. Chic rooms all have a high-style mix of traditional and contemporary furnishings, with facilities including CD players and fax machines.	AE DC MC V D	61 (2)	■		
LE MERIDIEN $$$$$ 250 Franklin Street. **Map** 2 E4. (800) 543-4300 or (617) 451-1900. FAX (617) 423-2844. W www.lemeridienboston.com This deluxe hotel in the heart of the Financial District often offers affordable weekend getaway packages.	AE DC MC V D	326 (26)	■	●	

Price categories for a standard double room per night, inclusive of breakfast, service charges, and any additional taxes:

$ under $100
$$ $100–$150
$$$ $150–$200
$$$$ $200–$250
$$$$$ over $250

CREDIT CARDS
Major credit cards accepted: *AE* American Express; *DC* Diners Club; *MC* MasterCard/Access; *V* Visa, *D* Discover Card.

NUMBER OF ROOMS
Number of rooms in the hotel (suites are shown in brackets).

RECOMMENDED RESTAURANT
Good restaurant within the hotel.

CHILDREN'S FACILITIES
Hotel has various facilities for young children.

GARDEN OR TERRACE
Hotel has a garden, courtyard, or terrace.

		CREDIT CARDS	NUMBER OF ROOMS	RECOMMENDED RESTAURANT	CHILDREN'S FACILITIES	GARDEN OR TERRACE
MILLENNIUM BOSTONIAN $$$$$ Faneuil Hall Marketplace. **Map 2 D3.** (800) 343-0922 or (617) 523-3600. FAX (617) 523-2454. W www.millenniumhotels.com Three mazelike redbrick former warehouse buildings opposite Faneuil Hall are home to this upscale traditional hotel. Rooms have small balconies. Complimentary airport limousine service.		AE DC MC V D	201 (13)	■		■
OMNI PARKER HOUSE $$$$$ 60 School Street. **Map 2 D4.** (800) 843-6664 or (617) 227-8600. FAX (617) 742-5729. W www.omnihotels.com Home of the Parker House Roll and Boston Cream Pie, this traditional and comfortable hotel has been open since 1855.		AE DC MC V D	551 (21)		●	
WYNDHAM BOSTON $$$$$ 89 Broad Street. **Map 2 E4.** (800) 996-3426 or (617) 556-0006. FAX (617) 556-0053. W www.wyndham.com This Art Deco former office building was converted to a hotel in 1999. The classy lobby and the bathrooms retain original marble floors; rooms are traditionally furnished with modern facilities.		AE DC MC V D	362 (66)		●	

NORTH END AND THE WATERFRONT

		CREDIT CARDS	NUMBER OF ROOMS	RECOMMENDED RESTAURANT	CHILDREN'S FACILITIES	GARDEN OR TERRACE
GOLDEN SLIPPER B&B AFLOAT $$$ Lewis Wharf. **Map 2 E3.** (781) 545-2845. This accommodation comprises a 40-ft (12-m) Chris Craft boat, docked at Lewis Wharf in Boston Harbor. Well equipped, it sleeps up to four and is available to guests from May through October. Owners provide a Continental breakfast.			2			
BOSTON HARBOR HOTEL $$$$$ 70 Rowes Wharf. **Map 2 E4.** (800) 752-7077 or (617) 439-7000. FAX (617) 330-9450. W www.bhh.com This opulent hotel with classically elegant furnishings overlooks the harbor. Although the "Big Dig" construction rumbles nearby, the hotel and its fine contemporary restaurant are oases of calm.		AE DC MC V D	230 (15)	■	●	■
MARRIOTT LONG WHARF $$$$$ 296 State Street. **Map 2 E3.** (800) 228-9290 or (617) 227-0800. FAX (617) 227-2867. W www.marriott.com An upscale, modern chain hotel in a great harborfront location, and which was completely renovated in 2001.		AE DC MC V D	400 (11)		●	■
SEAPORT HOTEL $$$$$ One Seaport Lane. **Map 2 F5.** (877) 732-7678 or (617) 385-4000. FAX (617) 385-4001. W www.seaporthotel.com A modern, towering business hotel next to the World Trade Center, every room has an internet hookup, plus in-room conferencing facilities. Weekend specials are attractive.		AE DC MC V D	426 (24)	■	●	

CHINATOWN AND THE THEATER DISTRICT

		CREDIT CARDS	NUMBER OF ROOMS	RECOMMENDED RESTAURANT	CHILDREN'S FACILITIES	GARDEN OR TERRACE
MILNER HOTEL $$ 78 Charles Street South. **Map 4 E2.** (800) 453-1731 or (617) 426-6220. FAX (617) 350-0360. Modest European-style budget hotel with basic rooms. Avoid the tiny standard rooms. Close to the heart of the Theater District.		AE MC V D	64			
RADISSON BOSTON $$$ 200 Stuart Street. **Map 4 D2.** (800) 333-3333 or (617) 482-1800. FAX (617) 451-2750. W www.radisson.com Comfortable mid-range hotel with lots of amenities. Standard rooms have no particular charm, but the location near to theaters and Back Bay is convenient for tourists and business travelers.		AE DC MC V D			●	

For key to symbols see back flap

Price categories for a standard double room per night, inclusive of breakfast, service charges, and any additional taxes: $ under $100 $$ $100–$150 $$$ $150–$200 $$$$ $200–$250 $$$$$ over $250	**CREDIT CARDS** Major credit cards accepted: *AE* American Express; *DC* Diners Club; *MC* MasterCard/Access; *V* Visa, *D* Discover Card. **NUMBER OF ROOMS** Number of rooms in the hotel (suites are shown in brackets). **RECOMMENDED RESTAURANT** Good restaurant within the hotel. **CHILDREN'S FACILITIES** Hotel has various facilities for young children. **GARDEN OR TERRACE** Hotel has a garden, courtyard, or terrace.			

	CREDIT CARDS	NUMBER OF ROOMS	RECOMMENDED RESTAURANT	CHILDREN'S FACILITIES	GARDEN OR TERRACE
BOSTON PARK PLAZA $$$$$ 64 Arlington Street. **Map 4 D2.** (800) 225-2008 or (617) 426-2000. FAX (617) 426-5545. W www.bostonparkplaza.com Opened in 1927, this grand luxury hotel is classically Bostonian. Elegantly appointed, the spacious rooms also boast many modern amenities, such as voice mail and dataports.	AE DC MC V D	95 (22)		●	
FOUR SEASONS $$$$$ 200 Boylston Street. **Map 4 D2.** (800) 332-3442 or (617) 338-4400. FAX (617) 423-0154. W www.fourseasons.com The ultimate in service and luxury, and consistently ranked among the top hotels in the city. It has grand reception rooms and sumptuous bedrooms, many overlooking the Public Garden.	AE DC MC V D	274 (72)	■	●	
RITZ-CARLTON BOSTON COMMON $$$$$ 10 Avery Street. **Map 4 E2.** (800) 241-3333 or (617) 574-7100. FAX (617) 574-7200. W www.ritzcarlton.com Opened in 2001, the ultra-contemporary "new" Ritz is among Boston's most stylish and sybaritic lodgings. The city's top sports club and a gourmet restaurant are both on the premises.	AE DC MC V D	193 (43)	■	●	
SWISSÔTEL $$$$$ One Avenue de Lafayette. **Map 4 D2.** (800) 621-9200 or (617) 451-2600. FAX (617) 451-0054. W www.swissotel.com A high-rise tower houses this modern, well-appointed hotel that caters to business travelers but also offers good-value weekend specials. The area is a bit seedy but close to Downtown Crossing.	AE DC MC V D	471 (30)		●	
TREMONT BOSTON WYNDHAM HOTEL $$$$$ 275 Tremont Street. **Map 4 E2.** (877) 999-3223 or (617) 426-1400. FAX (617) 338-1893. W www.wyndham.com The refurbished lobby of this imposing 1925 brick and stone building is decorated with pillars and carved granite. Rooms are more simple but have greater flair than those in a standard chain hotel.	AE DC MC V D	322		●	

BACK BAY AND SOUTH END

	CREDIT CARDS	NUMBER OF ROOMS	RECOMMENDED RESTAURANT	CHILDREN'S FACILITIES	GARDEN OR TERRACE
COPLEY HOUSE APARTMENTS $ 239 West Newton Street. **Map 3 B3.** (800) 331-1318 or (617) 236-8300. FAX (617) 424-1815. W www.copleyhouse.com Studio and one-bedroom apartments; weekly rentals only. Ask for details, as apartments vary significantly in style and quality.	AE DC MC V D	65		●	
CHANDLER INN $$ 26 Chandler Street. **Map 4 D3.** (800) 842-3450 or (617) 482-3450. FAX (617) 542-3428. W www.chandlerinn.com A simple but friendly inn in a former Coast Guard station, two blocks from most of the South End's restaurants. The small rooms with floral bed-spreads and simple motel-style furnishings sleep up to two people.	AE DC MC V D	56			
COLLEGE CLUB $$ 44 Commonwealth Avenue. **Map 3 C2.** (617) 536-9510. FAX (617) 247-8537. W www.thecollegeclubofboston.com A hidden gem and excellent value, this ornate Victorian townhouse near the Public Garden is home to a private club. It rents six lovely double rooms, and five more austere singles that share bathrooms.	MC V	11			
COMMONWEALTH COURT GUEST-HOUSE $$ 284 Commonwealth Avenue. **Map 3 A2.** (617) 424-1230. FAX (617) 424-1510, (888) 424-1230. W www.commonwealthcourt.com Some of the simple but comfortably furnished rooms in this 1882 redbrick townhouse retain carved wooden mantles or other original details; all have little kitchenettes. Twice-a-week maid service.	AE MC V	21		*	

COPLEY INN
$$ AE MC V   20
19 Garrison Street. **Map 3 B3.** ((800) 232-0306 or (617) 236-0300.
FAX (617) 536-0816. W www.copleyinn.com
Basic studio apartments with kitchens in an attractive Victorian building.
Children are welcome, but rooms only sleep up to three.

463 BEACON STREET GUEST-HOUSE
$$ DC MC V D   20
463 Beacon Street. **Map 3 A2.** ((617) 536-1302. **FAX** (617) 247-8876.
W www.463beacon.com
This stately five-story guest-house is good value. Rooms vary, but some have
bay windows, fireplaces, and other original features, plus microwaves and
fridges. Most rooms have a private bath. Weekly maid service only.

82 CHANDLER STREET B&B
$$$ 5
82 Chandler Street. **Map 4 D3.** ((617) 482-0408.
FAX (617) 482-0659. W www.channel1.com/82chandler
Located on a residential South End street, this long-established B&B in a
four-story row house has three guest rooms, plus two studio apartments.
All units are well furnished; four have kitchenettes; only two have TVs.

NEWBURY GUEST-HOUSE
$$$ AE DC MC V D   32
261 Newbury Street. **Map 3 B2.** ((617) 437-7666. **FAX** (617) 262-4243,
(800) 437-7668. W www.hagopianhotels.com
In Boston's chic shopping neighborhood, this brownstone guest-house caters
to business people and fashionable vacationers. Tasteful rooms are furnished
with Victorian-style reproductions. Book well in advance.

UNION PARK GUEST-HOUSE
$$$ AE MC V   3
12 Union Park. **Map 4 D4.** ((617) 421-1821. **FAX** (617) 421-1821.
W www.unionparkguesthouse.com
One block from Tremont Street and its many restaurants, this Victorian
townhouse has large rooms furnished with queen-sized beds. No breakfast is
served, but rooms have fridges, and there are several cafés nearby.

BACK BAY HILTON
$$$$ AE DC MC V D   384 (6)
40 Dalton Street. **Map 3 A3.** ((800) 874-0063 or (617) 236-1100.
FAX (617) 867-6104. W www.hilton.com
Modern 26-story tower hotel behind the Hynes Convention Center with
well-equipped rooms. Prices are often lower than at comparable Back
Bay hotels, especially on weekends.

CLARENDON SQUARE INN
$$$$ AE MC V   3
198 West Brookline Street. **Map 3 C4.** ((617) 536-2229. **FAX** (617) 266-2993.
W www.clarendonsquare.com
A stylish, professionally run B&B in an elegantly restored 1860s South
End townhouse. Rooms all have fireplaces and are decorated in a mix of
modern and traditional furnishings. There is a roof deck with hot tub.

MIDTOWN HOTEL
$$$$ AE DC MC V D   159 (2)
220 Huntington Avenue. **Map 3 B4.** ((800) 343-1177 or (617) 262-1000.
FAX (617) 262-8739. W www.midtownhotel.com
Family-friendly 1960s hotel near Symphony Hall. Simple, clean rooms. Front
and side rooms are more spacious than those in rear.

WHITAKER HOUSE B&B
$$$$ AE MC V   3
170 West Newton Street. **Map 3 C4.** ((617) 437-6464. **FAX** (617) 424-6833.
W www.whitaker-house.com
The rooms in this traditional but stylish 1868 townhouse have decorative
marble fireplaces, four-poster or brass beds, and other period features.
Breakfast is served in the kitchen or in the small garden.

COPLEY SQUARE HOTEL
$$$$$ AE DC MC V D   143 (11)
47 Huntington Avenue. **Map 3 C3.** ((800) 225-7062 or (617) 536-9000.
FAX (617) 267-3547. W www.copleysquarehotel.com
The rooms in this comfortably appointed older hotel have traditional
reproduction furnishings, including wing chairs and armoires. More
character than many nearby high-rise hotels.

ELIOT HOTEL
$$$$$ AE DC MC V D   95 (95)
370 Commonwealth Avenue. **Map 3 A2.** ((800) 443-5468 or
(617) 267-1607. **FAX** (617) 536-9114. W www.eliothotel.com
Graciously furnished, all-suite hotel, built in 1925. Rooms have separate
sitting rooms, plus business amenities including fax machines and dataports.
Home of the fine contemporary restaurant, Clio.

For key to symbols see back flap

Price categories for a standard double room per night, inclusive of breakfast, service charges, and any additional taxes:

Ⓢ under $100
ⓈⓈ $100–$150
ⓈⓈⓈ $150–$200
ⓈⓈⓈⓈ $200–$250
ⓈⓈⓈⓈⓈ over $250

CREDIT CARDS
Major credit cards accepted: *AE* American Express; *DC* Diners Club; *MC* MasterCard/Access; *V* Visa, *D* Discover Card.

NUMBER OF ROOMS
Number of rooms in the hotel (suites are shown in brackets).

RECOMMENDED RESTAURANT
Good restaurant within the hotel.

CHILDREN'S FACILITIES
Hotel has various facilities for young children.

GARDEN OR TERRACE
Hotel has a garden, courtyard, or terrace.

	CREDIT CARDS	NUMBER OF ROOMS	RECOMMENDED RESTAURANT	CHILDREN'S FACILITIES	GARDEN OR TERRACE
FAIRMONT COPLEY PLAZA HOTEL ⓈⓈⓈⓈⓈ 138 St. James Avenue. **Map 3 C2.** (800) 527-4727 or (617) 267-5300. FAX (617) 247-6681. W www.fairmont.com The gold lions guarding the hotel entrance are a city landmark. Known as the "grande dame" of Boston, this ornately appointed, palatial hotel is the epitome of luxury.	AE DC MC V D	379 (60)	■	●	
LENOX HOTEL ⓈⓈⓈⓈ 710 Boylston Street. **Map 3 B2.** (800) 225-7676 or (617) 536-5300. FAX (617) 267-1237. W www.lenoxhotel.com This highly regarded and recently refurbished 100-year-old hotel has sumptuously appointed rooms with all manner of luxuries. It is also home to the excellent Anago restaurant.	AE DC MC V D	212 (12)	■	●	
RITZ-CARLTON HOTEL ⓈⓈⓈⓈⓈ 15 Arlington Street. **Map 4 D2.** (800) 241-3333 or (617) 536-5700. FAX (617) 536-9340. W www.ritzcarlton.com This large luxury hotel, built in 1927 and overlooking the Public Garden, reopened in fall 2002 after extensive renovations. The tradition of excellent service remains unchanged.	AE DC MC V D	275 (42)	●		■
WESTIN COPLEY PLACE ⓈⓈⓈⓈⓈ 10 Huntington Avenue. **Map 3 C3.** (800) 228-3000 or (617) 262-9600. FAX (617) 424-7483. W www.westin.com This 36-story hotel buzzes with business traffic. Comfortable and upscale, it has excellent facilities and great views.	AE DC MC V D	800 (45)	■	●	
FARTHER AFIELD					
LONGWOOD INN Ⓢ 123 Longwood Avenue, Brookline. (617) 566-8615. FAX (617) 738-1070. W www.igo.boston.com/longwoodin Turn-of-the-century Arts and Crafts-style mansion, now a budget inn. It retains an air of faded elegance, although the rooms are quite basic.		22		●	■
CONSTITUTION INN ⓈⓈ 150 Second Avenue, Charlestown. (617) 241-8400. FAX (617) 241-2856. An economy inn run by the armed services, most of the rooms have two twin beds, although several have queen-sized ones.	AE MC V	149 (2)			
BROOKLINE MANOR INN ⓈⓈⓈ 32 Center Street, Brookline. (800) 535-5325 or (617) 232-0003. FAX (617) 734-5815. W www.brooklinemanorinn.com This tastefully refurbished Victorian guest-house has simple but comfortable rooms, all with modern *en-suite* bathrooms.	AE MC V	35		●	■
HARVARD SQUARE HOTEL ⓈⓈⓈ 110 Mt. Auburn Street, Cambridge. (800) 458-5886 or (617) 864-5200. FAX (617) 864-2409. W www.doubletreehotels.com Location is the best feature of this refurbished hotel in the heart of Harvard Square. The rooms are basic but comfortable.	AE DC MC V D	73		●	
HOLIDAY INN EXPRESS ⓈⓈⓈ 250 Monsignor O'Brien Highway, Cambridge. (888) 887-7690 or (617) 577-7600. FAX (617) 354-1313. W www.basshotels.com Basic, affordable, family-friendly chain hotel, but in a charmless location. Fridges, microwaves, voice mail, and dataports in rooms.	AE DC MC V D	112 (21)		●	
HOTEL@MIT – UNIVERSITY PARK ⓈⓈⓈ 20 Sidney Street, Cambridge. (800) 222-8733 or (617) 577-0200. FAX (617) 494-8366. W www.hotel@mit.com This hotel, owned by Massachusetts Institute of Technology, has in-room internet access and phones with voice mail.	AE DC MC V D	210 (28)	●		■

INN AT HARVARD $$$

	AE	113		●	
	DC	(1)			
	MC				
	V				
	D				

1201 Massachusetts Avenue, Cambridge. ☎ (800) 458-5886 or
(617) 491-2222. FAX (617) 520-3711. W www.theinnatharvard.com
Modern four-story hotel built around a sunny atrium, which blends well
with the nearby Harvard University buildings. The rooms are comfortably
appointed and filled with period furniture. 🔌 ⊞ ↕ ▮ 🔖 P ♿

IRVING HOUSE $$$

	AE	44		●	▪
	MC				
	V				

24 Irving Street, Cambridge. ☎ (877) 547-4600 or (617) 547-4600.
FAX (617) 576-2814. W www.irvinghouse.com
This wooden-framed Victorian house inn has simple rooms (some are quite
small) and an attractive terrace. Some rooms share baths. 🔌 ⊞ ▮ P ♿

A CAMBRIDGE HOUSE BED AND BREAKFAST $$$$

	AE	15			▪
	DC				
	MC				
	V				
	D				

2218 Massachusetts Avenue, Cambridge. ☎ (800) 232-9989 or (617) 491-6300.
FAX (617) 868-2848. W www.acambridgehouse.com
This enchanting bright yellow 1892 house is now an exquisitely restored
Victorian fantasy, complete with four-poster beds and working fireplaces.
🔌 P

BERTRAM INN $$$$

	AE	14			▪
	DC	(4)			
	MC				
	V				
	D				

92 Sewall Avenue, Brookline. ☎ (800) 295-3822 or (617) 566-2234.
FAX (617) 277-1887. W www.bertraminn.com
A meticulously restored 1907 Arts and Crafts-style home, with an elegant
parlor, sun porch, and cozy, antiques-filled rooms. 🔌 ⊞ 🔖 P

GRYPHON HOUSE $$$$

	AE	8			
	DC	(8)			
	MC				
	V				

9 Bay State Road, Boston. ☎ (877) 375-9003 or (617) 375-9003.
FAX (617) 425-0716. W www.gryphonhouseboston.com
This five-story 1895 bowfronted boutique hotel has gracious antiques-filled
public rooms and large guest suites furnished in a variety of styles. Bath-
rooms have whirlpool tubs, and some rooms have river views. 🔌 ⊞ 🔖 P

MARY PRENTISS INN $$$$

	AE	20			▪
	MC	(5)			
	V				

6 Prentiss Street, Cambridge. ☎ (617) 661-2929. FAX (617) 661-5989.
W www.maryprentissinn.com
An antiques-filled B&B in a Greek Revival-style house, with a spacious
sun deck and comfortable sitting rooms. Modern amenities include
dataports. 🔌 🔖 P

BOSTON MARRIOTT CAMBRIDGE $$$$$

	AE	431		●	
	DC	(13)			
	MC				
	V				
	D				

2 Cambridge Center, Cambridge. ☎ (800) 228-9290 or (617) 494-6600.
FAX (617) 494-0036. W www.marriott.com
Rising among the Kendall Square office towers, this upscale chain hotel
features modern, well-equipped rooms. Hosting a business crowd during the
week, it attracts leisure travelers on weekends. 🔌 ⊞ ↕ ▮ 🏊 🍽 🔖 P ♿

CHARLES HOTEL $$$$$

	AE	293	▪	●	▪
	DC	(44)			
	MC				
	V				
	D				

One Bennett Street, Cambridge. ☎ (800) 882-1818 or (617) 864-1200.
FAX (617) 864-5715. W www.charleshotel.com
This contemporary luxury hotel has rooms appointed with Shaker-style
furnishings and quilts. Home of the excellent modern-Mediterranean Rialto
restaurant and the Regattabar jazz club. 🕐 🔌 ⊞ ↕ ▮ 🏊 🍽 🔖 P ♿

HYATT REGENCY CAMBRIDGE $$$$$

	AE	469		●	▪
	DC	(10)			
	MC				
	V				
	D				

575 Memorial Drive, Cambridge. ☎ (800) 233-1234 or (617) 492-1234.
FAX (617) 491-6906. W www.hyatt.com
Modern pyramid-shaped hotel on the Charles River with a revolving
restaurant and great views of the Boston skyline. Slightly inaccessible for
those without a car, but there is a shuttle service for guests. Room rates
drop by as much as 50 percent on weekends. 🔌 ⊞ ↕ ▮ 🏊 🍽 🔖 P ♿

ROYAL SONESTA HOTEL $$$$$

	AE	400	▪	●	▪
	DC	(23)			
	MC				
	V				
	D				

5 Cambridge Parkway, Cambridge. ☎ (800) 766-3782 or (617) 806-4200.
FAX (617) 806-4232. W www.sonesta.com
Large modern hotel with panoramic views. Rooms are comfortable but
unfussy and have internet access, plus phones with voice mail. The Gallery
Café patio is pleasant for outside dining. 🕐 🔌 ⊞ ↕ ▮ 🏊 🍽 🔖 P ♿

SHERATON COMMANDER $$$$$

	AE	175		●	
	DC	(14)			
	MC				
	V				
	D				

16 Garden Street, Cambridge. ☎ (800) 535-5007 or (617) 547-4800.
FAX (617) 868-8322. W www.sheratoncommander.com
Chic, old-fashioned hotel opposite Cambridge Common. Rooms are
decorated in traditional colonial style. 🔌 ⊞ ↕ ▮ 🍽 🔖 P ♿

For key to symbols see back flap

RESTAURANTS, CAFÉS, AND BARS

OR A NUMBER of years Boston had a reputation of serving stodgy, old New England fare. Today, however, this is no longer the case, as the city now has a wide variety of exciting places to eat. Along with more traditional cuisine, Boston restaurants show many diverse influences, with immigrant restaurateurs and innovative chefs transforming local restaurant culture. Celebrated chefs also bring traditional

Sign for a downtown seafood restaurant

Boston cuisine to life for modern palates, and restaurants all delight in fresh New England produce. The top restaurants serve a medley of styles, such as French and Italian, often using other Mediterranean and Asian accents. For other flavors of the world, Boston has many Indian, Southeast Asian, Latin American, Caribbean, and Japanese restaurants, which are located in small neighborhoods and fashionable streets alike.

Murals at the Casablanca restaurant, a Cambridge institution

EATING THE BOSTONIAN WAY

IF YOUR LODGINGS don't include breakfast, join locals on their way to work and have a bagel and a cup of steaming coffee in one of the city's many delis and coffee bars. Most places also offer pastries, muffins, coffee cake, tea, and fruit juices. Diners offer richer, more substantial breakfasts of bacon, eggs, potatoes, and toast, with a "bottomless" cup of coffee – one with free refills.

Lunches in Boston may also be a simple sandwich or a larger meal in a restaurant, depending on how much time you have, and how hungry you are. Business districts abound with lunch options – join office workers Downtown at a lunch counter for a grinder (long filled roll).

Dinner is the biggest meal of the day for Bostonians. The most exclusive and elegant

restaurants are in the Financial District and Downtown. Those in the Back Bay and the South End tend to be more trendy and youthful. Cambridge restaurants are more relaxed, reflecting the area's laid-back atmosphere. (A very useful website for menus and prices is www.bostonchefs.com).

OPENING HOURS

THE TYPES OF MEALS served at many restaurants vary according to the type of establishment and its location. Many downtown lunch counters are open only for breakfast and lunch, while some finer restaurants are open only for dinner. Some restaurants close for a few hours between lunch and dinner, while smaller family-run places may stay open throughout the afternoon, making them a good bet for eating at more unusual times. Generally, lunch is served from 11:30am to 2:30pm, and dinner from 5:30 to 10:30pm. Massachusetts state law prohibits the sale of alcohol, including beer and wine, after 2am, so bars and most restaurants will close by then. There

are some very late night restaurants in Chinatown and Kenmore Square, supported mostly by the ravenous crowds leaving dance clubs and bars. Liquor sales are also restricted to dinner only on Sundays, although a few places (mostly in the South End) are allowed to serve cocktails with their amazing Sunday brunches.

Attractive exterior of the Terramia restaurant (see p136)

PAYING AND TIPPING

MOST RESTAURANTS with table service will bring you your bill at the end of the meal. The bill will have a 7 percent state meals tax added to the total. All restaurants with table service expect you to leave a tip for your waiter, who is paid a very low rate

The fashionable Sonsie restaurant in Boston's Back Bay (see p137)

A typically Italian atmosphere is created at Caffè Vittoria *(see p140)*

with the expectation that tips will fill out their salary. The standard tip is 15 percent of the pre-tax bill. If service is especially good or bad, adjust the tip accordingly. If paying by credit card, you may include the tip in the charged amount. Fast food restaurants may have optional tip jars next to the cashier.

BOOKING

FINER RESTAURANTS often require a reservation, though in most cases (especially on weeknights) reservations can be made at short notice. There are a few very popular places that do not accept reservations, and customers must put their names on the waiting list. The host will tell you how long you can expect to wait.

ALCOHOL AND SMOKING

THE CITY OF BOSTON has recently undertaken to prohibit smoking in all of its restaurants. The exception to this rule is if a restaurant has a bar area, where smoking is usually permitted. Boston's bars almost always have no restrictions on smoking.

Twenty-one is the legal drinking age, so under-age travelers should be aware that they will be denied access to most bars. They will not be able to order wine with dinner in restaurants, either. If there is any doubt that a person is old enough, proof will be required, so use your I.D. or passport if asked.

ETIQUETTE

FOR THE MOST PART, Bostonians dress on the casual side when dining out. The few restaurants that do have strict dress codes usually require a reservation, so ask when booking. For the top dining rooms, a jacket and tie for gentlemen and the equivalent for women is expected. Ladies may wear slacks, though skirts or dresses are more traditional. Formal evening wear is uncommon but not out of place in the finer restaurants.

CHILDREN

CHILDREN are welcome in most mid-range restaurants, although in the business areas restaurants are often

less accustomed to them. Avoid restaurants that feature a large bar and young crowds, as they are less likely to permit under 21's on the premises.

DISABILITIES

A NUMBER of restaurants in Boston and Cambridge are accessible by wheelchair *(see pp134–9)*, and many more are accessible to people with other disabilities. Doors may be fitted with an automatic opener, and rest rooms usually include the appropriate stalls and sinks.

FAST FOOD

BEING A COLLEGE CITY, Boston is teeming with fast food options. Sandwiches come in infinite varieties, the classic sandwich being found along with "wraps" (fillings wrapped up in a flatbread), "grinders" (long rolls stuffed with meats), and gourmet sandwiches on baguette or *focaccia*. Pizza is another ubiquitous meal, and bagels, spread with cream cheese, are a popular snack eaten on the go. Burritos are hearty portable meals of meat, beans, and cheese rolled into a flour tortilla. Downtown and Harvard Square are good places for fast food, with their many lunch counters catering to business people. These are reliable and easy on the wallet.

Enjoying a beer outside at one of Quincy Market's bars *(see p66)*

What to Eat in Boston

Ice cream

BOSTON'S CUISINE reflects the many cultures that have settled since the 17th century, when English pilgrims first adapted their tastes to include local ingredients. Ethnic foods are commonplace; the Irish brought corned beef and potatoes, the Italians pasta, and all adopted native ingredients. Many traditional dishes depended on foods that kept well – Boston was dubbed the "land of the bean and the cod," as both lasted well through winter. Today, it is not surprising to find elegant dining rooms, strongly influenced by tradition, serving variations on classical dishes.

Wild Blueberry Pancakes
Served in a stack with butter and maple syrup. Tiny wild blueberries from Maine are mixed in with the batter.

Deep Filled Sandwich
Huge, deep filled sandwiches are a Boston specialty. The choice of breads and fillings is almost endless.

Boston Baked Beans
White beans slow baked with salt pork and molasses are served with codfish cakes, brown bread, and beets.

Mustard seasoning

Beets

Small whole onions

Beef

Cabbage

Pickles

Carrots

Boiled potatoes

New England Boiled Dinner
Originally an Irish dish, this homestyle favorite consists of a large piece of beef, which is slow boiled with cabbage, potatoes, carrots, and onions. It is served with mustard seasoning and pickled beets and cucumbers on the side.

Chicken Pot Pie
Served as individual pies or by the wedge, the filling contains chunks of chicken and vegetables in a creamy sauce.

Calamari Italian Style
Whole, baked squid stuffed with breadcrumbs, herbs, and garlic are served in a rich tomato and herb sauce.

Sushi
Seasoned rice topped with thin sliced, raw fish such as tuna, yellowfin, and salmon, form nigiri sushi. Maki sushi is rolled in seaweed to enclose the fish and rice. Both types come with horseradish and pickled ginger.

Italian salami

SAUSAGES

Cured hard sausages, such as Italian salami, are eaten cold and are often found in sandwiches. Semi-cured and fresh sausages, including German *wurst* and Irish bangers, are served hot. Polish *kielbasa* can be chopped into omelets, while *linguica* is found in Portuguese soup.

Semi-cured Polish *kielbasa*

Semi-cured Portuguese *linguica*

German *wurst*

Irish banger

Boiled lobster

Steamer clams

Corn on the cob

Baked potato

Melted butter

Clam Chowder
This creamy soup contains chunks of potato and chopped clams. Corn, fish, and other chowders are also popular.

Clambakes
A boiled lobster and clams steamed with seaweed are served with fresh corn on the cob and baked potatoes. The lobster and clams are dipped into melted butter and eaten, usually, with the fingers.

Pretzel

Cookies

Muffin

Bagels

Wilted Spinach Salad
This side dish consists mainly of wilted spinach with crisp fried bacon crumbled on top. A light dressing may be added.

Baked Goods
Bagels and muffins are common breakfast foods. Cookies tend to be large, chewy, and hearty, with flavors such as oatmeal and chocolate chip. Large, soft pretzels are a ballpark treat.

Squash
Summer squashes come in two varieties – green zucchini and yellow squash. They are a common side dish in late summer.

Indian Pudding
Served with ice cream or cream, this slow baked, soft pudding is made of cornmeal, sugar, molasses, spices, and milk.

Pumpkin Pie
This pumpkin, milk, egg, and spice custard pie is often eaten at Thanksgiving and typically served in slices with cream.

DRINKS

As well as simple brewed cups of American-style coffee, espresso, cappuccino, and latte have become Bostonian favorites; decaffeinated coffee is also widely available. A host of microbreweries that brew beer to sell only in their restaurants have sprung up in the city. Sam Adams, on the other hand, is available on tap everywhere. Sakonnet Vineyards produces New England wines that can be found in some restaurants. Cranberry juice and frappés, a blend of ice cream and milk, are a refreshing alternative to alcoholic drinks.

Cranberry juice

Fruit frappé

A selection of microbrewery beers

Sam Adams beer

Sakonnet wine

Choosing a Restaurant

RESTAURANTS HAVE been selected across a wide range of price categories for their value, good food, atmosphere, and location. The chart below highlights some of the factors that may influence your choice of where to eat. Restaurants are listed by area, and within these by price. Opening times are indicated by a "B" for breakfast, "L" for lunch, and "D" for dinner.

	CREDIT CARDS	OUTDOOR TABLES	VEGETARIAN	GOOD WINE	LATE OPENING
BEACON HILL AND WEST END					
PANIFICIO $ 144 Charles St. **Map** 1 B3. (*(617) 227-4340.* Bakery and restaurant that serves a variety of unusual and delicious sandwiches, pizza, salads, and pastries. They also offer a few larger entrées, and serve Sunday brunch. No wine. B, L, D.			▦		
PARAMOUNT DELI-RESTAURANT $$ 44 Charles St. **Map** 1 B4. (*(617) 720-1152.* Imagine a diner-turned-gourmet, and you have the Paramount. The urban "home cooking" from their open kitchen includes chicken *picatta* and *farfalle* with sun-dried tomatoes, feta, and garlic. B, L, D. 🏃	AE MC V		▦		
FIGS $$$ 42 Charles St. **Map** 1 B4. (*(617) 742-3447.* A side project of famed chef Todd English, conceived as a similar but more affordable option to Olives in Charlestown. The Mediterranean influence shows in the huge array of pizza, pasta, and appetizers. L (Sat, Sun), D. 🏃	AE MC V		▦	●	
75 CHESTNUT $$$ 75 Chestnut St. **Map** 1 B4. (*(617) 227-2175.* The dark wood interior suggests an age-old private club; the menu, though, is anything but traditional. The focus is on delicious seafood, such as their pistachio-crusted salmon. Brunch Sun (mid-Sep–May), D. 🅿 🍸 🔥	AE DC MC V D		▦	●	
NO. 9 PARK $$$$ 9 Park St. **Map** 1 C4. (*(617) 742-9991.* The jazz-influenced retro decor here puts diners in a light-hearted mood. Carefully considered and well-executed modern American menu, including lobster, seafood, and game. L (Mon–Fri), D. 🅿 🍸 🍴 🔥 ● Sun.	AE DC MC V			●	
THE HUNGRY I $$$$$ 71 Charles St. **Map** 1 B4. (*(617) 227-3524.* Chef-owner Peter Ballarin has given this beloved institution a sophisticated facelift. The French-influenced food features fish and game. The enclosed terrace is a romantic oasis. L (Tue–Fri), D, Brunch Sun. ● Aug.	AE DC MC V	●	▦	●	
OLD BOSTON AND THE FINANCIAL DISTRICT					
DURGIN-PARK $$$ 340 North Market St. (Faneuil Hall Marketplace). **Map** 2 D3. (*(617) 227-2038.* A Boston institution, serving all the New England standards that no one else seems to cook any more – Indian pudding, baked beans, and baked scrod, dished up by a sharp-tongued staff. L, D. 🎵 🍸 🏃	AE DC MC V D				
UNION OYSTER HOUSE $$$$ 41 Union St. **Map** 2 D3. (*(617) 227-2750.* Boston's oldest restaurant, the Union Oyster House has managed to keep up with the times and features a respected updated menu of traditional New England seafood and more. Oyster bar is the best part. L, D. 🅿 🍸 🏃	AE DC MC V D			●	
JULIEN $$$$$ 250 Franklin St. (Hotel Meridien). **Map** 2 D4. (*(617) 451-1900.* Unadulterated French haute cuisine, exquisitely prepared. Julien has the comfort and grace of a classic dining room that is confident of its quality. Reservations are recommended. L, D. 🎵 🍴 🅿 🍸 🔥 ● Sun.	AE DC MC V D			●	
MAISON ROBERT $$$$$ 45 School St. **Map** 2 D4. (*(617) 227-3370.* This is *the* home of French cuisine in Boston, unfussy yet *au courant*. The café serves bistro fare for many budgets; the dining room is more expensive and requires reservations. L (Mon–Fri), D. 🅿 🍸 🍴 🔥 ● Sun.	AE MC V D	●	▦	●	

		Price categories / Legend	CREDIT CARDS	OUTDOOR TABLES	VEGETARIAN	GOOD WINE	LATE OPENING

Price categories include a three-course meal for one, half a bottle of house wine and all unavoidable extra charges such as sales tax and service.

$ under $20
$$ $20–30
$$$ $30–45
$$$$ $45–60
$$$$$ over $60

CREDIT CARDS
Major credit cards accepted: *AE* American Express; *MC* Master Card/Access; *DC* Diners Club; *V* Visa; *D* Discover Card.

OUTDOOR TABLES
Garden, courtyard, or terrace with outside tables.

VEGETARIAN
A good selection of vegetarian dishes available.

GOOD WINE
Extensive list of good wines, both native and international.

LATE OPENING
Full menu or light meals served after 11pm.

Restaurant	Credit Cards	Outdoor Tables	Vegetarian	Good Wine	Late Opening
THE VAULT $$$$ 105 Water St. **Map** 2 D4. (617) 292-9966. Upscale restaurant in the business district featuring both rustic Italian and southeast Asian fare. Dishes include shrimp pot stickers and *spaghettini* with lamb meatballs. L, D. ▼ ● Sun.	AE DC MC V D	●	■	●	■

NORTH END AND THE WATERFRONT

Restaurant	Credit Cards	Outdoor Tables	Vegetarian	Good Wine	Late Opening
ERNESTO'S PIZZERIA $ 69 Salem St. **Map** 2 D4. (617) 523-1373. Absolutely nothing fancy here, just a few tables, sawdust on the floor, and excellent fresh pizza. Perfect for lunch in a rush. No wine. L, D.			■		
MONICA'S $$ 67 Prince St. **Map** 2 E2. (617) 720-5472. An attractive pizza parlor in the North End, Monica's serves gourmet pizzas with seafood, chicken, vegetables, and scores of other combinations at cozy little tables. Good salads, too. No wine. D. 🚻	MC V		■		
RUDI'S $$ 30 Rowes Wharf (Boston Harbor Hotel). **Map** 2 E4. (617) 330-7656. Large delicatessen, where patrons order portions from the serving counter, and seat themselves at café tables. Beautiful pastries and gourmet food gifts to take home. No wine. B, L, D. 🅿 🚻	AE MC V D	●	■		
BARKING CRAB $$$ 88 Sleeper St. **Map** 2 E5. (617) 426-2722. Boston's classic shoreside seafood joint, facing the city across Fort Point Channel. Lobster, steamers, clamrolls, and chowder, all served along with plenty of paper napkins. L, D, Brunch Sun (winter only). ♪ 🅿 ▼ 🚻	AE MC V	●	■		
LA FAMIGLIA GIORGIO'S $$$ 112 Salem St. **Map** 2 D2. (617) 367-6711. Huge portions of well prepared pasta are the order of the day here, and La Famiglia is always ready to help you choose. Good value – you will leave full and happy. L, D. 🚻	AE DC MC V D		■		
POMODORO $$$ 319 Hanover St. **Map** 2 E2. (617) 367-4348. Crowded, raucous, and aromatic, the small storefront housing Pomodoro brims with patrons at all hours. The menu has real Italian dishes that are always well prepared. Try the monkfish with saffron risotto. L, D. 🚻			■		
ANTICO FORNO $$$$ 93 Salem St. **Map** 2 D2. (617) 723-6733. Menu featuring meals cooked in the large brick oven in the rear of the dining room. Excellent pizza and roasted meats. L (Mon–Sat), D. 🚻	MC V		■		
RABIA'S $$$$ 73 Salem St. **Map** 2 D2. (617) 227-6637. Romantic Italian restaurant, with helpful staff who combine with a talented chef to create a relaxed and convivial evening. D. ♪ 🚻	AE DC MC V D		■	●	
TAVERNA TOSCANA $$$$ 63 Salem St. **Map** 2 D2. (617) 742-5233. Frescoes and subtle, golden-hued walls create a comfortable setting in this intimate Italian restaurant. Good choice of seasonally inspired entrées. D.	AE MC V		■		
ROWES WHARF RESTAURANT $$$$$ 70 Rowes Wharf (Boston Harbor Hotel). **Map** 2 E4. (617) 439-3995. Elegant dining room overlooking the Boston Harbor. Serves excellent seafood and meats, prepared in a classical style with contemporary influences. Reservations recommended. L, D, Brunch Sun. 🅿 ▼ 🚻	AE DC MC V D		■	●	

Price categories include a three-course meal for one, half a bottle of house wine and all unavoidable extra charges such as sales tax and service.
$ under $20
$$ $20–30
$$$ $30–45
$$$$ $45–60
$$$$$ over $60

CREDIT CARDS
Major credit cards accepted: *AE* American Express; *MC* Master Card/Access; *DC* Diners Club; *V* Visa; *D* Discover Card.

OUTDOOR TABLES
Garden, courtyard, or terrace with outside tables.

VEGETARIAN
A good selection of vegetarian dishes available.

GOOD WINE
Extensive list of good wines, both native and international.

LATE OPENING
Full menu or light meals served after 11pm.

Restaurant	Credit Cards	Outdoor Tables	Vegetarian	Good Wine	Late Opening
TERRAMIA $$$$$ 98 Salem St. **Map** 2 D2. (617) 523-3112. Boisterous and mixed clientele line up nightly to dine on the trademark *gnocchi*, prepared daily, as well as on the sublime lobster fritters. Casual, friendly service and setting. D.	AE DC MC V D		■		
THE CHART HOUSE $$$$$ 60 Long Wharf. **Map** 2 E3. (617) 227-1576. A steak and seafood dining room frequented by tourists wandering the waterfront. Decor is quaintly old-fashioned, with ships' wheels and other nautical paraphernalia. Only snacks are served outside. D.	AE DC MC V D	●	■		
TRATTORIA A SCALINATELL $$$$$ 253 Hanover St. **Map** 2 E2. (617) 742-8240. A refreshingly original take on the age-old Italian trattoria. Diners may choose to eschew the menu in favor of host and owner Paolo's recommended progression of courses, chosen to suit your tastes. D.	AE MC V			●	

CHINATOWN AND THE THEATER DISTRICT

Restaurant	Credit Cards	Outdoor Tables	Vegetarian	Good Wine	Late Opening
BREW MOON $$$$ 115 Stuart St. **Map** 4 E2. (617) 742-2739. Thriving brew-pub serving very good modern American cuisine and a wide range of snacks to eat while sampling the award-winning beers. Also has a branch in Harvard Square. L, D, Brunch Sun.	AE DC MC V	●	■		■
CHINA PEARL $$$$ 9 Tyler St. **Map** 4 F2. (617) 426-4338. Boston's best dim sum, including seasonal favorites such as steamed dumplings and sesame balls. The atmosphere is noisy and exuberant. B, L, D.	AE MC V D		■		
EAST OCEAN CITY $$$$ 25-29 Beach St. **Map** 4 F2. (617) 542-2504. Tanks full of fish destined for diners' plates welcome visitors here. The menu includes seafood and much more, in portions meant to be shared. L, D.	AE MC V		■		■
IMPERIAL SEAFOOD RESTAURANT $$$$ 70 Beach St. **Map** 4 F2. (617) 426-8439. Friendly Cantonese restaurant serving tasty seafood, vegetable, and meat dishes, as well as dim sum, selected from a roving trolley. L, D.	AE MC V		■		
JACOB WIRTH COMPANY RESTAURANT $$$$ 31-37 Stuart St. **Map** 4 E2. (617) 339-8586. Built by German Jacob Wirth, the 19th-century decor remains unaltered. Delicious *wursts* and *schnitzel*. Great selection of beer. L, D.	AE DC MC V D				
LEGAL SEAFOODS $$$$$ 26 Park Square. **Map** 4 E2. (617) 426-4444. Legal has many locations throughout the city, all serving the freshest and best prepared fish and seafood available. Try their raw bar for oysters, then one of their superb entrées. L, D.	AE DC MC V D		■	●	■
LOCKE-OBER $$$$$ 3 Winter Place. **Map** 1 C4. (617) 542-1340. New owners have breathed excitement into one of America's most legendary restaurants, founded in 1875. Inventive twists enliven European and American classic dishes. Reservations essential. L, D.	AE DC MC V			●	

BACK BAY AND SOUTH END

Restaurant	Credit Cards	Outdoor Tables	Vegetarian	Good Wine	Late Opening
FIREFLY $$ 130 Dartmouth St. **Map** 3 C3. (617) 262-4393. A casual, contemporary restaurant with modern deco. It excels at salads, risottos, pizzas and desserts (such as an eight-layer chocolate trifle). B, L, D.	MC V		■		

MEN TEI NOODLE HOUSE $$
66 Hereford St. **Map** 3 A2. **(** *(617) 425-0066.*
Osaka-style *udon* noodles and an array of snack foods and entrées for a
low budget. Efficient staff and mixed, lively clientele. No wine. L, D.

STEVE'S $$
316 Newbury St. **Map** 3 A3. **(** *(617) 267-1817.*
This casual Greek restaurant is a bargain among its more glamorous neighbors. All the Greek classics, and retsina to wash it down with. B, L, D.

DC
MC
V
D

THE OTHER SIDE COSMIC CAFE $$
407 Newbury St. **Map** 3 A3. **(** *(617) 536-9477.*
Avant-garde juice bar and sandwich restaurant with cheerful staff. Bever-
ages dominate, from health-conscious wheat grass to potent black coffee.
Hip, artsy crowd makes anyone feel at home. No wine. L, D.

CIAO BELLA $$$
240 Newbury St. **Map** 3 A3. **(** *(617) 536-2626.*
This restaurant serves good quality southern Italian dishes. The main
feature, however, is the outside seating, which attracts a lively crowd,
including sports figures and celebrtities L, D.

AE
MC
V

THE POUR HOUSE $$$
907-909 Boylston St. **Map** 3 B3. **(** *(617) 236-1767.*
Casual and popular place, with typical bar menu and simple, well-
cooked food. Burgers, fries, and beer are the things to have here. B, L, D.

MC
V

CHARLEY'S SALOON $$$$
284 Newbury St. **Map** 3 B2. **(** *(617) 266-3000.*
Typical American food, well prepared, is what Charley's does best.
Large outdoor seating area is cool and shady in the afternoon. The
bar is busy from after work onward. L, D, Brunch Sun.

AE
DC
MC
V
D

GYUHAMA OF JAPAN $$$$
827 Boylston St. **Map** 3 B3. **(** *(617) 437-0188.*
One of the best sushi bars in Boston, with both tables and chairs and tatami
rooms. Drop by late-night for the surreal Rock-n-Roll Sushi, when waitresses
change from kimonos to dancing gear, with music to match. L, D.

AE
DC
MC
V
D

METROPOLIS $$$$
584 Tremont St. **Map** 4 D4. **(** *(617) 247-2931.*
A very pleasant environment in which to dine. The Sunday brunch
is festive, and dinner unassuming and tasty. Modern American cuisine
with Mediterranean influences. D, Brunch Sat and Sun.

AE
MC
V

SAMUEL ADAMS BREW HOUSE $$$$
710 Boylston St. **Map** 3 B2. **(** *(617) 536-2739.*
The brew-pub outlet for the national microbrewed beer, it attracts
a big after-work and tourist crowd. Food is decent, with the generic
menu including burgers and plenty of appetizers. L, D.

AE
DC
MC
V
D

TAPEO $$$$
266 Newbury St. **Map** 3 B2. **(** *(617) 267-4799.*
A wonderfully earthy tapas bar in the middle of pretentious Newbury Street.
Regulars are devoted to the sangria and a dinner of tiny dishes, though
there is a full menu. Lunch is served only at weekends. L, D.

AE
MC
V

THE JEWEL OF NEWBURY $$$$
254 Newbury St. **Map** 3 B2. **(** *(617) 536-5523.*
An elegant, friendly, and charming restaurant serving beautiful Moroccan
cuisine, especially the couscous and tagine. L, D. Mon (Nov–Mar).

MC
V

AMBROSIA ON HUNTINGTON $$$$$
116 Huntington Ave. **Map** 3 B3. **(** *(617) 247-2400.*
The warm-toned decor and high ceilings lend a spacious feel that is
rare in urban restaurants. The chef uses classic French methods fused
with Asian flavors; sorbets are his signature dish. L, D.

AE
DC
MC
V

ANAGO $$$$$
65 Exeter St (Lenox Hotel). **Map** 3 B2. **(** *(617) 266-6222.*
This bistro is host to the cuisine of a top American chef. The "global"
menu is both fresh and creative, while avoiding being too trendy.
D, Brunch Sunday.

AE
MC
V

For key to symbols see back flap

	CREDIT CARDS	OUTDOOR TABLES	VEGETARIAN	GOOD WINE	LATE OPENING

Price categories include a three-course meal for one, half a bottle of house wine and all unavoidable extra charges such as sales tax and service.
$ under $20
$$ $20–30
$$$ $30–45
$$$$ $45–60
$$$$$ over $60

CREDIT CARDS
Major credit cards accepted: *AE* American Express; *MC* Master Card/Access; *DC* Diners Club; *V* Visa; *D* Discover Card.

OUTDOOR TABLES
Garden, courtyard, or terrace with outside tables.

VEGETARIAN
A good selection of vegetarian dishes available.

GOOD WINE
Extensive list of good wines, both native and international.

LATE OPENING
Full menu or light meals served after 11pm.

AUJOURD'HUI $$$$$ — *AE MC V* — VEGETARIAN, GOOD WINE
200 Boylston St. (Four Seasons Hotel). **Map** 4 D2. **(** *(617) 451-1392.*
Arguably one of the best dining experiences in Boston, the excellent contemporary cuisine includes rack of lamb and medallions of veal. This is complemented both by a lovely ambience, and a view of the Public Garden. There is also an alternative healthy cuisine menu. B, L, D.

CLIO $$$$$ — *AE DC MC V* — GOOD WINE
370A Commonwealth Ave. (Eliot Hotel). **Map** 3 A2. **(** *(617) 536-7200.*
It is hard to say whether the wonderful food or the Parisian dining-club ambiance is responsible for the popularity of this French-inspired modern American restaurant. *Foie gras*, caramelized swordfish, and seared spiced steak are highlights. B, D, Brunch Sun. **P Y Y &** ⬤ Mon.

HAMERSLEY'S BISTRO $$$$$ — *AE MC V* — OUTDOOR TABLES, VEGETARIAN, GOOD WINE
553 Tremont St. **Map** 4 D4. **(** *(617) 423-2700.*
Top chef Gordon Hamersley consistently receives rave reviews for his convivial French provincial cuisine, which includes a stunning lemon–garlic chicken. L, D. **Y**

L'ESPALIER $$$$$ — *AE DC MC V* — VEGETARIAN
30 Gloucester St. **Map** 3 B2. **(** *(617) 262-3023.*
In the absolute top tier of Boston restaurants, with impeccably classic decor, excellent service, and New England-influenced European cuisine. Reservations recommended. D. **P Y Y** ⬤ Sun.

MISTRAL $$$$$ — *AE MC V* — VEGETARIAN, LATE OPENING
223 Columbus Ave. **Map** 3 C3. **(** *(617) 867-9300.*
Like the wind in the south of France, Mistral's waiting list shows no sign of dwindling. The cellar is as thoughtfully assembled as the menu, and the fashionable wine bar is always busy. Reservations essential. D. **P Y Y &**

SONSIE $$$$$ — *AE DC MC V* — LATE OPENING
327 Newbury St. **Map** 3 A3. **(** *(617) 351-2500.*
For supermodels and aspiring actors, this is the hip place to go. The open-front dining room is good for people-watching while you sip a cocktail and nibble gourmet pizza or tequila-battered shrimp. L, D, Brunch Sun. **Y &**

STEPHANIE'S ON NEWBURY $$$$$ — *AE MC V D* — OUTDOOR TABLES, GOOD WINE
190 Newbury St. **Map** 3 B2. **(** *(617) 236-0990.*
A large patio offers good people-watching potential, the favorite pastime on Newbury Street. Menu mainly has lighter fare, such as salads, inventive sandwiches, and good pizzas. L, D. **Y &**

TREMONT 647 $$$$$ — *AE DC MC V* — VEGETARIAN
647 Tremont St. **Map** 3 C4. **(** *(617) 266-4600.*
Pushing the boundaries of new and old American food alike, this youthful and unpretentious restaurant enjoys innovation, and succeeds. Try the sea bass on jasmine rice or the spice-rubbed steak. Sundays' Pajama Brunch is a must, if solely for the cinnamon rolls. D, Brunch Sun. **P Y ⬥ &**

FARTHER AFIELD

CAMPO DE FIORI $ — *AE MC V D* — VEGETARIAN
Holyoke Center Arcade, 1350 Massachusetts Ave., Cambridge. **(** *(617) 354-3805.*
Subtly delicious Roman flatbread sandwiches. Fillings include avocado, grilled mushrooms, and fresh mozzarella. No wine. L. **⬥ &** ⬤ Sun.

ONE ARROW ST. CRÊPES $ — *MC V* — OUTDOOR TABLES, VEGETARIAN
1 Arrow St., Cambridge. **(** *(617) 661-2737.*
Nestled off Massachusetts Avenue and serving sweet and savory crêpes. Sip homemade lemonade and try a spiced pear, blue cheese, arugula, and walnut crêpe, or something more simple. No wine. L, D. ⬤ Mon.

PINOCCHIO'S   ⑤
74 Winthrop St., Cambridge. ☏ (617) 876-4897.
Excellent value and terrific pizza – Sicilian style pizza rectangles heaped
with toppings are an unbeatable fast meal, night or day. No wine. L, D.

| | MC | | | |
| | V | | | |

MR. BARTLEY'S BURGER AND SALAD COTTAGE   ⑤⑤
1246 Massachusetts Ave., Cambridge. ☏ (617) 354-6559.
Hamburgers in such glorious profusion and variety that you will dwell
over their chalk-board menu despite the reigning chaos around you.
Excellent burgers, and great sweet potato fries. No wine. L, D. 🏃 ● Sun.

SOUTH STREET DINER   ⑤⑤
178 Kneeland St. **Map 4 F2.** ☏ (617) 350-0028.
A true American greasy spoon, in the most endearing sense. This 24-hour
diner next to the transportation hub of South Station serves sandwiches,
frappés, and omelets fresh from the griddle. No wine. B, L, D. 🏃

	AE			
	MC			
	V			
	D			

JOHN HARVARD'S BREW HOUSE   ⑤⑤⑤
33 Dunster St., Cambridge. ☏ (617) 868-3585.
Features their excellent microbrewed beer on tap. Publike decor and a
menu of inspired American staples, such as buttermilk-fried chicken with
spiced cornbread. Try the beer sampler if indecisive. L, D. 🍷 🏃 &

	AE			
	DC			
	MC			
	V			
	D			

PHO PASTEUR   ⑤⑤⑤
36 Dunster St., Cambridge. ☏ (617) 864-4100.
Pho is a Vietnamese noodle dish, prepared with sublime complexity at
this stylish restaurant in Harvard Square. While other dishes are excellent,
the grilled pork *pho*, with mint and a delicate sauce, is definitive. L, D. 🏃

	AE			
	MC			
	V			

R. WESLEY'S   ⑤⑤⑤
31 Cambridge St., Charlestown. ☏ (617) 242-7202.
It's worth going out of the way for the homey hipster atmosphere, unusual wine and beer selections, and inventive chef's fare. R. Wesley's also
serves generous portions at good prices. L (Thu & Fri only), D. ● Mon.

	AE			
	MC			
	V			

STARS ON HUNTINGTON   ⑤⑤⑤
393 Huntington Ave, Boston. ☏ (617) 536-3232.
Bright and cheerful, Stars features the obligatory meatloaf and gravy as
well as grilled salmon or steak with "tater tots". B, L, D, Brunch Sun.

	AE			
	DC			
	MC			
	V.			
	D			

HOUSE OF BLUES   ⑤⑤⑤⑤
96 Winthrop St., Cambridge. ☏ (617) 491-2583.
Music hall and restaurant devoted to bringing the beauty of Southern
music and food to the rest of the country. Succulent barbecue fare and
moist cornbread, adapted to Northern tastes. L, D, Brunch Sun. 🎵 🍷

	AE			
	MC			
	V			
	D			

CHEZ HENRI   ⑤⑤⑤⑤⑤
1 Shepard St., Cambridge. ☏ (617) 354-8980.
The offspring of French bistro and Cuban café, the relaxed and
romantic Chez Henri mixes classical methods with fresh Caribbean
and local ingredients. Try the nightly fixed-price menu. D. 🍷 🏃 &

	AE			
	DC			
	MC			
	V			
	D			

LES ZYGOMATES   ⑤⑤⑤⑤⑤
129 South St. **Map 4 F2.** ☏ (617) 542-5108.
Wine is the *raison d'être* here, with delicious bistro fare, such as rabbit
pâté and venison *vol-au-vents* to complement it. L, D. 🎵 🍷 🍴 ● Sun.

	AE			
	DC			
	MC			
	V			

OLIVES   ⑤⑤⑤⑤⑤
10 City Square, Charlestown. ☏ (617) 242-1999.
Mediterranean-influenced cuisine by local celebrity chef Todd English,
served in a bistro-like setting. Perpetually crowded, they do not accept
reservations. Dress well to minimize your wait. D. 🅿 🍷 🍴 & ● Sun.

	AE			
	DC			
	MC			
	V			
	D			

RIALTO   ⑤⑤⑤⑤⑤
1 Bennett St. (Charles Hotel), Cambridge. ☏ (617) 661-5050.
Rarely do the top restaurants create an atmosphere so down to earth. The
menu of seasonal dishes may include *foie gras* with dried fruit compote,
tender roast duckling, or simple tomatoes with fresh mozzarella. D. 🅿 🍷 &

	AE			
	DC			
	MC			
	V			
	D			

THE HARVEST   ⑤⑤⑤⑤⑤
44 Brattle St., Cambridge. ☏ (617) 868-2255.
A favored haunt of university professors, The Harvest is one of the finest
restaurants in Harvard Square. Modern American cuisine bursting with
fresh flavors and local produce. Reservations suggested. L, D. 🍷 🍴 &

	AE			
	DC			
	MC			
	V			

For key to symbols see back flap

Cafés and Bars

THE SOCIAL FABRIC OF BOSTON is held together through its abundance of places to meet with friends and while away the hours. A city with a rich mix of students, working folk, and executives provides a selection of cafés and bars that cater to all tastes, and to people who keep all hours. There are places where you can find a pick-me-up, rest your feet, and meet local people. A further selection of bars is listed on pp152–3.

CAFÉS

CAFÉS TEND TO CLUSTER in a few areas of the city, most notably Harvard Square and its environs, the South End, the North End, and Beacon Hill. **Café Pamplona** in Harvard Square is a cramped nook of a café with European pretensions that has served Harvard students for generations. The Italian-style **Café Paradiso** features light food and Italian sodas in a trendier, more hurried atmosphere. For an especially genteel treat, make your way to **L.A. Burdick's Handmade Chocolates** and order a sampler plate of their innovative chocolates or one of their superb buttery fruit tarts. They also have some fine teas, including herbals. There are two branches of the **1369 Coffeehouse**, which are spacious, upbeat and frequented by a clientele of all ages, who come mainly for the excellent cookie bars.

The South End's secluded cafés are home to a thriving café society. Many are popular with the vibrant gay community *(see p153)* that has made its home in this neighborhood, but also happily welcome all visitors, regardless of sexual preference. **The Garden of Eden**, with its cozy, provincial decor, is a perfect place to start the day, reading the newspapers and enjoying the croissants they bake for breakfast daily, or one of their many original sandwiches. **XII Church** is a tiny place, which has primarily a take-out business of coffee, breakfast pastries, and assorted lunch foods. **To Go** offers a full range of coffee, tea, pastries, and lunch foods. **Berkeley Perk** is colorful

and spacious, with a wide selection of juices, quality sodas, and sweet treats.

Cafés cluster around the main thoroughfares of the North End, where many local restaurants do not even bother to serve coffee or dessert because the cafés in this lively Italian neighborhood do it so much better – espresso or cappuccino with *tiramisu* or *cannoli* are a must. **Caffe Vittoria**, decorated in marble and chrome, has a wide array of pastries and liqueurs, and its own cigar parlor. **Caffe Pompei** is a more chaotic place, which features murals of its doomed namesake crowding the walls. While many like **Mike's Pastry** for their *cannoli*, it is said that the best are found alongside the nougat at **Maria's Pastry Shop**, which sadly does not have seating. On Beacon Hill, **Café Vanille** has a range of exquisite Parisian pastries.

TEA ROOMS

A COUPLE OF grand hotels have preserved a genteel tradition of offering afternoon tea: **The Bristol Lounge** at the Four Seasons Hotel serves a lovely tea, while the **Ritz-Carlton** (closed until fall 2002) lavishes tea-drinkers with their signature dish of swan-boat shaped, cream-filled puff pastry, though you must arrange in advance to have tea there. More recently, tea has found aficionados among the college-aged crowd, and a number of tea houses designed for the younger and more budget-conscious flourish in Harvard Square and on Newbury Street. **Tea-luxe**, which has a branch on Newbury Street

and in Harvard, lets its customers peruse their impressive catalog of hundreds of teas from around the world. At **Tea Tray in the Sky**, which is situated near Harvard, the renowned pastry chef makes sure the food matches the tea in quality. They also serve high tea. At **Finale**, which is close to the Theater District and Back Bay, they are famous for specializing in producing the most delicious desserts.

ICE CREAM PARLORS

BOSTONIANS eat more ice cream, per person, year round, than anyone else in America. They are highly discerning customers, and fiercely loyal to their favorite parlor. Many restaurants make a point of serving one of the locally made ice creams with their dessert menus. When ordering ice cream, you can get it served in a dish with a spoon, or in a cone to lick. You get a choice of wafer cone (light, crispy, slightly bland) or a sugar cone (thin, crisp, sweet cookie wafer). Some may decide to order one of the enormous waffle cones, which is really just an overgrown sugar cone custom-made for the truly indulgent. Parlors are open most of the day and late into the evening. In central Boston the best ice creams are hard to find, but Newbury Street *(see p95)* has some of the best options. **J.P. Licks** is an old favorite, its bizarre tiled decor a landmark. The New England ice cream giant **Ben and Jerry's** has several parlors featuring all their flavors.

Farther out of town, Cambridge has some great parlors, and old college friends often reunite over a heaped cone at **Herrell's** in Harvard Square, trying the latest flavors while chatting in what was once a bank vault. Massachusetts Institute of Technology *(see p111)* students wax nostalgic for **Toscanini's** ice cream, and its popularity has spread into other locations. Tosci's, as it's known, is perhaps the most daring in inventing new flavors, though competition for this particular accolade is very stiff. For example, **Christina's** in Inman Square makes the best green tea ice cream in the city, as well as a wide range of other flavors, ranging from the sublime to the simply gooey.

A little farther afield, **Ron's Gourmet Homemade Ice Cream & Bowling** features specialty flavors such as peanut sunrise, as well as a chance to work off some calories on their candlepin bowling lanes.

BARS

THE LEGAL DRINKING AGE in Boston is 21, and you may be asked to show proof of identification *(see p164)*.

Boston has scores of bars which offer live music and other types of entertainment *(see also pp152–3)*. Those listed here are a good place to relax and simply have a drink, though some of them can still be quite lively.

For good, down-to-earth bars, you cannot go wrong with the youthful **Shay's Pub**

and Wine Bar, **The Sevens**, the slightly tacky **Purple Shamrock**, the well-heeled **21st Amendment**, or the kitschy lounge paradise of **The Good Life**. **Parker's Bar** at the Omni Parker House Hotel has the atmosphere of a gentleman's club, while around the city are dotted a number of good wine bars, notably **Les Zygomates** and **The Vault**. **Jacob Wirth's** *(see p87)*, which is also a restaurant, is situated in the Theater District and has good beer and a lively ambience.

DIRECTORY

CAFÉS

Berkeley Perk
69 Berkeley St. **Map** 4 D3.
((617) 426-7375.

Café Pamplona
2 Bow St., Cambridge.

Café Paradiso
1 Elliot Square,
Cambridge.
((617) 868-3240.

Caffe Pompei
280 Hanover St.
Map 2 E2.
((617) 227-1562.

Café Vanille
119 Mount Vernon St.
Map 1 B4.
((617) 523-9200.

Caffe Vittoria
290–296 Hanover St.
Map 2 E2.
((617) 227-7606.

**The Garden
of Eden**
571 Tremont St.
Map 4 D4.
((617) 247-8377.

**L.A. Burdick's
Handmade
Chocolates**
52 Brattle St.,
Cambridge.
((617) 491-4340.

**Maria's
Pastry Shop**
46 Cross St. **Map** 2 D3.
((617) 523-1196.

Mike's Pastry
300 Hanover St.
Map 2 E2.
((617) 742-3050.

To Go
314 Shawmut Ave.
Map 4 D4.
((617) 482-1015.

**1369
Coffeehouse**
1369 Cambridge St.,
Cambridge.
((617) 576-1369.

757 Massachusetts Ave.
((617) 576-4600.

XII Church
12 Church St.
Map 4 D2.
((617) 348-0012.

TEA ROOMS

The Bristol Lounge
200 Boylston St.
Map 4 D2.
((617) 351-2072.

Finale
15 Columbus Ave.
Map 1 B5.
((617) 423-3184.

Ritz-Carlton
15 Arlington St. **Map** 4 D2.
((617) 536-5700.

Tea-Luxe
Brattle Square,
Cambridge.
((617) 441-0077.

108 Newbury St.
Map 3 C2.
((617) 927-0400.

Tea Tray in the Sky
1796 Massachusetts Ave.,
Cambridge.
((617) 492-8327.

ICE CREAM
PARLORS

Ben and Jerry's
174 Newbury St.
Map 3 B2.
((617) 536-5456.

20 Park Plaza.
Map 4 D2.
((617) 426-0890.

36 John F. Kennedy St.,
Cambridge.
((617) 864-2828.

Christina's
1255 Cambridge St.
((617) 492-7021.

Herrell's
15 Dunster St., Cambridge.
((617) 497-2179.

J.P. Licks
352 Newbury St.
Map 3 A3.
((617) 236-1666.

**Ron's Gourmet
Homemade Ice
Cream & Bowling**
1231 Hyde Park Ave.,
Hyde Park, MA 02136.
((617) 364-5274.

Toscanini's
899 Main St, Cambridge.
((617) 491-5877.

1310 Massachusetts Ave.,
Cambridge.
((617) 354-9350.

BARS

The Good Life
28 Kingston St.
Map 2 D5.
((617) 451-2622.

Jacob Wirth
33 Stuart St.
Map 4 E2.
((617) 338-8586.

Parker's Bar
60 School St.
Map 2 D4.
((617) 227-8600.

**Purple
Shamrock**
1 Union St.
Map 2 D3.
((617) 227-2060.

The Sevens
77 Charles St.
Map 1 B3.
((617) 523-9074.

**Shay's Pub
and Wine Bar**
58 John F. Kennedy St.,
Cambridge.
((617) 864-9161.

21st Amendment
150 Bowdoin St.
Map 1 C3.
((617) 227-7100.

The Vault
105 Water St.
Map 2 D4.
((617) 292-9966.

Les Zygomates
129 South St.
Map 4 F2.
((617) 542-5108.

SHOPPING IN BOSTON

Shopping in Boston has evolved dramatically in recent years. Long known as an excellent center for antiques, books, and quality clothing, the city's shopping options now cover a much broader spectrum, influenced both by its booming economy and its large, international student population. From the fashionable boutiques of Newbury Street, to the many stores selling cosmopolitan home furnishings

Red Sox baseball cap

or ethnic treasures, to the varied art and crafts galleries, Boston caters to every shopping need. Whether you are looking for the latest fashion accessory, an unusual antique, or a special souvenir, choices abound to accommodate every sense of style and budget. Boston is no longer simply traditional, and now holds its own in providing a vibrant, eclectic and world-class shopping experience.

Large glass atrium of the busy Prudential shopping mall

SALES

There are two major sale seasons in Boston: July, when summer clothes go on sale to make room for fall fashions, and January, when any winter clothing and merchandise is cleared after the holidays. Most stores also have a sale section or clearance rack throughout the year.

PAYMENT AND TAXES

Major credit cards and traveler's checks with identification are accepted at most stores. There is a tax of 5 percent on all purchases except groceries and clothing, although any item of clothing over $175 will be taxed.

OPENING HOURS

Most stores open at 10am and close at 6pm from Monday to Saturday, and from noon to 5 or 6pm on Sunday. Many stores stay open later on Thursday nights,

and most department stores stay open until 7:30 or 8pm throughout the week. Weekday mornings are the best times to shop. Saturdays, lunch hours, and evenings can be very busy.

SHOPPING MALLS

Shopping malls – clusters of shops, restaurants, and even cinemas all within one large and open complex – have become top destinations for shopping, offering variety, dining, and entertainment. With long winters and a fair share of bad weather, New Englanders flock to malls to

Farm produce on display on Charles Street

shop, eat, and, in the case of teenagers, simply hang out.

Copley Place, with its 11-screen cinema complex, elegant restaurants, and more than 100 shops, is based around a dazzling 60-ft (18-m) atrium and waterfall. Across a pedestrian overpass, **Shops at Prudential Center** encompasses two department stores, a huge food court, and a multitude of smaller specialty shops. The most upscale mall in town, **Heritage on the Garden** looks out over Boston's Public Garden, and features the boutiques of top European designers, fine jewelers, and stores selling other luxury goods. Outside the center of town, across the Charles River, **Cambridgeside Galleria** has over 100 shops and a waterfront food court. For last-minute purchases, **Boston Landing**, at Logan Airport, has two dozen shops, restaurants, and a hair salon.

DEPARTMENT STORES

There are five major department stores in Boston, each offering a large and varied selection of clothing, accessories, cosmetics, housewares, and gifts. They also have restaurants and beauty salons, and provide a variety of personal shopping services. For those wanting to shop at several stores, **Concierge of Boston** provides a shopping service in metropolitan

Boston. At Downtown Crossing *(see p84)*, a bustling shopping district between Boston Common and the Financial District, generations of Bostonians have shopped at **Filene's** *(see p84)*, founded in 1881. Featuring apparel from some of the best known American designers, as well as major brand labels for women, men and children, Filene's offers six floors of high quality merchandise. It is known, perhaps, for its famous bargain basement, now owned and operated separately.

Directly across the street, **Macy's**, the legendary New York emporium, offers an equally impressive array of fashions, cosmetics, housewares, and furnishings.

Heading uptown, through Boston Common and Public Garden to Boylston Street, you can spot the Prudential Tower, centerpiece of a once nondescript but recently revitalized complex of shops, offices, and restaurants. This includes the venerable and elegant **Saks Fifth Avenue**, which caters to its upscale clientele with renowned service, a luxurious ambiance, and strikingly stylish displays. For the ultimate high fashion, high profile shopping experience, stop by

Neiman Marcus, which specializes in haute couture, precious jewelry, furs, and gifts. The store is well known for its Christmas catalog, with presents that have included authentic Egyptian mummies, vintage airplanes, a pair of two-million-dollar diamonds, and robots to help out around the house – or mansion. Next door is **Lord and Taylor**, well known for its classic American designer labels, juniors, and children's departments, and menswear, also carries crystal, china, and gifts.

DISCOUNT AND OUTLET STORES

DEDICATED BARGAIN hunters may want to consider making a day trip to one of New England's famed outlet centers, where many top designers and major brand manufacturers offer last-season and overstocked clothing and goods at big discounts. Generally sold at 20 to 30 percent less than their regular retail prices, some items can be found reduced by as much as 75 percent.

Brattle Bookshop's sign

Wrentham Village

Boutiques of genteel Newbury Street

Premium Outlets are about 40 miles (65 km) south of Boston. The stores here sell designer clothing, housewares, and accessories from many of the leading manufacturers.

Kittery, 50 miles (80 km) north of Boston, is an even larger outlet destination, with more than 125 shops selling everything from footwear and designer clothes, to sports equipment, perfume, books, china, glass, and gifts. There are also numerous restaurants.

Freeport, Maine, is one of the largest and most famous outlet centers, being home to the renowned outdoor equipment specialist **L.L. Bean**. Over two hours' drive from Boston, it is only worth the journey for the dedicated shopper, or for those already visiting Maine.

Fashion

FROM CHAIN STORES stocked with popular brand labels to specialists selling vintage clothing, Boston offers choices in every area of fashion. Well-heeled shoppers frequent high-fashion boutiques, students flock to vintage emporiums, bargain hunters converge at Filene's Basement, and businessmen visit both traditional outlets and the many fashionable men's outfitters. In this stylish, international city, many stores feature fine clothes from Italy, France, England, and Japan, along with the more prevalent fashions from top American designers.

MIXED FASHION

MANY STORES in Boston offer quality clothing for both men and women. **Louis Boston**, housed in an elegant building on Berkeley Street that once contained Boston's Museum of Natural History, has long been known as the city's most exclusive men's outfitters. It now also features similarly beautiful clothing for women, ranging from the traditional look of Ralph Lauren to contemporary styles from Jil Sander and Kiton. Its award-winning café serves lunch and dinner.

Nearby on Newbury Street, **Giorgio Armani**, **Riccardi**, and **Gianni Versace** all cater to the well-heeled, who love to browse through their extravagantly stylish and outrageously expensive clothing and accessories. **Alan Bilzerian** attracts celebrities in search of both his own label and the latest avant-garde looks from Europe and Japan. Donna Karan's **DKNY** features a wider range of fashion, from casual sportswear to glamorous evening attire, as well as housewares and baby clothes. **Urban Outfitters** offers an eclectic collection of clothing and accoutrements for the young and trendy, and stocks Kikit, Girbaud, and Esprit. America's favorite chain, **Gap**, has simple styles which remain stylish enough for movie stars, yet affordable for the masses. **Banana Republic** is ideal for those after a sleeker more modern look.

In other areas, popular stores include **Abercrombie and Fitch**, favored by teens and college students for its range of street fashion, and the original **Levi's Store**, which put denim on the map and carries jeans in every size, shape, and color. For clothing more suited to the great outdoors, visit **Eddie Bauer**, which sells a range of no-nonsense sporting gear, or **Patagonia**, a mecca for serious climbers, skiers, and sailors, which also carries sophisticated, high-tech sporting equipment.

WOMEN'S FASHION

NO WOMAN need leave Boston empty-handed, whether her taste is for the *haute couture* of **Chanel** in Boston's Ritz-Carlton Hotel or the earthy ethnic clothing at **Nomad**. Newbury Street is filled with sumptuous, high-fashion boutiques, including **Bijoux**, **Betsy Jenney**, and **Max Mara**, Italy's largest and most luxurious ready-to-wear manufacturer for women. Natural-fiber separates with a simple, relaxed style are the specialty at **CP Shades**, while **Oilily**, the Dutch boutique, blazes with colorful prints and youthful designs. On Boylston Street, **Ann Taylor** is the first choice for refined, modern career clothes, while **Talbots**, a Boston institution, features enduring classics. **Anthropologie** stocks an eclectic mix of exotic and whimsical clothing and accessories from around the world, while **The Limited** has a huge selection of affordable options for all occasions.

In Cambridge, popular stores include **Jasmine Sola**, which sells chic, flirtatious clothing, **April Cornell**, with its richly hued folkwear, and **Settebello**, which carries elegant European apparel, accessories, and shoes.

MEN'S FASHION

GENTLEMEN SEEKING a quintessential New England look need go no farther than **Brooks Brothers** on Newbury Street, longtime purveyors of traditional, high-quality men's and boys' wear.

America's foremost fashion house, **Polo/Ralph Lauren** offers top-quality and highly priced sporting and formal attire, while **Jos. A. Bank Clothiers** and **Simon's** sell private label merchandise as well as most major brands at discounted prices. **Stonestreets** carries a wide variety of European sportswear, accessories and shoes.

Academics and college students alike head to Cambridge, where the venerable **Andover Shop** and **J. Press** provide a selection of Ivy-League essentials of impeccable quality.

While visitors may not expect to find Western wear in Boston, a large selection of cowboy boots, jeans, leather jackets, Stetson hats, and Harley-Davidson gear is available at **Walkers Riding Apparel**, suppliers of Western and riding gear, both Western and English.

DISCOUNT AND VINTAGE CLOTHES

THE LEGENDARY Boston bargain emporium **Filene's Basement** (*see p84*) has been selling a broad selection of discounted clothing for over 90 years. It is still unique among other discount stores for its frenzied atmosphere and its discount system, which reduces prices by 25% after 14 days, 50% after 21 days, and 75% after 28 days. After 35 days the clothes go off to charity. Bargain hunters vie for everything from designer wedding dresses to everyday fashions, with daily specials advertised in the local newspapers. First among the other discount chains is **Marshall's**, promising "brand names for less" and offering bargains on clothing, shoes, housewares, and accessories.

Vintage aficionados will love the vast collections at **Bobby**

from Boston, a longtime costume source for Hollywood and top fashion designers. In Cambridge, **Keezer's** has provided generations of Harvard students with everything from used tuxedos to sports jackets and loafers. **Second Time Around**, with consignment shops in both Cambridge and Boston, offers a select array of top-quality, gently worn contemporary clothing for women.

SHOES AND ACCESSORIES

Many stores in Boston specialize in accessories and footware. **Helen's Leather** on Charles Street is well known for leather jackets, briefcases, purses, shoes, and Birkenstock sandals, as well as its huge selection of Western boots. At Downtown Crossing, **Foot Paths** carries a range of shoes from Timberland, Kenneth Cole, Rockport, and others.

Stylish Italian shoes and bags are the specialty at **Joan and David** at Copley Place, while the more adventurous will find more fashionable and unusual shoes at **Berk's**, **Jasmine Sola**, and **Sola Men** in Cambridge. For sports gear, the large and opulent **Niketown** on Newbury Street shows video re-runs of sports events while shoppers peruse the latest designs in athletic clothing and footwear.

DIRECTORY

MIXED FASHION

Abercrombie and Fitch
Faneuil Hall Marketplace.
Map 2 D3.
(617) 742-6838.

Alan Bilzerian
34 Newbury St. Map 4 D2.
(617) 536-1001.

Banana Republic
28 Newbury St. Map 4 D2.
(617) 267-3933.

DKNY
37 Newbury St. Map 3 C2.
(617) 236-0476.

Eddie Bauer
500 Washington St. Map 2 D4.
(617) 423-4722.

Gap
201 Newbury St. Map 3 C2.
(617) 267-4055.

Gianni Versace
12 Newbury St. Map 3 C2.
(617) 536-8300.

Giorgio Armani
22 Newbury St. Map 3 C2.
(617) 267-3200.

Levi's Store
Prudential Center.
Map 3 B3.
(617) 375-9010.

Louis Boston
234 Berkeley St. Map 3 C2.
(617) 262-6100.

Patagonia
346 Newbury St. Map 3 A3.
(617) 424-1776.

Riccardi
116 Newbury St. Map 3 C2.
(617) 266-3158.

Urban Outfitters
361 Newbury St. Map 3 A3.
(617) 236-0088.

WOMEN'S FASHION

Ann Taylor
800 Boylston St. Map 3 B3.
(617) 421-9097.

Anthropologie
799 Boylston St. Map 3 B3.
(617) 262-0545.

April Cornell
43 Brattle St, Cambridge.
(617) 661-8910.

Betsy Jenney
114 Newbury St. Map 3 C2.
(617) 536-2610.

Bijoux
141 Newbury St. Map 3 C2.
(617) 424-8877.

Chanel
5 Newbury St. Map 4 D2.
(617) 859-0055.

CP Shades
139 Newbury St. Map 3 C2.
(617) 421-0846.

Jasmine Sola
37 Brattle St, Cambridge.
(617) 354-6043.

Max Mara
69 Newbury St. Map 3 C2.
(617) 267-9775.

Nomad
1741 Massachusetts Ave, Cambridge.
(617) 497-6677.

Oilily
32 Newbury St. Map 4 D2.
(617) 247-2386.

Settebello
52c Brattle St, Cambridge.
(617) 864-2440.

Talbots
500 Boylston St. Map 3 C2.
(617) 262-2981.

The Limited
Copley Place. Map 3 C3.
(617) 236-1883.

MEN'S FASHION

Andover Shop
22 Holyoke St, Cambridge.
(617) 876-4900.

Brooks Brothers
46 Newbury St. Map 4 D2.
(617) 267-2600.

Jos. A. Bank Clothiers
399 Boylston St.
Map 4 D2.
(617) 536-5050.

J. Press
82 Mount Auburn St, Cambridge.
(617) 547-9886.

Polo/Ralph Lauren
100 Huntington Ave.
Map 3 C3.
(617) 266-4121.

Simon's
220 Clarendon St.
Map 3 C2.
(617) 266-2345.

Stonestreets
133 Newbury St. Map 3 C2.
(617) 450-0001.

Walkers Riding Apparel
122 Boylston St. Map 4 E2.
(617) 423-9050.

DISCOUNT AND VINTAGE CLOTHES

Bobby from Boston
19 Thayer St. Map 4 E4.
(617) 423-9299.

Filene's Basement
426 Washington St.
Map 4 F1.
(617) 542-2011.

Keezer's
140 River St, Cambridge.
(617) 547-2455.

Marshall's
500 Boylston St. Map 3 C2.
(617) 262-6066.

Second Time Around
167 Newbury St. Map 3 B2.
(617) 247-3504.

SHOES AND ACCESSORIES

Berk's
50 John F. Kennedy St, Cambridge.
(617) 492-9511.

Foot Paths
489 Washington St.
Map 4 F1.
(617) 338-6008.

Helen's Leather
110 Charles St. Map 1 B3.
(617) 742-2077.

Jasmine Sola/Sola Men
37 Brattle St, Cambridge.
(617) 354-6043.

Joan and David
100 Huntington Ave.
Map 3 C3.
(617) 536-0600.

Niketown
200 Newbury St. Map 3 B2.
(617) 267-3400.

Antiques, Fine Crafts, and Gifts

VISITORS HOPING TO take home a special memento will find an enormous number of antique, craft, and gift stores in Boston. From the huge antique markets and cooperatives, to specialty shops selling everything from rugs to rare books, there are abundant opportunities to indulge a passion for the past. Those favoring more contemporary *objets d'art* will find crafts guilds, galleries, and gift shops selling unique glassware, ceramics, textiles, jewelry, and much more produced by New England artisans, as well as items from every corner of the world.

ANTIQUES

CHARLES STREET is Boston's antiques Mecca, with more antique stores than any other part of town. The neighborhood is extremely affluent with many exclusive and expensive stores, though the occasional bargain may be found in some of the larger stores. One of the larger places is **Antiques at 80 Charles**, which has three floors of merchandise ranging from silver tea sets to jewelry, paintings, clocks, and collectables. **Upstairs Downstairs** also sells "affordable antiques," and has four rooms full of furniture, lamps, prints, and a large selection of smaller items.

Collectors of fine Asian antiques should not miss **Alberts-Langdon, Inc.** and **Judith Dowling Asian Art**, for everything from screens and scrolls to lacquerware, ceramics, paintings, and furniture from all over Asia. A prime source for antique pine and painted furniture, **Danish Country** carries antique *armoires* and other furniture from Scandinavia, as well as Royal Copenhagen china and tall case clocks.

Antique jewelry from around the world is a specialty at **Marika's Antiques Shop**, along with paintings, porcelain, glass, and silver. Across Boston Common, venerable **Shreve, Crump & Low, Inc.** also deals in jewelry, having been Boston's reigning jeweler since 1796. They now offer antiques as well, including 17th- and 18th-century English and American furniture, prints, paintings, silver, and porcelain. **Twentieth Century Ltd** excels particularly in glittery costume jewelry from top designers. They also offer pieces in sterling silver.

Elsewhere, French and Italian furnishings, including mirrors and lighting, can be found at **Autrefois Antiques** on Newbury Street. For an eclectic mix of antiques both fine and funky from the 19th century to the 1950s, head to **Easy Chairs** in Cambridge.

ANTIQUE MARKETS AND COOPERATIVES

IF BROWSING through mountainous inventories with the broadest range of quality, price, and stock is your idea of heaven, then there are several multi-dealer antiques emporiums worth exploring. On Charles Street, **Boston Antiques Cooperative I and II** has everything from quilts, candlesticks, and wicker furniture to chandeliers and furniture. In the Leather District, situated near South Station, is **JMW Gallery** which specializes in fine 19th- and early 20th-century American furniture, ceramics, and printed materials associated with the Arts and Crafts Movement. In Cambridge, **Antiques on Cambridge Street** and **Cambridge Antique Market** each encompasses over 100 dealers, offering estate antiques, collectibles, furniture, jewelry, and a vast selection of many other items.

If you have scoured Charles Street and scrutinized the Cooperatives and still have not found what you are looking for, try **Skinner Inc.**, Boston's foremost auctioneers and appraisers of antiques and fine arts, with 60 auctions annually for those seeking the crème de la crème.

SPECIALTY DEALERS

COLLECTORS IN PURSUIT of more specific pieces will find shops in Boston that specialize in everything from nautical antiques to rare books, maps, jewelry, and rugs. Fine antiques and jewelry featuring Victorian and Art Nouveau designs are beautifully displayed and described by the knowledgeable staff at **Small Pleasures**. Vintage watches from Rolex, Cartier, Vacheron, Constantia, and others are a specialty at **Time and Time Again** watch emporium; while **The Bromfield Pen Shop** has been purveyor of thousands of new, antique, and limited edition pens for over 50 years. For nautical antiques, including model ships and marine paintings, **Lannan Ship Model Gallery** boasts an extensive and high quality inventory. Antique rugs, carpets, and tapestries from around the world are the mainstay at **Decor International**, and at **Mario Ratzki Oriental Rugs**, which has a discriminating selection of antique Persian carpets and tribal rugs from the 1860s to the 1930s. Bibliophiles will also find an extraordinary range of stores in Boston. In business since 1825, **Brattle Book Shop** *(see p85)* is the oldest and best known, with a huge selection of used, out-of-print and rare books, magazines, and photo albums. Rare and scholarly books in the fine arts are the focus of **Ars Libri Ltd.**, while **Eugene Galleries** features antiquarian maps, prints, and etchings, in addition to its comprehensive selection of books. Old magazines, biographies, science fiction, and mysteries are a specialty at **Avenue Victor Hugo**, which offers a search service if the title you are looking for cannot be found among the 100,000 in stock. In Cambridge, **James & Devon Gray Booksellers**, and **Canterbury's Book Shop** offer a wide selection of antiquarian scholarly books. The **Bryn Mawr Bookstore** stocks used books and some rare volumes covering every conceivable subject.

FINE CRAFTS

Collectors with a more contemporary bent will find several distinguished galleries and shops featuring a wide variety of American crafts by both local and nationally recognized artists. **Alianza** carries contemporary glassware, jewelry, clocks, and boxes made of exotic woods. The **Society of Arts and Crafts**, established in 1897, has a shop and gallery, with exhibits from the 350 artists it represents. Works are largely in wood, fiber, metal,

glass, and mixed media. The **Cambridge Artists' Co-operative**, owned and run by over 200 artists, offers an eclectic collection of items, ranging from hand-painted silk jackets to ornaments and other larger items. **The Artful Hand Gallery** also has a range of fine items, again crafted primarily by American artists.

GIFTS

In addition to the plethora of souvenir shops that threaten to drown tourists in tasteless, predictable merchandise,

Boston has numerous shops specializing in original and distinctive gifts that you will not find anywhere else. In Newbury Street browse the **International Poster Gallery**, for original, vintage posters from the 19th and 20th centuries. In Cambridge, **Joie de Vivre** has a fantastic collection of toys, clocks, jewelry, jack-in-the-boxes, and much more beside. Next door, **Paper Source** carries a selection of fine handmade papers, gift wrap, rubber stamps, and other materials for creative indulgence.

DIRECTORY

ANTIQUES

Alberts-Langdon, Inc.
126 Charles St. **Map** 1 B3.
(617) 523-5924.

Antiques at 80 Charles
80 Charles St. **Map** 1 B4.
(617) 742-8006.

Autrefois Antiques
125 Newbury St. **Map** 3 C2. (617) 424-8823.

Danish Country
138 Charles St. **Map** 1 B3.
(617) 227-1804.

Easy Chairs
375 Huron Ave, Cambridge.
(617) 491-2131.

Judith Dowling Asian Art
133 Charles St. **Map** 1 B3.
(617) 523-5211.

Marika's Antiques Shop
130 Charles St. **Map** 1 B3.
(617) 523-4520.

Shreve, Crump & Low, Inc.
330 Boylston St. **Map** 4 D2.
(617) 267-9100.

Twentieth Century Ltd
73 Charles St. **Map** 1 B4.
(617) 742-1031.

Upstairs Downstairs
93 Charles St. **Map** 1 B4.
(617) 367-1950.

ANTIQUES MARKETS AND COOPERATIVES

Antiques on Cambridge Street
1076 Cambridge St, Cambridge.
(617) 234-0001.

Boston Antiques Cooperative I and II
119 Charles St. **Map** 1 B3.
(617) 227-9810.

Cambridge Antique Market
201 Msgr. O'Brien Highway, Cambridge.
(617) 868-9655.

JMW Gallery
144 Lincoln St.
Map 4 F2.
(617) 338-9097.

Skinner Inc.
63 Park Plaza. **Map** 1 C4.
(617) 350-5400.

SPECIALTY DEALERS

Ars Libri Ltd.
560 Harrison Ave.
Map 4 E4.
(617) 357-5212.

Avenue Victor Hugo
339 Newbury St. **Map** 3 B2. (617) 266-7746.

Brattle Book Shop
9 West St. **Map** 1 C4.
(617) 542-0210.

The Bromfield Pen Shop
5 Bromfield St. **Map** 1 C4.
(617) 482-9053.

Bryn Mawr Bookstore
373 Huron Ave., Cambridge.
(617) 661-1770.

Canterbury's Book Shop
1675 Massachusetts Ave, Cambridge.
(617) 864-9396.

Decor International
141 Newbury St. **Map** 3 C2. (617) 262-1529.

Eugene Galleries
76 Charles St. **Map** 1 B4.
(617) 227-3062.

James & Devon Gray Booksellers
12 Arrow St, Cambridge.
(617) 868-0752.

Lannan Ship Model Gallery
540 Atlantic Ave. **Map** 2 E5. (617) 451-2650.

Mario Ratzki Oriental Rugs
76 Charles St. **Map** 1 B4.
(617) 742-7850.

Small Pleasures
142 Newbury St.
Map 3 C2.
(617) 267-7371.

Time and Time Again
172 Newbury St.
Map 3 B2.
(617) 266-6869.

FINE CRAFTS

Alianza
154 Newbury St.
Map 3 B2.
(617) 262-2385.

The Artful Hand Gallery
100 Huntington Ave.
Map 3 C3.
(617) 262-9601.

Cambridge Artists' Cooperative
59a Church St, Cambridge.
(617) 868-4434.

Society of Arts and Crafts
175 Newbury St.
Map 3 B2.
(617) 266-1810.

GIFTS

International Poster Gallery
205 Newbury St.
Map 3 B2.
(617) 375-0076.

Joie de Vivre
1792 Massachusetts Ave, Cambridge.
(617) 864-8188.

Paper Source
1810 Massachusetts Ave, Cambridge.
(617) 497-1077.

ENTERTAINMENT IN BOSTON

F ROM AVANT-GARDE performance art to serious drama, and from popular dance music to live classical performances, Boston offers an outstanding array of entertainment options, with something to appeal to every taste: the Theater District offers many excellent plays and musicals throughout the year; the Wang Center hosts the Boston Ballet; and Symphony Hall is the

Quincy Market entertainer

home of the renowned Boston Symphony Orchestra. Boston is also well acquainted with jazz, folk music, and blues as well as being a center for more contemporary music, played in big city nightclubs. During the summer, entertainment often heads outdoors, with a number of open-air plays and concerts, such as the famous Boston Pops at the Hatch Shell.

PRACTICAL INFORMATION

T HE BEST SOURCES for information on current films, concerts, theater, dance, and exhibitions include the Thursday *Calendar* section of the *Boston Globe* and the Friday entertainment weekly, the *Boston Phoenix*. Even more up-to-date listings can be found on the Web at the following sites: **Ticketmaster** (www.boston.city search.com); the *Boston Globe* (www. boston.com); *Boston Phoenix* (www.bostonphoenix.com).

Boston entertainment listings magazines

BOOKING TICKETS

T ICKETS TO POPULAR musicals, theatrical productions, and touring shows often sell out far in advance, although theaters sometimes have a few returns

or restricted-view tickets available. You can either get tickets in person at theater box offices, or use one of the ticket agencies in Boston. For advance tickets these are **Ticketmaster** and **NEXT Ticketing**. Tickets can be purchased from both of these agencies over the telephone, in person, or online. Half-price tickets to most noncommercial arts events as well as to some commercial productions are available from 11am on the day of the performance at **BosTix** booths. Purchases must be made in person and only cash is accepted. BosTix also sells advance full-price tickets. Special Boston entertainment discount vouchers, available from hotel lobbies and tourist offices, may also give a saving on some shows.

Tchaikovsky's *Nutcracker,* **danced by the Boston Ballet (***see p150***)**

DISTRICTS AND VENUES

M USICALS, PLAYS, comedies, and dance are generally performed at venues in the Theater District, although larger noncommercial theater companies are distributed throughout the region, many being associated with colleges and universities.

The area around the intersection of Massachusetts and Huntington Avenues hosts a concentration of outstanding concert venues, including Symphony Hall, Berklee Performance Center at Berklee College of Music, and Jordan Hall at the New England Conservatory of Music.

The major nightclub and dance venues are on Lansdowne Street by Fenway Park and around Boylston Place near the Theater District. The busiest areas for bars and small clubs offering live jazz and rock music are Central and Harvard Squares in Cambridge, Davis Square in Somerville, and Allston. The principal gay scene in Boston is found in the South End, with many of the older bars and clubs in neighboring Bay Village.

Boston's Symphony Orchestra performing at Symphony Hall (*see p150***)**

OPEN-AIR AND FREE ENTERTAINMENT

THE BEST FREE outdoor summer entertainment in Boston is found at the Hatch Shell *(see p94)* on the Charles River Esplanade. The Boston Pops *(see p150)* performs here frequently during the week around July 4, and all through July and August jazz, pop, rock, and classical music is played. On Friday evenings from late June to the week before Labor Day, the Hatch Shell also shows free big-screen family films.

Music is also performed during the summer months at the **FleetBoston Pavilion** on the waterfront, which holds live jazz, pop, and country music concerts. City Hall Plaza and Copley Plaza have music concerts at lunchtimes and in the evenings, and the **Museum of Fine Arts** *(see pp106–109)*

Free open-air music concert outside New City Hall

operates a summer musical concert series in its courtyard. Most of the annual concerts and recitals of the **New England Conservatory of Music** are also free, although some require advance reservations.

Other open-air entertainment includes a series of free plays staged on Boston Common by the **Commonwealth Shakespeare Company** in July and August, and ticketed performances of various plays by the **Publick Theater** at Christian Herter Park on the Charles River.

An area that has more unusual open-air entertainment is Harvard Square, famous for its nightly and weekend scene of street performers.

Entrance to the Shubert Theatre *(see p150)*

Many recording artists paid their dues here, and other hopefuls still flock to the square in the vain hope of being discovered – or at least of earning the cost of dinner.

Details of all free entertainment happening in the city are listed in the *Calendar* section of Thursday's *Boston Globe*.

DISABLED ACCESS

MANY ENTERTAINMENT venues in Boston are wheelchair accessible. **Very Special Arts Massachusetts** offers a full Boston arts access guide. Some places, such as **Jordan Hall**, the **Emerson Majestic Theater**, and the **Wheelock Family Theater**, have listening aids for the hearing impaired, while the latter also has signed and described performances.

The Arts in Boston

Performing arts are vital to Boston's cultural life. Since the 1880s, the social season has revolved around openings of the Boston Symphony Orchestra and many Brahmins *(see p47)* occupy their grand-parents' seats at performances. In the past, theaters in Boston were heavily censored *(see p89)*, but today's Bostonians are avid theatergoers, patronizing commercial venues for plays bound to, or coming from, Broadway and attending ambitious contemporary drama at repertory theaters. Many noncommercial theater and dance companies perform in smaller venues in local neighborhoods and at the colleges. Although some theaters are closed on Mondays, there is rarely a night in Boston without performing arts.

CLASSICAL MUSIC AND OPERA

Two cherished Boston institutions, the **Boston Symphony Orchestra** and its popular-music equivalent, the Boston Pops, have a long history of being led by some of America's finest conductors. The BSO performs a full schedule of concerts at Symphony Hall from October through April. The Boston Pops takes over for May and June, performing at the Charles River Esplanade *(see p94)* for Fourth of July festivities that are the highlight of the summer season.

The students and faculty of the **New England Conservatory of Music** present more than 450 free classical and jazz performances each year, many in Jordan Hall. **Boston Lyric Opera** has assumed the task of reestablishing opera in Boston, through small-cast and light opera at venues around the city.

Boston's oldest musical organization is the **Handel & Haydn Society**, founded in 1815. As the first American producer of such landmark works as Handel's *Messiah* (performed annually since 1818), Bach's *B-Minor Mass* and *St. Matthew Passion*, and Verdi's *Requiem*, H & H is one of the country's musical treasures. Since 1986, the society has focused on performing and recording Baroque and Classical works using the period instruments for which the composers wrote. H & H gives regular performances at Symphony Hall, Jordan Hall, and the New Old South Church *(see p98)* in Copley Square.

Classical music is ubiquitous in Boston. **Emmanuel Music**, for example, performs the entire Bach cantata cycle at regular services at Emmanuel Church on Newbury Street. The Isabella Stewart Gardner Museum *(see p105)* hosts a series of chamber music concerts, continuing a 19th-century tradition of professional "music room" chamber concerts in the homes of the social elite.

The **Celebrity Series of Boston** brings world-famous entertainers, orchestras, soloists, and dance companies to Boston, often to perform in the Wang Center for the Performing Arts *(see p88)*.

THEATER

Though much diminished from its heyday in the 1920s *(see p89)*, when more than 40 theaters were in operation throughout Boston, the city's Theater District *(see pp80–89)* today still contains a collection of some of the most architecturally eminent, and still commercially productive, early theaters in the United States. Furthermore, during the 1990s, many of the theaters that are currently in use underwent programs of restoration to their original grandeur, and visitors today are bound to be impressed as they catch a glimpse of these theaters' past glory.

The main, commercially run theaters of Boston – the **Colonial**, **Wilbur**, and **Shubert** theaters, and the **Wang Center for the Performing Arts** *(see pp86–9)* – generally program Broadway productions that have aleady premiered in New York and are touring the United States. Nevertheless, some shows still "try out" in Boston before appearing on Broadway.

In stark contrast to some of the mainstream shows on offer in Boston, the most avant-garde contemporary theater in the city is performed at the **American Repertory Theater (ART)**, an independent, non-commercial company associated with Harvard University *(see pp112–3)*. ART often premieres new plays, particularly on its second stage, but is best known for its often radical interpretations of traditional and modern classics. By further contrast, the **Huntington Theatre**, allied with Boston University, is widely praised for its traditional direction and interpretation. Most recently, for example, the Huntington has been the co-developer of Pulitzer-Prize winning plays detailing 20th-century African American life, by the important chronicler of American race relations, August Wilson.

Several smaller companies, including **Lyric Stage**, devote their energies to showcasing local actors and directors and often premiere the work of Boston-area playwrights. Many of the most adventurous companies perform on one of the three stages at the **Boston Center for the Arts**.

DANCE

The city's largest and most popular resident dance company, the **Boston Ballet** performs a five-ballet season of classics and new choreography between October and May at the Wang Center for the Performing Arts and at the Shubert Theater *(see p88)*. The annual performances of the *Nutcracker* during the Christmas season are a

Boston tradition. The somewhat more modest **José Mateo's Ballet Theater of Boston** has developed a strong and impressive body of repertory choreography. The company performs in the neo-Gothic Old Cambridge Baptist church, which is situated near Harvard Square. Modern dance in Boston is represented by many small companies, collectives, and independent choreographers, who often perform in the **Dance Complex** and **Green Street Studios** in Cambridge. Boston also hosts many other visiting dance companies, who often put on performances at the **Emerson Majestic Theater**.

CINEMA

Situated in Harvard Square, close to Harvard Yard *(see pp112–3)*, the **Brattle Theater**, one of the very last repertory movie houses in the Greater Boston area, primarily shows classic films on a big screen. For example, the Brattle was instrumental in reviving moviegoers' interest in the Humphrey Bogart, black-and-white classic *Casablanca*. Something of a Harvard institution, the Brattle has long served as a popular "first date" destination for couples with a shared passion for the movies.

Serious students of classic and international cinema patronize the screening programs of the **Harvard Film Archive**. The **Kendall Square Cinema** multiplex is the city's chief venue for non-English language films, art films and documentaries. Multiplex theaters showing mainstream, first-run Hollywood movies are found throughout the Boston area. Two of the most popular showing mainstream, first-run Hollywood movies are found throughout the Boston area. Two of the most popular are **Loews Theaters**, located at Copley Place in the Back Bay, and the **Fenway Theater General Cinema** in the suburb of Brookline. Tickets for every kind of movie in Boston are discounted for first shows of the day on weekends and all weekday shows before 5pm.

DIRECTORY

CLASSICAL MUSIC AND OPERA

Boston Lyric Opera
various venues.
(617) 542-4912.
w www.blo.org

Boston Symphony Orchestra
Symphony Hall,
301 Massachusetts Ave.
Map 3 A4.
(617) 266-1200, (617) 266-1492.
w www.bso.org

Celebrity Series of Boston
various venues.
(617) 482-6661.
w www.celebrityseries.org

Emmanuel Music
Emmanuel Church,
15 Newbury St.
Map 4 D2.
(617) 536-3355.

Handel & Haydn Society
various venues.
(617) 266-3605. w
www.handelandhaydn.org

New England Conservatory of Music
Jordan Hall,
30 Gainsborough St.

Map 3 A4.
(617) 585-1122.
w www.newenglandconservatory.edu

THEATER

American Repertory Theater
Loeb Drama Center,
64 Brattle St.,
Cambridge.
(617) 547-8300.
w www.amrep.org

Boston Center for the Arts
539 Tremont St.
Map 4 D3.
(617) 426-2787.
w www.bcaonline.org

Colonial Theater
106 Boylston St.
Map 4 E2.
(617) 426-9366.

Huntington Theatre
264 Huntington Ave.
Map 3 B4.
(617) 266-0800.
w www.bu.edu/huntington

Lyric Stage
140 Clarendon St.
Map 3 C3.
(617) 437-7172.
w www.lyricstage.com

Shubert Theater
265 Tremont St.
Map 4 E2.
(617) 482-9393.

Wang Center for the Performing Arts
270 Tremont St.
Map 4 E2.
(617) 482-9393.

Wilbur Theater
246 Tremont St.
Map 4 E2.
(617) 423-4008.

DANCE

José Mateo's Ballet Theater of Boston
1151 Massachusetts Ave.
Cambridge
(617) 354-7467.
w www.btb.org

Boston Ballet
various venues.
(617) 695-6950.
w www.boston.com/bostonballet

Dance Complex
536 Massachusetts Ave,
Cambridge.
(617) 547-9363.

Emerson Majestic Theater

219 Tremont St.
Map 4 E2.
(617) 824-8000.
w www.maj.org

Green Street Studios
185 Green St.,
Cambridge.
(617) 864-3191.

CINEMA

Brattle Theater
40 Brattle St.,
Cambridge.
(617) 876-6837.

Harvard Film Archive
24 Quincy St.,
Cambridge.
(617) 495-4700.

Kendall Square Cinema
1 Kendall Square,
Cambridge.
(617) 494-9800.

Loews Theaters
Copley Place, 100
Huntington Ave. Map 3
C3. (617) 266-1300.

Fenway Theater General Cinema
201 Brookline Ave.
(617) 424-6266.

Music and Nightlife

Boston's mix of young professionals and tens of thousands of college students produces a lively nightlife scene, focused on live music, clubs, and bars. Ever since the 1920s, Boston has been especially hospitable to jazz, and Boston still has an interesting jazz scene, with Berklee College of Music playing an important part. Cambridge is an epicenter of folk and acoustic music revivals, while Lansdowne Street near Fenway Park (see p156) is the city's main district for nightclubs and discos. Virtually every neighborhood has a selection of friendly bars, often with live music.

ROCK MUSIC

Situated on Lansdowne Street, and its most important music venue, the **Avalon Ballroom** hosts concerts by established and up-and-coming rock bands, though the musicians play earlier in the night to clear the house out for a late-night dance crowd. Sunday is gay night. The **Middle East** in Cambridge's Central Square leads the alternative rock scene, featuring both local bands and touring newcomers. Larger rock concert venues are the **Orpheum Theater** and the arena seating of **Fleet Center**, used at other times for hockey and basketball games.

JAZZ AND BLUES

The city's premier, large concert venue for jazz is **Berklee Performance Center** in Back Bay, which draws on faculty and students from Berklee College of Music as well as touring performers. More intimate settings include **Scullers Jazz Club** overlooking the Charles River in Brighton, the upscale martini-Scotch-cigar scene of the **Oak Bar** at the Fairmont Copley Plaza Hotel, and the suave elegance of the **Regatta Bar** just off Harvard Square. No-frills, neighborhood jazz thrives at **Ryles Jazz Club** in Cambridge's Inman Square. The musical parent of jazz, the blues, is also alive and well. The charter room of the **House of Blues** chain in Harvard Square has a Hollywood ambience, but the music is genuine and the Sunday gospel-music brunch is legendary. The **Cantab Lounge** in Cambridge's Central Square is a blues lover's gem, with Wednesday and Sunday blues jams. Musician-owner "Little" Joe Cook occasionally performs his 1950s R&B to an enthusiastic audience. The Cantab also runs popular Wednesday night poetry "slams."

FOLK AND WORLD MUSIC

Harvard Square's **Club Passim** is a folk music legend, the hangout in the late 1950s and early 1960s for the likes of Joan Baez and Van Morrison, and still one of the United States' key clubs in the touring life of singer-songwriters. **Bishop's Pub** in the Theater District is a good place to catch unplugged rock, the occasional lounge act, and some good acoustic and moderately amplified R&B. Davis Square is a couple of Red Line stops farther out from Harvard station, but well worth the trip for **Johnny D's Uptown Restaurant & Music Club**, where the program offers an eclectic mix ranging from solo singer-songwriters, to zydeco bands, and acoustic and amplified rockabilly. To enjoy some local Caribbean tunes and dancing, one of the best options is a weekend night at **Rhythm & Spice Caribbean Grill** located in Cambridge's Central Square.

International acts ranging from Afro-pop to ska play at many large venues across Boston in a concert series presented by the music promoters **World Music**.

NIGHTCLUBS AND DISCOS

Boston has a club for just about every type of dance music. Like club scenes everywhere, little happens until late; in Boston nothing gets going until at least 11pm. **Axis** is one of the edgier Lansdowne Street choices, with several nights of trance, techno, and house, and gay night on Sundays. At the other end of the spectrum, **The Big Easy** in the Theater District spins rock and pop music for young urban professionals. Located in the rear of a stylish restaurant, **Pravda 116** has a Latin night as well as house and techno music. The extravagant and upscale **Aria** on Tremont Street draws a moneyed Euro-crowd. **ManRay Night Club** in Central Square attracts a gothic crowd, with several fetish-themed nights exhibiting a different extreme in club-going. More middle-of-the-road is the **Roxy** in the Theater District, with classy touches such as doormen instead of bouncers, marble walls, and a vast dance floor.

BARS

The legal drinking age in Boston is 21, and you may be asked to show proof of identification (see p164).

Boston has many bars (see also p141), but many, such as those listed below, offer live entertainment, or place a strong emphasis on being "party" venues. The bar at **Mistral** is typical of the increasingly upscale places springing up in Boston, where the young and the beautiful like to meet and play. More down to earth are some of Boston's Irish bars offering live music and the obligatory pints of Guinness. Among these are **The Phoenix Landing Bar and Restaurant**, a mock Irish pub in Central Square lined with mahogany and featuring English football on cable television as well as Celtic and dance rock performances on weekend nights, **The Burren** that features some of the finest musicians in the city, and the smaller **Druid**, where as the evening wears on, crowds of young professionals give way to recent Irish immigrants.

Bostonians love sports, and the city has dozens of sports bars. The **Cask 'N' Flagon** is adjacent to Fenway Park, perfect for celebrating victory or drowning the pain of defeat. The **Red Line** glorifies the Ivy League, while the **Sports Depot** is just mammoth. The area immediately around North Station is filled with bars catering to Boston Celtics and Boston Bruins fans.

GAY CLUBS AND BARS

BOSTON'S GAY SCENE comes into sharpest focus in the South End and Bay Village, but gay and gay-friendly bars and clubs are found throughout the city. The perpetually packed **Fritz Lounge**, which is attached to the Chandler Inn, is a stalwart South End bar. Boston's longest-running gay club, **Jacques**, features rock acts Friday through Monday and female impersonator cabaret during the rest of the week. The weekly *Bay Windows* newspaper provides wider information as do other Boston listings.

COMEDY CLUBS

MANY CLUBS and bars program occasional evenings of standup comedy, and several specialize in this form of entertainment. The **Comedy Connection** at Quincy Market, which some feel is an unlikely venue, nevertheless presents an impressive line-up of comedians, who are familiar from their work on national television. **Nick's Comedy Stop** in the Theater District, on the other hand, tends to focus on homegrown talent, grooming performers who often go on to the "big time."

SPORTS AND OUTDOOR ACTIVITIES

BOSTONIANS HAVE a wealth of recreational opportunities, thanks largely to the city's many spacious parks, its long, well-maintained riverfront, sizeable harbor, and excellent sports facilities. Visitors can enjoy many outdoor activities, whether it is going for an early morning jog on Boston Common, sailing on the

Charles River, taking to one of the extensive cycle paths, or playing a round at a public golf course. In the winter there is also outdoor ice-skating, and farther afield, skiing. For those who watch sports rather than participate, major-league baseball, football, soccer, basketball, and ice-hockey are played at different times through the year.

Rollerblading

WATER SPORTS

DURING ALL BUT the winter months, dozens of small pleasure craft can be seen navigating the Charles River between Cambridge and Boston. At long-established **Community Boating**, visitors can rent sailboats, kayaks, and windsurfers, while farther upriver at the **Charles River Canoe & Kayak Center**, canoes, racing shells, rowboats, and adult and children's kayaks can be rented.

For those who enjoy swimming or sunbathing, there are a number of good beaches near Boston. Carson Beach and the beach at Castle Island in South Boston are two of the closest, while Revere Beach to the north is larger and busier and served by the subway. There are beaches along the Charles River, although many are badly polluted. From June to September swimmers can use any of the **Metropolitan District Commission** outdoor swimming pools.

BICYCLING, JOGGING, AND SKATING

THE GENTLE BOSTON topography makes sightseeing by bicycle ideal. A number of good trails and bicycle paths crisscross the city, the most popular of which is the Dr. Paul Dudley White Bike Path. This links central Boston with outlying Watertown via a circular 17-mile (27-km) trail that runs along both sides of the Charles River. The Southwest Corridor cycle route links the Back Bay with Roxbury along a section of the Emerald Necklace *(see p105)*, and the recently extended Boston harborfront pathways also attract many cyclists. Farther afield, an old railroad line has been transformed into the Minuteman Bikeway, which runs between Cambridge and Bedford via historic Lexington. **Boston Bike Tours** offers cycle tours along with rental bikes, while other rental stores include **Back Bay Bicycles** and **Community Bicycle Supply**.

In-line skating and jogging are also popular activities in Boston, with riverside esplanades and Boston Common being the favorite areas. In-line skates can be rented from **Blades, Board and Skate**.

Cyclist on the Dr. Paul Dudley White Bike Path

GOLF AND TENNIS

ALONG WITH ITS many excellent private golf clubs, the Boston area also boasts a number of public courses, including some municipal links. A couple of the best include **William J. Devine Golf Course** in Franklin Park and **George Wright Golf Course** in Hyde Park. There is also the nine-hole **Fresh Pond Golf Course** in Cambridge.

The **Metropolitan District Commission** maintains a dozen public tennis courts in Boston. Those in North End Park on Commercial Street and Charlesbank Park on the Charles River Esplanade are the most central. Court time can't usually be reserved, so availability is on a first-come-first-served basis.

Sailboats on the Charles River with Back Bay in the distance

WINTER SPORTS

Freezing winter weather sees large groups of heavily clothed ice skaters heading for the Frog Pond on Boston Common. A modest fee is charged for skating, and skate rental is available in the pavilion by Frog Pond, or else a few blocks away at the **Beacon Hill Skate Shop**. Each winter, the **Metropolitan District Commission** also opens its many indoor rinks in Boston and Cambridge to the public.

Most of the best skiing in New England is found a long way from Boston, in Vermont, Maine, and New Hampshire. If you have enough time it is well worth planning a trip, but otherwise, closer options include **Blue Hills Ski Area** in Canton for downhill skiing, and **Middlesex Fells Reservation** in Stoneham for cross-country. These areas depend a lot on the weather, however, and have only a few slopes.

Tentative ice-skaters take to the frozen Boston Common pond

FITNESS FACILITIES

Amenities at most of Boston's large hotels include fitness facilities. Those hotels that don't have facilities on-site usually have an arrangement whereby guests can use a private club in the immediate area. Otherwise, choose from the many other public gyms and health clubs found throughout the city. **Fitcorp** has excellent, modern exercise facilities at its four city branch locations, while **Boston Athletic Club** in Downtown has both a well-equipped gym, and also a swimming pool, tennis, and squash courts. Across the river, **Cambridge Racquet & Fitness Club** offers various racquet sports and a good gym.

DIRECTORY

WATER SPORTS

Community Boating
21 Embankment Rd.
Map 1 A3.
(617) 523-1038.
www.state.ma.us/mdc

Charles River Canoe & Kayak Center
Soldiers Field Rd., Brighton.
(617) 965-5110.
www.ski-paddle.com

Boston Harbor Islands National Park Area
(617) 223-8666.
www.bostonislands.com

BICYCLING AND SKATING

Boston Bike Tours
Boston Common. **Map** 1 C4. *(617) 308-5902.*
www.bostonbike tours.com

Back Bay Bicycles
336 Newbury St.
Map 3 A3.
(617) 247-2336.
www.backbaybicycles.com

Community Bicycle Supply
496 Tremont St. **Map** 4 D3.
(617) 542-8623.
www.communitybicycle .com

Blades, Board and Skate
38 JFK St., Cambridge.
(617) 491-4244.
www.blades.com

GOLF COURSES

Fresh Pond Golf Course
691 Huron Ave., Cambridge. *(617) 349-6282.*

William J. Devine Golf Course
1 Circuit Drive, Dorchester.
(617) 265-4084.

George Wright Golf Course
420 West St., Hyde Park.
(617) 361-8313.

WINTER SPORTS

Beacon Hill Skate Shop
135 South Charles St.
Map 4 E2.
(617) 482-7400.

Blue Hills Ski Area
Canton, MA 02021.
(781) 828-8171.

Middlesex Fells Reservation
MDC, 4 Woodland Rd., Stoneham, MA 02180.
(781) 322-2851.

FITNESS FACILITIES

Boston Athletic Club
653 Summer St.
(617) 269-4300.
www.bostonathletic club.com

Cambridge Raquet and Fitness Club
215 First St., Cambridge.
(617) 491-8989.
www.cambridgefitness .com

Fitcorp

1 Beacon St.
Map 1 C4.
(617) 248-9797.

Prudential Center.
Map 3 B3.
(617) 262-2050.

350 Longwood Ave.
(617) 732-7111.

133 Federal St.
Map 1 D4.
(617) 542-1010.
www.fitcorp.com

USEFUL ADDRESSES

Boston Parks and Recreation Department
1010 Massachusetts Ave.
(617) 635-4505.
www.ci.boston.ma .us/park

Metropolitan District Commission
20 Somerset St.
Map 1 C3.
(617) 727-5114.
www.state.ma .us/mdc

Spectator Sports

BOSTONIANS WATCH sporting events with a passion that is unmatched in most other U.S. cities. Boston has had a team in every major professional league for many years, and some of popular sports' greatest athletes have played for home sides. Moreover, such widely known annual competitions as the Boston Marathon and the Head of the Charles Regatta draw amazingly large and enthusiastic crowds, as do the metropolitan area's many college teams, which have long traditions and avid fans.

A Boston Bruin waiting for the pass during a game at the FleetCenter

BASEBALL

NO MATTER whether they win or lose, the **Boston Red Sox** have always had an emotional following, especially when their local rivals, the New York Yankees, come to town. The Red Sox beloved Fenway Park stadium is the oldest in the country, and is famous for its enormous 37-ft (11-m) left-field wall known as the "Green Monster." The small seating capacity, however, means that tickets can be difficult to obtain for the bigger games. Tickets are sold at the gate on **Red Sox** the day of the game **baseball** and are also available **player** from the Fenway Park hotline. The "Bosox" are in the Eastern Division of the American League, one of the country's two major professional leagues. The baseball season runs from early April to the end of September, with post-season championship playoffs, culminating in the World Series (last won by Boston in 1918), extending the action well into October.

BASKETBALL

DESPITE A FLUCTUATING record, the **Boston Celtics** have been the most successful of all of Boston's major-league sports teams. They were the dominant team during the 1960s and 80s, winning 16 National Basketball Association (NBA) championships. Banners hung above their home court, the modern 19,000-seat FleetCenter

arena, pay testament to this record. Even with their recent mediocre level of success the Celtics normally draw big crowds, hoping to see the team rekindle past glories. Tickets are usually available for most games, although they can be pricey – good seats cost around $50. The basketball season extends from October through to April.

AMERICAN FOOTBALL

THE HOME FOOTBALL team, the **New England Patriots** has shown much improved form in recent times, winning the 2002 Superbowl Championship. They play against their National Football League (NFL) opponents in the new CMGI Field, about an hour's drive south of downtown Boston. Most NFL games are played during the fall on Sundays, or sometimes on Monday evenings to attract a national television audience. Tickets sell out a long way in advance, so the chances of picking one up are remote.

New England Revolution playing soccer against Miami Fusion

ICE HOCKEY

FIVE STANLEY CUP wins make the **Boston Bruins** one of the most successful teams in National Hockey League (NHL) history, although their recent form has been changeable. The hockey season runs from September to April, with the hard-charging "B's" playing in the NHL's Eastern Conference. End-of-season Stanley Cup Championship games are often sold out well in advance, but for other games, tickets are usually available for between $30 and $75. Games are played at the FleetCenter.

OTHER SPORTS

BOSTON'S MAJOR-league professional soccer team, the **New England Revolution**, plays all of its home games at CMGI Field after the New England Patriots have finished their season. The soccer season runs from April through to July, and the game is slowly gaining more widespread support, due partly to its increasing popularity as a college sport.
   Suffolk Downs is the Boston area's main thoroughbred racetrack, where bets are taken on both live and simulcast races. The year's biggest attraction is the Massachusetts Handicap or "Mass 'Cap" race in July.

Greyhound racing takes place at **Wonderland Park** in north-suburban Revere. The track can be reached on the subway's Blue Line, and dog racing is held year-round.

Each August, many of the world's top-seeded players compete in the week-long U.S. Pro Tennis Championships at Brookline's **Longwood Cricket Club**. Despite the suggestive name, no cricket is actually played here.

Each year on Patriot's Day (a city holiday on the third Monday of April,) the largest event on the sports calendar takes place. The **Boston Marathon** has burgeoned since its inception in 1897, and now approximately 15,000 participants, including many top runners from all over the world, take on the challenge of the 26.2-mile (42.2-km) course. The marathon starts in the town of Hopkinton, west of Boston, and finishes Downtown at the Boston Public Library on Boylston Street. More than half a million people line the entire length of the course to cheer on the runners.

Boats taking part in the Head of the Charles Regatta in October

Detail from plaque celebrating the Boston Marathon

The other major event of the sporting year is the **Head of the Charles Regatta**. The world's largest rowing event, this is a huge two-day competition held annually during the third weekend of October on the Charles River. It involves more than 6,000 crew members, who represent clubs, universities, and colleges from around the world. The 3-mile (5-km) course runs upstream from Boston University boathouse to Eliot Bridge. With up to 80 boats in each race, crews set off at short intervals and are timed along the course.

This is a major social event, as well as a sports one, with as many as 300,000 spectators crowding both banks of the river, spread out on blankets and enjoying picnics and beer as they cheer on the rowers.

COLLEGE SPORTS

Boston's major colleges actively compete in a number of sports, with the major events occurring during the winter and fall. The annual Harvard–Yale football game takes place on the Saturday before Thanksgiving and is usually a fun and spirited event, both on and off the field. The sport that Boston colleges are best at, however, is ice-hockey, and the biggest event on the calendar is the fiercely contested "Beanpot" hockey tournament. This is held at the FleetCenter over two weekends at the beginning of February and involves most of the area's major colleges.

CHILDREN'S BOSTON

FIRST-TIME VISITORS to Boston may wonder what this city, famous for its history and learning, has to offer families with children. The answer is more than can possibly be explored in one visit, with an enormous variety of children's attractions and entertainment, as well as many helpful services and facilities. Whether you begin your adventure at Boston's acclaimed Children's Museum, head out to sea on a whale-watching expedition, take a specially designed children's walking

Giant teddy outside F.A.O. Shwarz store

tour of The Freedom Trail, or visit Franklin Park Zoo, families will soon discover that Boston's unique heritage has as much to interest children as it does adults. A good starting point is the Prudential Center Skywalk *(see p100)*, a 360-degree observatory from where children can locate the city's major landmarks, parks, and attractions. For parents hoping to find some time on their own, a few attractions have supervised children's activities and entertainment, and there are also various baby-sitting agencies.

Boston's Duck Tours – from dry land to the Charles River

PRACTICAL ADVICE

A USEFUL MONTHLY publication, found free at many local children's attractions, is *The Boston Parent's Paper*. This has detailed listings of events, attractions, and activities for kids throughout the Boston region. Children's events are also listed in the Calendar section of Thursday's *Boston Globe*. Short-term baby-sitting can be arranged through **Parents-in-a-Pinch**. **CVS Pharmacy** *(see p167)* is open until late for supplies. Boston is easy to explore on foot, but be cautious before crossing streets with children, as Boston's drivers can be very assertive. Boston's subway system *(see pp172–3)*, is free for children under 5, and half-price for 5- to 11-year-olds.

TOURS AND HISTORICAL SIGHTS

THERE ARE MANY tours and historical sights in Boston which children will find both fun and interesting. They can board an amphibious World

War II vehicle for a land and water tour of historic Boston with **Boston Duck Tours** *(see p165)*. These drive past the city's attractions' neighborhoods and landmarks and then splash into the Charles River for a spectacular view of the Boston skyline. Boston's inner harbor and islands can be explored with **Boston Harbor Cruises**, whose cruises also stop at the *U.S.S. Constitution*, commonly known as "Old Ironsides" *(see p117)*. Even more breathtaking are the whale-watching trips, run all through the summer by the New England Aquarium *(see pp78–9)*.

Even if tickets to see the Red Sox games are sold out, baseball fans can still take the 40-minute tour of **Fenway Park** for a behind-the-scenes glimpse of the press box, private suites, and dugouts of this historic ballpark.

The experienced guides of **Boston by Foot** conduct special 60-minute family walking tours of the heart of The Freedom Trail *(see pp32–5)*. History comes alive for children as they walk along the old cobblestone streets, and visit many sites of architectural and historical significance. Tours begin and end in front of the statue of Samuel Adams at Faneuil Hall. This is the gateway to **Quincy Market** *(see p66)*, a lively emporium that sees flocks of tourists and locals alike, attracted by the enormous array of restaurants, shops, and entertainment. Children in particular will enjoy the jugglers, mime artists, musicians, and magicians who perform all around the attractive and traffic-free cobblestone marketplace.

Street entertainer, Quincy Market

Museums

K NOWN AS A PIONEER of hands-on interactive learning, **Boston Children's Museum** *(see p77)* calls itself "Boston's Best Place for Kids." Offering four floors of fun-filled education for toddlers to pre-teens, few will disagree. Children can do make-believe building work in the Construction Zone, explore an authentic 170-year-old house transplanted from Tokyo, experience contemporary Japanese youth culture in Teen Tokyo, and create giant bubbles or conduct experiments in Science Playground. Children aged under three have their own Playspace, a stimulating second-floor area designed especially for them. The **Museum of Science** *(see p55)* could be another full-day stop, housing over 600 permanent exhibits exploring astronomy, energy, industry, anthropology, and nature. Younger children will enjoy the Human Body Discovery Space, while older kids can explore basic scientific principles in Investigate. All will be impressed by the

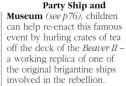
Playspace activity, Children's Museum

life-sized Tyrannosaurus Rex and the Hall of Electricity, with spectacular lightning displays created by a giant Van de Graaff generator. Attached to the museum there is also a Planetarium and an Omni IMAX film theater.

Few art museums have made their collections so accessible to families as Boston's **Museum of Fine Arts** *(see pp106–9)*. During weekday afternoons the Children's Room offers a combined gallery exploration and studio project for children aged 6 to 12. Children can be dropped off at 3:30pm and picked up an hour later, giving parents a chance to explore the museum on their own. At weekends you can visit Family Place, with self-guided activities including

games, puzzles, sketching materials, and scavenger hunt clues to help explore the Museum's exhibits.

The unique history of Boston's African-American community is presented at two sites. **The African Meeting House** *(see p51)* is the oldest black church in the United States and the **Abiel Smith School** *(see p51)* was the first schoolhouse for black children in America. Recently renovated, the schoolhouse has interactive computer stations where children can learn about slavery, the American abolitionist movement, and the Underground Railroad *(see p51)*, as well as more contemporary issues affecting African-Americans in New England. Older children may be interested in the **Black Heritage Trail** *(see p51)*, a 1.5-mile (2.5-km) guided walking tour that visits 14 sites significant to the history of free African-Americans. At the **Boston Tea Party Ship and Museum** *(see p76)*, children can help re-enact this famous event by hurling crates of tea off the deck of the *Beaver II* – a working replica of one of the original brigantine ships involved in the rebellion.

Sports enthusiasts will want to make a trip to the **Sports**

Hands-on exhibit at Boston's Museum of Science

Having fun, Boston Museum of Science

Museum of New England, where interactive exhibits, mini-presentations, and a vast collection of sports memorabilia chronicle the region's sporting history. Children will be fascinated by the life-size wooden statues of Larry Bird, Carl Yastremsky, and Bobby Orr, and enthusiastically take the chance to try out a variety of sports equipment.

Capybara, some of the many fascinating animals at Franklin Park Zoo

AQUARIUMS, ZOOS, AND PARKS

VISITORS are greeted by a group of harbor seals at the entrance to the **New England Aquarium** *(see pp 78–9)*, but once inside, all eyes are transfixed by the huge 200,000 gallon (900,000 liter) saltwater tank, which teems with tropical fish, sharks, sea turtles, and even the occasional scuba diver. The gently inclined wheelchair-friendly ramp winds up and around the three-story cylindrical tank, giving a fascinating view of this simulated marine environment. Young children will also enjoy getting their hands wet in the huge indoor tide pool and watching the penguins and the sea lion presentations. Naturalists aboard the Aquarium's Science-at-Sea cruise teach older children about navigation, water testing, and lobstering. Animal lovers will want to

head directly to **Franklin Park Zoo** *(see p104)*, with its collection of native and exotic fauna. Don't miss the African Tropical Forest, a re-created savanna with gorillas, monkeys, and pygmy hippos, the Children's Zoo, and Bird's World. For a wildlife trip in the middle of town, no visit to Boston is complete without a ride on the famous **Swan Boats** *(see p48)* in the Boston Public Garden. Immortalized in Robert McCloskey's 1941 children's classic, *Make Way for Ducklings (see p48)*, the pedal propelled boats gently circle a lovely pond as ducks clamor alongside for a snack. Nearby are large bronze sculptures of Mrs. Mallard and family. Crossing Charles Street, visitors will come to **Boston**

Bronze duck sculpture, Boston Public Garden

Common *(see pp48–9)*, which separates Downtown from Beacon Hill and Back Bay. There is a playground here, as well as Frog Pond, which is a huge wading pool in the summer and a skating rink in the winter. Boston's most attractive park, the highlight of the Emerald Necklace, is **Arnold Arboretum** *(see p104)*, in Jamaica Plain. With plenty of opportunity for exploration, it is a good place for children to let off steam.

CHILDREN'S THEATER

CHILDREN'S THEATER thrives in Boston. The **Boston Children's Theater** celebrated its 50th season in 2000, with its acclaimed "live theater for children by children." Main-stage productions run from December through April, and its Stagemobile takes performances outside to Boston's parks in the summer. The **Wheelock Family Theater**, another highly acclaimed company, uses multi-ethnic and inter-genera-tional casting, with performances on most weekends from September to May. Fables and fairy tales come to life at the **Puppet Showplace Theater**, with shows for pre-schoolers on Wednesday and Thursday, and performances for the over-5s on weekends from September to May.

Swan Boats on a relaxing cruise around the pond, Boston Public Garden

Exterior of legendary toy store F.A.O. Schwarz, Boylston Street

CHILDREN'S SHOPPING

WHILE KEEPING children entertained can often be a challenge, in Boston you will find that even shopping can hold their interests. With enticing window displays, and stores overflowing with desirable goods, do not, however, expect to survive such an outing without spending any money. For pure fun and fantasy, visit **F.A.O. Schwarz**, the legendary toy store. Life-sized stuffed animals stand guard, wind-up toys patrol the aisles, and there is even a giant floor keyboard where

kids can pound out tunes with their feet. **Susie's Gallery** has bright and innovative goods, and the **Discovery Channel Store** is good for educational toys and videos. Movie fans will love the memorabilia, toys, and clothing at **The Disney Store**. **Newbury Comics** features posters, CDs, and the best selection of comic books in Boston. **Zoinks!** stocks a huge assortment of toys and games. The latest in cool clothes

can be found at **Gap Kids**, and outdoor gear at **Patagonia**. It is well worth the trip to Brookline Village for **The Children's Book Shop**, with an excellent selection of books for infants to young-adults, and **No Kidding!**, an award-winning toy store. Kids will also enjoy the shops, stalls, and street vendors at **Quincy Market** *(see p66)*.

EATING OUT WITH CHILDREN

THOUGH CHILDREN never seem to tire of fast food, adults generally long for something more substantial and memorable. Both needs can be catered for in many of Boston's restaurants. Children will enjoy sampling Chinese delicacies at **The Golden Palace** in Chinatown. For pizza in an authentic Italian atmosphere, try the North End's **Pizzeria Regina**. At the Prudential Center, **Marché Mövenpick**'s international food stations have something for every member of the family. In the Huron Avenue shopping district in Cambridge, the friendly restaurant **Full Moon** has a children's play area as well as a varied children's menu.

Popcorn, a favorite snack

DIRECTORY

CHILDREN'S THEATER

Boston Children's Theater
321 Columbus Ave.
Map 3 C3.
(617) 424-6634.

Puppet Showplace Theater
32–33 Station St.,
Brookline.
(617) 731-6400.

Wheelock Family Theater
200 The Riverway,
Brookline.
(617) 734-4760.

CHILDREN'S SHOPPING

The Children's Book Shop
237 Washington St.,
Brookline.
(617) 734-7323.

Discovery Channel Store
40 South Market Building,
Quincy Market. **Map** 2 D3.
(617) 227-5005.

The Disney Store
6 North Market, Quincy
Market. **Map** 2 D3.
(617) 248-3900.

F.A.O. Schwarz
440 Boylston St. **Map** 3 C2.
(617) 262-5900.

Gap Kids
201 Newbury St. **Map** 3
B2. *(617) 424-8778.*

Newbury Comics
332 Newbury St. **Map** 3
A3. *(617) 236-4930.*

No Kidding!
19 Harvard St., Brookline.
(617) 739-2477.

Patagonia
346 Newbury St. **Map** 3
A3. *(617) 424-1776.*

Susie's Gallery for Children
348 Huron Ave.,
Cambridge.
(617) 876-7874.

Zoinks!
8 North Market Building,
Quincy Market. **Map** 2 D3.
(617) 227-6266.

EATING OUT WITH CHILDREN

Full Moon
344 Huron Ave.,
Cambridge.
(617) 354-6699.

The Golden Palace
14–20 Tyler St.
Map 4 F2.
(617) 574-8822.

Marché Mövenpick
800 Boylston St.
Map 3 B3.
(617) 354-6699.

Pizzeria Regina
11 1/2 Thacher St.
Map 2 D2.
(617) 227-0765.

SURVIVAL
GUIDE

PRACTICAL INFORMATION

ORE THAN MOST American cities, Boston is built to human scale. With the main parts of the city all within a relatively small area, Boston is ideal for the visitor, with walking not only possible, but often preferable, despite a modern and efficient transit system. Boston is also one of the safest cities in the U.S., and one of the most friendly, making it

Trolley bus logo

very easy to feel at home here. So long as visitors take a few sensible precautions, they should enjoy a trouble-free stay. Boston's excellent visitor information centers help people get the most from their stay, and the city also deals better than most with the needs of children and the disabled. Other useful services in the city include many banks and foreign exchanges.

FOREIGN VISITORS

THE CONDITIONS for entering Boston are the same as for entering other parts of the United States. Citizens of the U.K., most western European countries, Australia, New Zealand, and Japan need a valid passport but do not require a visa if their stay is less than 90 days and they hold a return ticket. Canadian citizens require only proof of residence. Citizens of all other countries require a valid passport and a tourist visa, which can be obtained from a U.S. consulate or embassy.

VISITOR INFORMATION

VISITOR INFORMATION desks at the airport can provide guides and maps, answer questions, and make hotel reservations. The **Greater Boston Convention and Visitors Bureau** offers a more comprehensive service, and

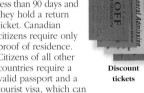

Discount tickets

can help with arrangements before you travel. Major hotels also have helpful guest service desks. All of these places also hold a range of discount tickets offering savings at many of Boston's major museums and attractions, night-life spots, theaters and restaurants.

OPENING HOURS

FOR THE most part Boston's stores keep a 10am to 6pm schedule from Monday to Friday. Many stores also open at weekends, although those open on Sundays often open later. Some gas stations and convenience stores stay open 24 hours. July 4, Thanksgiving, Christmas Day, and New Year's Day are the only retail holidays observed.

ETIQUETTE

SMOKING IS prohibited in many buildings, stores and restaurants in the Boston area. Check for no-smoking signs before lighting up, or else

smoke outside if you are not sure. Tipping is expected for most services: in restaurants tip 15–20 percent of the bill, give $1 per bag to porters, and $2 to valet parking attendants. Bartenders expect 50 cents to $1 per drink.

TAX

IN BOSTON and the surrounding area be aware that taxes will be added to hotel and restaurant charges and most retail purchases, except all clothing items and groceries priced under $150. State sales tax is 5 percent, and hotel tax in the Boston metropolitan area is 12.45 percent.

ALCOHOL AND CIGARETTES

THE LEGAL AGE for drinking alcohol in Boston is 21, and most young people will be required to show photo identification (I.D.) as proof of age in order to get into bars and to purchase alcohol. It is illegal to drink in public spaces, and penalties for driving under the influence of alcohol are severe. The legal age for buying cigarettes is 18, and I.D. may also be required. It is illegal to smoke in public buildings and also in many restaurants (*see p131*).

ELECTRICITY

ELECTRICITY FLOWS at 110–120 volts, and a two-prong plug is used. Non-U.S. appliances will need a plug adaptor and a voltage converter. Most hotel rooms, however, have hairdriers as well as dedicated sockets for electric shavers.

Visitor Information Center on Boston Common

STUDENTS

STUDENTS FROM ABROAD should purchase an International Student Identification Card (I.S.I.C.) before traveling to Boston, as there are many discounts available to students in the city. The I.S.I.C. handbook lists many places and services offering discounts to card holders, including hotels, hostels, museums, and theaters. The **Student Advantage Card** is a similar card available to all American undergraduates.

International Student Identity Card, recognized student I.D. in America.

CHILDREN

BOSTON IS A reasonably child-friendly city, boasting its own **Children's Museum** *(see p77)*, as well as other museums and attractions that offer interesting hands-on exhibits and activities for children *(see pp158–61)*.

Families with children will find that the casual and fast-food restaurants cater best to their needs, with menus often tailored to children's tastes and appetites. Well-behaved children are welcome at most of Boston's restaurants, however.

SENIOR CITIZENS

ANYONE OVER the age of 65 is eligible for various discounts with proof of age. Contact the **American Association of Retired Persons** for further information. Also, try the international senior travel organization **Elderhostel**, which has programs in Boston.

DISABLED VISITORS

MASSACHUSETTS and U.S. law mandate accessibility for persons with handicaps, but wheelchair accessibility is sometimes limited in Boston's historic buildings. Most hotels and restaurants, however, are wheelchair accessible. **Very Special Arts – Massachusetts** provides useful information on disabled-accessible entertainment. For other information contact the **Society for Accessible Travel and Hospitality**.

Trolley bus outside Trinity Church, Back Bay

Disabled sign

GUIDED TOURS

MANY CITY TOURS depart from the Visitor Information Center on Boston Common, including **Old Town Trolley Tours**, which offers narrated sightseeing tours in an old-fashioned trolley bus, as well as theme tours, such as one featuring Boston beers. For something a bit different try the **Boston Duck Tours**, which use an open-air amphibious vehicle that tours the streets and navigates the Charles River. Also, **National Park Service** rangers offer free walking tours of Boston's parks, the Freedom Trail *(see pp32–35)*, and the Black Heritage Trail *(see p51)*.

Personal Security and Health

Hospital sign

BOSTON'S CRIME RATE started to drop in the early 1990s, and the trend has continued ever since. This has made its police force and community relations programs models for other American cities. Nonetheless, it is still prudent to take a few simple precautions and to keep to the tourist areas. The main sights are all located in safe parts of the city with lots of people and where major crime is rare. If you are unfortunate enough to be taken ill during your visit, healthcare in Boston is world class. This does not come cheaply, however, and it is essential to have adequate insurance coverage before you travel.

LAW ENFORCEMENT

THE MOST VISIBLE uniformed law enforcement personnel in Boston are the National Park Service or Boston Park Service rangers (usually dressed in olive green or khaki) and the members of the Boston Police Department (BPD), dressed in blue. You will also see City Parking and Traffic officers, who deal exclusively with traffic violations.

Should you encounter any trouble as a visitor, approach any of the blue-uniformed BPD officers who regularly patrol the city streets. Park rangers are often useful sources of information.

GUIDELINES ON SAFETY

SERIOUS CRIME is rarely witnessed in the main sightseeing areas of Boston. However, avoid wandering into areas that are off the beaten track, during the day or at night. Pickpockets operate in the city and will target anyone who looks like a tourist. Police officers regularly patrol the tourist areas, but it is still advisable to use common sense, and to stay alert. Try not to advertise the fact that you are a visitor; prepare the day's itinerary in advance, and study your map before you set off. Avoid wearing expensive jewelry, and carry your camera or camcorder securely. Only carry small amounts of cash; credit cards and traveler's checks are a more secure option. Keep these close to your body in a money belt or inside pocket.

Before you leave home, take a photocopy of important documents, including your passport and visa, and keep them with you, separate from the originals. Also make a note of your credit card numbers, in the event of their being stolen. Keep an eye on your belongings at all times, whether checking into or out of the hotel, standing in the airport, or sitting in a bar or restaurant. Keep any valuables in your hotel safe, as most hotels will not guarantee their security if they are left in your room. Also be careful not to tell strangers where you are staying or to let anyone you do not know into your room.

LOST PROPERTY

Boston police officer

ALTHOUGH THE CHANCES of retrieving lost property are slim, you should report all stolen items to the police. Use the **Police Non-Emergency Line**. Make sure you keep a copy of the police report, which you will need for your insurance claim. In case of loss, it is useful to have a list of your valuables' serial numbers or a photocopy of any relevant documents or receipts as proof of possession. This should be kept separately. It is also useful to try and remember the taxi companies or bus routes you use, as it might make it easier to retrieve lost items. If your passport is lost or stolen, get in touch with your country's embassy or consulate immediately.

If you lose your credit cards, most card companies have toll-free numbers for reporting a loss or theft, as do Thomas Cook and American Express for lost traveler's checks (*see p168*).

TRAVEL INSURANCE

TRAVEL INSURANCE is not compulsory but strongly recommended when traveling to the United States. It is particularly important to have insurance for emergency medical and dental care, which can be very expensive in the U.S.. Even with medical coverage you may have to pay for the services, then claim reimbursement from your insurance company. If you take medication, bring a

Mounted Boston Park Service ranger, Copley Square

Police car

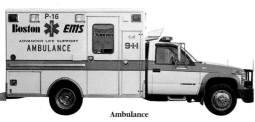

Ambulance

back-up prescription with you. In addition, it is advisable to make sure your personal property is insured and to obtain coverage for lost or stolen baggage and travel documents, as well as trip cancellation fees, legal advice, and accidental death or injury.

EMERGENCIES

IF YOU ARE involved in a medical emergency, go to a hospital emergency room. Should you need an ambulance, call 911 (toll-free) and one will be sent. Also call 911 for police or fire department assistance.

If you have your medical insurance properly arranged, you need not worry about medical costs. Depending on the limitations of your insurance, it is better to avoid the overcrowded city-owned hospitals listed in the phone book Blue Pages, and opt instead for one of the private hospitals listed in the Yellow Pages. Alternatively ask at your hotel desk or at the nearest pharmacy for information. You can also ask your hotel to call a doctor or dentist to visit you in your room.

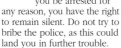

Pharmacy sign

PHARMACIES

IF YOU NEED a prescription dispensed, there are plenty of pharmacies (drugstores) in and around the city, some staying open 24 hours. Ask your hotel for the nearest one.

LEGAL ASSISTANCE

NON-U.S. CITIZENS requiring legal assistance should telephone their consulate if there is an office in Boston, or their embassy in Washington, DC. These offices will not lend you money but can help with legal advice in emergencies. Should you be arrested for any reason, you have the right to remain silent. Do not try to bribe the police, as this could land you in further trouble.

PUBLIC RESTROOMS

ALL VISITORS' CENTERS, museums, and galleries have public restrooms, and invariably offer disabled and baby-changing facilities as well. All restaurants and hotels also have restrooms, but these may be available only to paying customers.

DIRECTORY

LOST PROPERTY

Police Non-Emergency Line

Ⓒ Boston (617) 343-4200.
Ⓒ Cambridge (617) 349-3300.

EMERGENCIES

Police, Fire, Medical (all emergencies)

Ⓒ Call 911 (toll-free), or dial 0 for the operator.

Dental Referrals

Ⓒ (800) 342-8747.
Ⓦ www.massdental.org

Medical Referrals

Ⓒ (781) 893-4610.
Ⓒ (800) 322-2303.

Area Hospitals

Ⓒ Call 411 for directory assistance.

PHARMACIES

CVS Pharmacy

155 Charles St., Boston.
Map 1 B3. (Open until midnight Mon–Fri, until 9pm Sat & Sun.)
Ⓒ (617) 523-1028.

35 White St., Cambridge.
(Open 24 hours.)
Ⓒ (617) 876-5519.

CONSULATES

Australia

150 East 42nd St, 34th floor, New York, NY 10017.
Ⓒ (212) 351-6530.
Ⓦ www.australianyc.org

Canada

3 Copley Place.
Map 3 C3.
Ⓒ (617) 262-3760.
Ⓦ www.boston.gc.ca

Ireland

535 Boylston St. **Map** 3 C2.
Ⓒ 267-9330.
Ⓦ irelandemb.org

New Zealand

37 Observatory Circle, NW Washington, DC 20008.
Ⓒ (202) 328-4800.
Ⓦ www.nzemb.org

United Kingdom

1 Memorial Drive, Cambridge.
Ⓒ (617) 248-9555.
Ⓦ www.britainusa.com

Fire engine

Banking and Currency

T HROUGHOUT BOSTON there are various places to access and exchange your money, from the numerous banks and automatic teller machines (cash machines) to the foreign currency exchanges. The most important things to remember are not to carry all your money and credit cards with you at one time, and to be aware that most banks and currency exchanges are closed on Sundays.

One of Fleet Bank's many Boston branches in Chinatown

BANKING AND ATM'S

G ENERALLY, MOST BANKS are open Monday through Friday from 9am to 2 or 3pm, although some may open earlier and close later. Most banks also open Saturday mornings from 9am to noon or 1pm. All banks are closed on Sundays and Federal holidays (see p39).

Always ask if there are any special fees before you make your transaction. At most banks, traveler's checks in U.S. dollars can be cashed with any photo identification, although passports are usually required if you want to exchange any foreign money. Foreign currency exchange is available at the main branches of large banks, which often have a separate dedicated area or teller window.

Automated Teller Machines (ATMs) are found throughout Boston, usually near the entrance to banks, or inside some convenience stores and supermarkets. Widely accepted bank cards include Cirrus, Plus, NYCE, and some credit cards such as VISA or MasterCard. Note that a fee may be levied on your withdrawal depending on the bank. Check with your bank

American Express charge cards

which machines your card can access and the various fees charged. To minimize the risk of robbery, avoid using ATMs in isolated areas, and be aware of the people around you.

CREDIT CARDS

A MERICAN EXPRESS, VISA, MasterCard, Diner's Club, and the Discover Card are accepted almost everywhere in Boston, from theaters and hotels to restaurants and shops. Besides being a much safer alternative to carrying a lot of cash, credit cards also offer some useful additional benefits, such as insurance on your purchases. They are also essential if you want to reserve a hotel or book a rental car. Credit cards can also be useful in emergencies when cash may not be readily available.

CURRENCY EXCHANGE

F OREIGN CURRENCY exchanges are generally open week-days from 9am to 5pm, but some, especially those in shopping districts, may have extended opening hours.

Among the best known are the American Express Travel Service and Thomas Cook

Currency Services, both of which have branches in and around Boston. Major banks also offer exchange services. Most currency exchanges charge a fee or commission, so it is worth looking around to get the best value rates. Hotels may also exchange money, but their fees will be much higher.

TRAVELER'S CHECKS

T RAVELER'S CHECKS in U.S. dollars issued by American Express and Thomas Cook are accepted as payment without a fee by most shops, restaurants, and hotels. It is often simpler to pay by U.S. dollar travelers' checks, where possible, rather than cashing them in advance. Traveler's checks in foreign currencies can be cashed at a bank or with a cashier at a major hotel. Exchange rates are posted wherever currency exchange is offered, along with the commission charges. Check these before you exchange your money – it may be prudent to shop around for the best deal as commission rates can vary.

Personal checks issued by foreign banks are rarely accepted in the United States, so cannot be relied upon as a means of obtaining cash.

DIRECTORY

CURRENCY EXCHANGES

American Express Travel Service
1 State Street.
Map 2 D3.
(*(617) 723-8400.*

432 Stuart Street.
Map 4 D2.
(*(617) 439-4400.*

222 Berkeley Street.
Map 4 D2.
(*(617) 236-1331.*

39 J.F.K. Street, Cambridge.
(*(617) 868-2600.*

Thomas Cook Currency Services
Logan International Airport,
Terminals C & E.
(*(800) 287-7362.*

Communications and Media

Phone card

BOSTON'S COMMUNICATIONS infrastructure is modern and well developed. Coin or card operated public payphones are easy to find on many streets and in restaurants, theaters, bars, department stores, hotel lobbies, and gas stations. News is readily available from Boston's many television and radio stations, newspapers, and magazines, and the postal service is quick and efficient – whether you are sending mail within the United States or abroad.

TELEVISION AND RADIO

THE BOSTON MEDIA market is highly competitive, and saturated with television and radio broadcasters. Major network television stations include CBS (channel 4), ABC (channel 5), NBC (channel 7), and Fox (channel 25). Public television station PBS is on Channel 2. Popular radio stations include NPR (National Public Radio) on WBUR (91.9 FM), WFNX (101.7 FM) for rock music, WCRB (102.5 FM) for classical music, and WMJX (106.7 FM) for easy listening.

TELEPHONES

PUBLIC TELEPHONES are usually found on street corners or in stores all over the Boston area. Most accept coins as well as phone cards, which can be purchased at gas stations, convenience stores, and newsstands. Credit card calls can be made by calling 1-800-225-5288. Local calls cost 25–35 cents for three minutes from pay-phones, while long-distance call rates vary, and include both a fixed call charge and a per-minute charge. All numbers with a **1-800**, **888 or 877** prefix, however, are free of charge. Direct calls can also be made from hotel rooms but usually carry hefty surcharges. Unless you are using your own international telephone card, it is better to use the payphone in the lobby.

Directory assistance is free of charge by dialing 411 (local) or 00 (international.) **Operator assistance** is available by dialing 0 (local) or 01 (international.) All operator assisted calls carry a surcharge. For **emergency services** (fire, police, or ambulance) call 911.

AREA CODES

THE AREA CODE for central Boston is **617** or **857**, which must be included when dialing local calls. If dialing out of the local area (but within the U.S. or Canada) dial **1**, then the area code.
For international calls dial **011**, followed by the appropriate country code, the area code (omitting the first 0), and then the local number.

POSTAL SERVICE

POST OFFICES are open from 9am to 5pm, Monday through Friday, and most are open Saturday from 9am to noon. They close on Sundays and for all Federal holidays.

If the correct postage is attached, letters and parcels of less than 16 oz (500 g) can be put in any blue mailbox. Pickup times are written inside the lid. Always use a zip code to insure delivery, and send all overseas mail by airmail to avoid long delays.

NEWSPAPERS

THE MOST WIDELY read newspaper in the Boston area is the *Boston Globe*, which is also thought of as one of the best newspapers produced in the United States. The other local daily widely available around the city is the *Boston Herald* tabloid. Other U.S. newspapers, found at most newsstands, are *USA Today*, the *New York Times* and *The Wall Street Journal*. Thursday's edition of the *Boston Globe*, and the *Boston Phoenix (see p148)*, published on Friday, contain exhaustive listings of entertainment and cultural events in Boston.

Boston newspapers

Boston post office, Charles Street

DIRECTORY

POST OFFICES

Beacon Hill
136 Charles St.
Map 1 B3.

West End
25 New Chardon St.
Map 1 C3.

Financial District
90 Devonshire St.
Map 2 D4.

Back Bay
390 Stuart St.
Map 3 C3.

Cambridge
125 Mt. Auburn St.,
Cambridge.

South Station
(main city post office)
25 Dorchester Ave.
Map 2 E5.

GETTING TO BOSTON

United
Airlines plane

Arriving in Boston is relatively easy. It is served by Logan International Airport as well as by the smaller satellites, Worcester and Green Airports, which are both located within 50 miles (80 km) of the city center. Greyhound Bus Lines, Peter Pan Trailways, and Amtrak trains come into Boston's South Station. From here the subway, known as the "T," connects to almost every part of the city. Boston also makes an ideal base from which to take day or weekend trips to the numerous places of interest throughout the New England area.

Control Tower at Boston's Logan International Airport

ARRIVING BY AIR

SITUATED IN East Boston, **Logan International Airport** is the major airport serving Boston, although some international charter flights and several domestic carriers use the less crowded **Worcester Airport** in Worcester, Massachusetts, and **T. F. Green Airport** in Warwick, Rhode Island. Both are a bus ride of around an hour from Boston. Boston is served directly by almost all North American airlines and by most international airlines, either directly or in partnership with U.S. carriers. Often the least expensive flights, especially between continental Europe and Boston, require making connections in New York. Frequent direct service is available between Boston and the United Kingdom and Ireland on U.S. carriers as well as British Airways

and Aer Lingus. Logan lies within Boston city limits on an island across the inner harbor from the central city. Harbor tunnel crossings tend to act as a bottleneck, which slows taxi services between the airport and downtown. At busy times, a taxi ride ($15–$25) can take 30 minutes or more, with much of the wait spent in bumper-to-bumper traffic. The least expensive means ($1) of

Bus from South Station to Logan

getting from the airport to downtown Boston is via the M.B.T.A. subway *(see p172)*. Free, continuously running buses connect the airport's air terminals to its subway terminal. There is also a bus service that runs between the airport and Boston's South Station. Arguably the most scenic approach into Boston is M.B.T.A.'s Water Shuttle ($10), which crosses the harbor between the Harborview Hilton and Rowes Wharf *(see p76)*.

AIR FARES

FOR CHEAP AIR FARES check with the various airlines and travel agents. The more you shop around, the better deal you will get, and it is worth taking the time to do some research, or to trust a reliable agent to do it for you. For inexpensive consolidated tickets, contact **Expedia.com** online or **Consolidators: Air Travel's Bargain Basement**. Finding the best published fare available at any time can be accomplished through **Lowestfare.Com**, online or on the telephone.

High season runs from June to August as well as around Easter and Christmas, when flights are most expensive. May, September, and October are less expensive, and any other time of the year is considered off-peak. Flights are usually least expensive for travel from Tuesday to Thursday. APEX tickets, usually the best deal, must be booked a few weeks in advance and must include a Saturday night.

M.B.T.A. water shuttle, which runs from Logan Airport across the harbor to Rowes Wharf

PACKAGE DEALS

BOSTON PACKAGES are sometimes available in the U.S. as part of a fall foliage bus tour or through AAA (American Automobile Association). Several airlines arrange packages including travel and lodging. Boston hotels generally post their special event packages on the web site of the **Greater Boston Convention and Visitors Bureau** *(see p165).*

ARRIVING BY TRAIN

A TRAIN SERVICE between New York and Boston via coastal Connecticut and Rhode Island is provided by **Amtrak**. Conventional train services take 4–5 hours, and arrive and depart from Boston's South Station. A high-speed service which takes 3 hours is now also available but is somewhat more expensive.

In November 2001 a new Amtrak train service between Boston and Portland, Maine was inaugurated. During the summer months, there is a useful stop at Old Orchard Beach in Maine.

ARRIVING BY CAR

BOSTON IS NOT CALLED "The Hub" for nothing, as most routes in the Northeast converge here. Principal routes from the north are I-95 from the coast and I-93 from northern New England. I-90 comes

Amtrak train waiting to depart from Boston's South Station

in from the west as the Massachusetts Turnpike. I-93 approaches from the south as the Southeast Expressway. I-95, also known as Rte 128, circumvents Boston. All highway approaches are being considerably slowed at present until the completion of the "Big Dig" sometime before 2010. The largest public works project in human history, the "Big Dig" will bury most of interstate I-93 under the city.

Greyhound Lines

TICKETS

Greyhound Bus Lines logo

ARRIVING BY BUS

ALTHOUGH taking a bus is easily the slowest and usually cheapest way to get to Boston, it need not be unpleasant. **Greyhound Bus Lines** and **Peter Pan Trailways** both serve Boston as long-distance carriers, sharing quarters at the South Station bus terminal. Both offer routes around the country and provide discounts for children, senior citizens, and U.S. military personnel on active duty. Both also offer bargain excursion tickets for unlimited travel within a certain time period for a single fixed rate.

Main concourse of Boston's South Station

DIRECTORY

AIRPORTS

Logan International Airport
East Boston, Massachusetts.
C (617) 561-1800.
W www.massport.com/logan

T. F. Green Airport
Warwick, Rhode Island.
C (401) 737-8222.

Worcester Airport
Worcester, Massachusetts.
C (508) 799-1741.

AIR FARES

Consolidators: Air Travel's Bargain Basement
Intrepid Traveler, PO Box 438, New York, New York 10034.
C (212) 569-1081.
W www.intrepidtraveler.com

Expedia.com
13810 SE Eastgate Way, Suite Bellevue, WA 98005.
C (800) 397-3342.
W www.expedia.com

Lowestfare.Com
980 Kelly Johnson Dr., Las Vegas, Nevada 89119.
C (888) 333-0440.
W www.lowestfare.com

PUBLIC TRANSPORTATION

Amtrak
South Station. **Map** 2 D5.
C (617) 345-7460.
C (800) 872-7245.

M.B.T.A. Water Shuttle
(Route and schedule information)
10 Park Plaza.
Map 1 B5.
C (617) 222-3200.
W www.mbta.com

Greyhound Bus Lines
700 Atlantic Ave. **Map** 2 D5.
C (617) 526-1800.
C (800) 231-2222.

Peter Pan Trailways
700 Atlantic Ave. **Map** 2 D5.
C (800) 343-9999.

Getting Around Boston

Public transportation in Boston and Cambridge is very good. In fact it is considerably easier to get around by public transportation than by driving, with the added benefit of not having to find a parking space. All major attractions in the city are accessible on the subway, by bus, or by taxi. The central sections of the city are also extremely easy to navigate on foot.

M.B.T.A. commuter bus, with distinctive yellow paintwork

FINDING YOUR WAY IN BOSTON

The more planning you do before your trip, the easier it will be to locate sights and find your way around the city. The **Greater Boston Convention and Visitors Bureau** *(see p165)* will be a helpful contact point, and your hotel is also likely to be able to offer advice. To find out about any upcoming cultural events, check websites for **Boston CitySearch** and the **Boston Globe** *(see p165)*.

Most of Boston is laid out "organically" rather than in the sort of strict grid found in most American cities. When trying to orient yourself, it helps to think of Boston as enclaves – of neighborhoods around a few central squares. In general, uphill from Boston Common is Beacon Hill, downhill is Downtown. Back Bay begins west of Arlington Street. The North End sticks out from the north side of Boston, while the Waterfront is literally that, where Boston meets the sea.

M.B.T.A. SUBWAY AND TROLLEY BUSES

Boston's subway system is the oldest in North America, but has been vastly expanded and modernized since the first cars rolled between Park Street and

Visitor's Passport, valid on all M.B.T.A. services

Boylston Street on September 1, 1897. The street trolley system is even older, having begun in 1846 with trolleys drawn along tracks by horses. The system was electrified in 1889. The combined subway and trolley lines (most lines move above ground when they leave the city center) are generally known as the "T." The "T" operates Monday through Saturday, 5am to 12:45am, and Sunday 6am to 12:45am. Weekday service is officially every three to 15 minutes; on weekends less frequent. There are four lines. The Red Line runs from south of the city to Cambridge. The Green Line runs from the Museum of Science westward into the suburbs. The Blue Line begins near Government Center and goes to Logan Airport and on to Revere. The Orange Line connects the northern suburbs to southwest Boston. Maps of the system are available at the Downtown Crossing M.B.T.A. station.

Admission to subway stations is via turnstiles into which you insert a $1 "T" token or swipe an electromagnetic pass card. Visitor's Passport passes for unlimited travel for one, three, or five days ($6/$11/$22) can be purchased at Downtown Crossing and Airport stations or at **Greater Boston Convention and Visitors Bureau** information booths.

M.B.T.A. BUSES

The bus system complements the subway system and in effect enlarges the entire transit network to cover more than 1,000 miles (1,600 km). However, buses are often crowded and schedules can be hard to obtain. Two useful routes for sightseeing are Charlestown-Haymarket, (from Haymarket, near Quincy Market, to Bunker Hill) and Harvard-Dudley (from Harvard Square via Massachusetts Avenue, through Back Bay and the South End, to Dudley Square in Roxbury.) Exact change (75 cents) or a pass is required for the fare.

TAXIS

Finding a taxi in Boston and Cambridge is rarely difficult except when it is raining. They can be found at taxi stands in tourist areas and can be hailed on the street. Taxis may only pick up fares in the city for which they are licensed – Cambridge taxis only in Cambridge, Boston taxis only in Boston. If you need to be somewhere on time, it is advisable to call a taxi company and arrange a definite pickup time and place.

Rates are calculated by both mileage and time, beginning with a $1.10 "pick-up" fee when the meter starts running. In general, the taxis in Boston and Cambridge are more

Boston taxis waiting for fares at one of the city's many taxi stands

expensive than those in other U.S. cities. Taxis to Logan Airport are required to charge customers an airport use fee ($2), while those coming from the airport charge for the harbor tunnel toll ($3). Additional surcharges may apply late at night. A full schedule of fares should be posted inside the vehicle.

Boston parkland, ideal for walking

The driver's photograph and permit and the taxi's permit number will also be posted inside all legitimate taxicabs, along with directions for reporting complaints.

WALKING IN BOSTON

Boston is considered North America's premier walking city, partly because it is so compact, and partly because virtually all streets are flanked by sidewalks. It is nonetheless essential to wear comfortable walking shoes with adequate cushioning and good support.

Because Boston is principally a city of neighborhoods, it is often simplest to use public transportation to get to a particular neighborhood, and then to walk to soak up the atmosphere. Walking also allows you to see parts of the city that are impractical to explore by car as the streets are too narrow; for example Beacon Hill, parts of the North End, and Harvard Square.

DIRECTORY

M.B.T.A.

M.B.T.A.
(Route and schedule information)
10 Park Plaza.
(617) 222-3200.
www.mbta.com

TAXIS

Boston Cab Dispatch, Inc.
262-2227.

Checker Taxi
(617) 536-7000.

Town Taxi
(617) 536-5000.

Yellow Cab
(Cambridge).
(617) 547-3000.

THE BOSTON "T"

KEY

- ▬ Red line
- ▬ Green line (including green lines B, C, D, & E)
- ▬ Orange line
- ▬ Blue line
- ○ Terminal station
- •—• Interchange with other lines

M.B.T.A. website: www.mbta.com
© MBTA 2000

Driving in and Around Boston

DESPITE HEAVY TRAFFIC and restricted parking, having your own vehicle in Boston can, at times, be an undeniable convenience. For example, visiting some of the outlying sights of Boston, which may be difficult to reach by public transportation, is much easier with a car. Many U.S. visitors to the city arrive with their own cars, and overseas visitors can rent one quite easily. Even so, driving in and around Boston requires patience, good humor, good maps, good driving skills, and the ability to read the road swiftly and take decisive actions.

Boston traffic by night – with the Financial District in the background

DRIVING AND PARKING IN THE CITY

DESPITE BOSTON'S comparatively small size, its traffic can at times rival a much larger "world city" such as Rome or Hong Kong. Like those cities, Boston has far too many vehicles for its roads, and the city's many one-way streets can prove confusing to everyone except the locals, who will honk at befuddled visitors. A new subterranean highway is planned for late 2005, so expect waterfront area detours from "Big Dig" construction until then. Use the Street Finder *(see pp178–81)* or other good map (the best show the direction of one-way streets) to help you get around. Also avoid the rush hours of 8–9:30am and 4–6pm and plan your route in advance so you can concentrate on traffic.

Curbside parking is hard to find at the most popular locations, and during morning

"Tow Zone" sign

and afternoon rush hours curbside parking is banned in some areas. If you do manage to find a space on the street, be sure to feed the meter with coins, or you might face a hefty fine. Vehicles parked near fire hydrants, alleyways, in spaces reserved for the handicapped, or at overland "T" and bus stops may be towed away, and can be retrieved only at considerable cost and inconvenience. Parking at meters is free on Sundays and public holidays, and many downtown areas allow parking in loading zones on Sunday as well. Read posted signs carefully. Parking in a public lot or garage can cost more than $10 per hour or $40 per day, but is sometimes the only choice. Valet parking is available at some restaurants, hotels, and malls for a fee. Visitors may consider parking near a "T" or bus stop in the city's suburbs, and continuing their journey into town by public transportation.

RULES OF THE ROAD

THE HIGHWAY SPEED limit in the Boston area is 55 mph (88 km/h) – much lower than in many European countries. In residential areas the speed limit ranges from 20–35 mph (32–48 km/h). Near schools it can be as low as 15 mph (24 km/h). It is important to obey all signs or you will risk getting a ticket. If you are stopped by the police, be courteous or you may face a larger fine. In addition, all drivers are required to carry a valid driver's license and registration documents for their vehicle.

CAR RENTAL

YOU MUST be at least 25 years old with a valid driving license (plus an international driver's license if from outside the U.S.) to rent a car. All rental agencies require a credit card or a cash deposit. Collision and liability insurances are recommended, but are sometimes offered free with certain credit cards. Return the car with a full tank of gas to avoid paying inflated agency fuel prices. You can rent (and return) a car at the airport, but may save paying airport fees if you pick up and drop off downtown.

GAS

COMPARED to prices worldwide, gas (petrol) is relatively inexpensive in the U.S. However, with the large engines that are found in older American cars, any savings on

Boston street signs, usually posted very clearly

fuel may be partially offset.
Gas comes in three grades:
economy, super, and premium.
There are many gas stations
in and around Boston, which
often have self-service pumps.
The gas at these is often a
few cents cheaper per gallon
than at pumps with attendants.

BREAKDOWNS

I N THE UNLUCKY event of a
breakdown, the best course
of action is to pull off the
road completely and put on
the hazard lights to alert other
drivers that you are stationary.
There are emergency phones
along some major interstate
highways, but in other situa-
tions breakdown services or
even the police can be con-
tacted from land or cellular
(mobile) phones. In case of
breakdown, drivers of rental
cars should contact the car
rental company first. Members
of the **American Automobile**

Cycle path along the Boston side of the Charles River

Association (AAA) can contact the association to have
the car towed to the nearest
service station to be repaired.

CYCLING

I T IS PERHAPS surprising that
a city in which driving can
be so difficult has an extensive network of bike paths.
Cycling is actually a very
useful way to see some of the
outlying attractions. Cycling

on the highways is illegal,
and cycling city streets can be
hazardous, but dedicated bike
paths are generally very safe.
Cycle shops and some newsstands carry the Boston Bike
Map, which details trails and
paths throughout the met-
ropolitan region *(see p154).*

TIPS AND SAFETY FOR DRIVERS

- Traffic moves on the right-
  hand side of the road.
- Seat belts are compulsory
  in the front seats and
  suggested in the back
  seats; children under three
  must ride in a child seat.
- You can turn right at a red
  light as long as you first
  come to a complete stop,
  and if there are no signs
  that prohibit it.
- A flashing yellow light
  at an intersection means
  slow down, look for
  oncoming traffic, and
  proceed with caution.
- Passing (overtaking) is
  allowed on any multi-
  lane road, and you must
  pass on the left.
- Crossing a double-yellow
  line, either by U-turn or
  by passing the car in front,
  is illegal, and you will be
  charged a fine if caught.
- If a school bus stops, all
  traffic from both directions
  must stop completely
  and wait for the bus
  to drive off.
- Driving while intoxicated
  (DWI) is a punishable
  offense that incurs heavy
  fines or even a jail

  sentence. Do not drink
  if you plan to drive.
- Avoid driving at night if
  unfamiliar with the area.
  Boston's streets can
  change from safe to dan-
  gerous in a single block,
  so if you don't know
  where you are going it is
  better to take a taxi than
  to get lost in your own car.
- Single women should be
  especially careful driving
  in unfamiliar territory,
  day or night.
- Keep all doors locked
  when driving around.
  Do not stop in a rural
  area, or on an unlit block
  if someone tries to get
  your attention. If a fellow
  driver points at your car,
  suggesting something is
  wrong, drive to the
  nearest gas station and
  get help. Do not get out
  of your car.
- Avoid sleeping in your car.
- Avoid short cuts and stay
  on well-traveled roads.
- Avoid looking at a map
  in a dark, unpopulated
  place. Drive to the nearest
  open store or gas station
  before pulling over.

BOSTON STREET FINDER

THE KEY MAP BELOW shows the area of Boston covered by the *Street Finder* maps, which can be found on the following pages. Map references, given throughout this guide, for sights, restaurants, hotels, shops, and entertainment venues refer to the grid on the maps. The first figure in the map reference indicates which *Street Finder* map to turn to (1 to 4), and the letter and number that follow refer to the grid reference on that map.

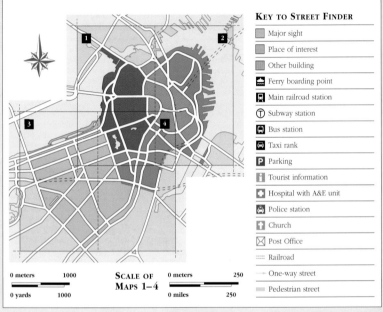

KEY TO STREET FINDER

▦	Major sight
▦	Place of interest
▦	Other building
⚓	Ferry boarding point
🚆	Main railroad station
Ⓣ	Subway station
🚌	Bus station
🚕	Taxi rank
P	Parking
🛈	Tourist information
✚	Hospital with A&E unit
🛡	Police station
🛕	Church
✉	Post Office
═══	Railroad
⟶	One-way street
▬▬	Pedestrian street

SCALE OF MAPS 1–4

0 meters — 1000
0 yards — 1000

0 meters — 250
0 miles — 250

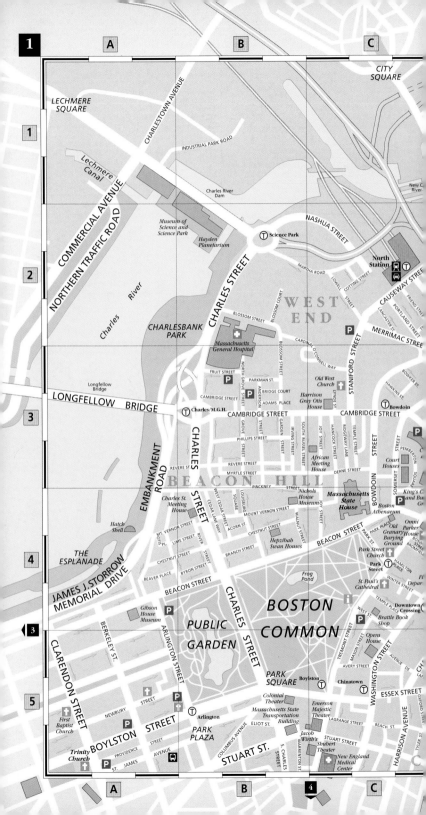

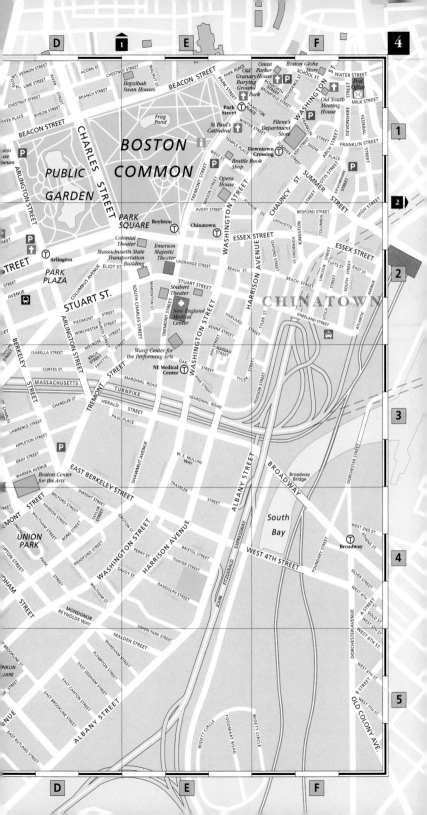

General Index

Page numbers in bold type refer to main entries.

Acknowledgments

DORLING KINDERSLEY would like to thank the following people whose contributions and assistance have made the preparation of this book possible.

MAIN CONTRIBUTORS

PATRICIA HARRIS AND DAVID LYON are journalists and critics. They review art and restaurants and write extensively about travel, food, and popular culture from their home in Cambridge, Massachusetts. In addition to their books on art and travel, their essays, narratives, and photographs have appeared in a wide variety of online and print publications, including Expedia.com, the *Boston Globe*, the *Los Angeles Times*, *American Craft*, *Food Arts*, and *Travel Holiday*. They are also online restaurant reviewers for Boston.CitySearch.com.

TOM BROSS has lived in Massachusetts since 1965 and now lives in Boston's North End, virtually next door to Old North Church. During the past 25 years as a freelance travel journalist Tom has written extensively about U.S., Canadian, and overseas destinations for various guidebooks, national magazines, newspapers, newsletters, and on-line publications. His domestic specialties are New England and California; overseas, Germany, Belgium, and Luxembourg. He is, in addition, a professional photographer and spent several years in the 1980s as staff photographer of his home city's American League baseball team, the Boston Red Sox.

KEM SAWYER lives in Washington DC and has written children's books, feature articles, and book reviews. She particularly enjoys writing about history and has written the history feature for the *DK Eyewitness Travel Guide to Washington DC* as well as for this guide.

ADDITIONAL CONTRIBUTORS
Brett Cook, Carolyn Heller, Juliette Rogers.

ADDITIONAL ILLUSTRATIONS
Christopher King.

ADDITIONAL PHOTOGRAPHY
Peter Anderson, Clive Streeter.

MANAGING EDITOR
Helen Townsend.

MANAGING ART EDITOR
Kate Poole.

SENIOR MANAGING EDITOR
Louise Lang.

ART DIRECTOR
Gillian Allan.

DESIGN AND EDITORIAL ASSISTANCE
Sam Borland, Katherine Mesquita, Lynne Robinson.

PROOFREADER
Stewart J. Wild.

INDEXER
Hilary Bird.

RESEARCHER
Timothy Kennard.

SPECIAL ASSISTANCE
Aimee O'Brien at the Greater Boston Convention and Visitors Bureau, who provided invaluable assistance establishing contact with many of Boston's sights.
Rosemary Barron for acting as food consultant, and for food preparation.

PHOTOGRAPHY PERMISSIONS

DORLING KINDERSLEY would like to thank the following for their assistance and kind permission to photograph at their establishments:

Courtesy COMMONWEALTH OF MASSACHUSETTS ART COMMISSION: *George Washington* Sir Francis Chantrey, 1827 – 53bl; *Civil War Army Nurses Memorial* Bela Pratt, 1911 – 53ca; *John Hancock Memorial* artist unknown, 1915 – 19cl; *Return of the Colours to the Custody of the Commonwealth*, December 22, 1986, mural by Edward Simmons, 1902 – 53tl; Stained glass window, Main Stair Hall, 1900/details: *Magna Carta seal* 43, *Seal of the Commonwealth* (pre-1898) 52b.

Museum of Fine Arts, Sackler Museum, Harvard Museum of Natural History, the Fogg Art and Busch- Reisinger Museums, and Franklin Park Zoo.

All other churches, museums, hotels, restaurants, shops, galleries and sights too numerous to thank individually.

PICTURE CREDITS

t = top; tl = top left; tlc = top left centre; tc = top centre; tr = top right; cla = centre left above; ca = centre above; cra = centre right above; cl = centre left; c = centre; cr = centre right; clb = centre left below; cb = centre below; crb = centre right below; bl = bottom left; b = bottom; bc = bottom centre; bcl = bottom centre left; br = bottom right; d = detail.

The publisher would like to thank the following individuals, companies and picture libraries for permission to reproduce their photographs.

ALLSPORT USA: 156t/c/b; THE ART ARCHIVE: 89bc; AXIOM: 36cl.

BOSTON BALLET: Farnsworth/Blalock Photography 148cr; BOSTONIAN SOCIETY/OLD STATE HOUSE: 55b, 89cb; *Boston Harbor*, 1853, John White Allen Scott. Purchase 1884 – 8-9; DAVID J. BOOKER: 68.

CORBIS: 22t, Bettmann 23t, 29t/b, 74b, 89cra/bl, 100b; Edifice, Philippa Lewis 34c; Kevin Fleming 39b, 148b, 174t; Todd Gypstein 160b; Robert Holmes 102; Hulton-Deutsch Collection 47t; Richard T. Nowitz 75c; Lee Snider 1; CULVER PICTURES, INC.: 20c, 22c.

GRANGER COLLECTION, NEW YORK: 9 (insert), 14, 15t, 16t/c/b, 17t/c/b, 18tr/cl/b, 18-19c, 19t/cra/crb, 20t, 21t/c, 23cl, 28t/b, 29c, 41 (insert), 67tl, 77b/c, 85b, 163 (insert).

HARVARD UNIVERSITY ART MUSEUMS: © President and Fellows of Harvard College, courtesy of the Busch-Reisinger Museum, Gift of Mrs. Gordon Dexter *Colonel Ernst August von Hugo and Lt. Colonel von Schlepegrell*, John Singleton Copley, 1787 - 114cr; courtesy of the Busch-Reisinger Museum, Gift of Sibyl Moholy-Nagy, © DACS, London 2000 *Light-Space Modulator*, Laszlo Moholy-Nagy, 1930 - 114b; courtesy Fogg Art Museum, Gift of Lawrence Rubin © ARS, N. Y. and DACS, London 2000 *Red River Valley*, Frank Stella, 1958 - 115cl; courtesy Fogg Art Museum, Bequest: Collection of Maurice Wertheim *Skating* Edouard Manet, 1877 - 115b; HULTON GETTY COLLECTION: 60b.

IMAGE BANK: Archive Photos 28c. LEBRECHT COLLECTION: The Rodgers

& Hammerstein Organization 89t/br; James Lemass: 6cl, 23crb, 36t/b, 37t/c/b, 38b, 39t, 56, 80, 93crb, 154c, 155, 157t, 158c/b, 162-163.

Mary Evans: 121 (insert); Massachusetts Bay Transportation Authority: 173b; Museum of Fine Arts, Boston: Gift of Egypt Exploration Fund *Egypt, Deir el-Bahri* painted wood 22b; HU-MFA Expedition *Shawabtis of Taharka* 26b; 106t; Bequest of Mrs. Beatrice Constance (Turner) Maynard in Memory of Winthrop Sargent *Revere Silver Teapot* 106ca; Egypt Exploration Fund *Inner Coffin of Nes-mut-aat-neru* 106cb; 1951 Purchase Fund *La Japonaise* Claude Monet, 1876 – 107t; Ruth and Carl J. Shapiro Colonnade and Vault *John Singer Sargent Murals* 107c; Henry Lillie Pierce Fund *Ram's Head* 107b; George Nixon Black Fund *Ewer and basin* 108t; M. and M. Karolik Collection of American Paintings, 1815 – 1865, by exchange, *Boston Harbor* Fitz Hugh Lane 108c; Bequest of John T. Spaulding *La Berceuse* Vincent van Gogh, 1889 – 108b; Maria Antoinette Evans Fund *Babylonia: Nebuchadnezzar II* 109t; Gift by Contribution *Horse, early 8th century, China* 109c; Richard Norton Memorial Fund *Fragment of fresco from villa at Contrada Bottaro* 109b; Museum of Science: George Kiley 159t; Andrew Brilliant 159b; Kindra

Clineff 26t; New England Aquarium: Bob Kramer 78t/b, 79t; David Noble: 40-41.

Omni Parker House: 58clb.

Peabody Museum of Archaeology and Ethnology/Harvard University: © President and Fellows of Harvard College 1976. All Rights Reserved. Photos Hillel Burger 116c. Courtesy Paul Revere Memorial Association: 75t.

Science Photo Library: CNES, 1986 Distribution Spot Image 11t. Swissôtel Boston: © René Staud 122b.

Topham Picturepoint: 23b.

United Airlines: 170t.

Front Endpaper: All special photography except David J. Brooker: cr; James Lemass: bl/bc.

Jacket Front - DK Picture Library: Alan Keohane bl; Karl Shone br; Peter Wilson bc; Getty Images: Ron Thomas main image. Back - DK Picture Library: Alan Keohane b; Francesca York t. Spine - Getty Images: Ron Thomas.

All other images ©Dorling Kindersley. See www.dkimages.com for further information.

Further Reading

NON-FICTION

A Guide to Public Art in Boston: from Newburyport to Plymouth. Carlock, Marty. (Harvard Common Press, 1993.)

AIA Guide to Boston. Southworth, Michael and Susan. (Globe Pequot Press, 1996.)

All about Boston Harbour Islands. Kales, Emily and David. (Hewitts Cove Publishing Co. Inc., 1983.)

Boston Sites and Insights. Wilson, Susan. (Beacon Hill Press, 1994.)

Exploring in and Around Boston on Bike and Foot. Sinai, Lee. (Appalachian Mountain Club Books, 1996.)

Imagining Boston: A Literary Landscape. O'Connell, Shaun. (Beacon Press, 1990.)

Paul Revere's Ride. Fischer, David Hackett. (Oxford University Press, 1994.)

Romantic Days and Nights in Boston. Harris, Patricia and Lyon, David. (Globe Pequot Press, 1997, 1999.)

The Fitzgeralds and the Kennedys: an American Saga. Goodwin, Doris Kearns. (Simon and Schuster, 1987.)

26 Miles to Boston: the Boston Marathon Experience from Hopkinton to Copley Square. Connelly, Michael. (Parnassus Imprints, 1998.)

FICTION

The Godwulf Manuscript. Parker, Robert. (Delacorte Press, 1974.)

Make Way for Ducklings. McCloskey, Robert. (Viking Press, 1941.)

Mortal friends. Carroll, James. (Little Brown & Company, 1978.)

The Last Hurrah. O'Connor, Edwin. (Little Brown & Company, 1956.)

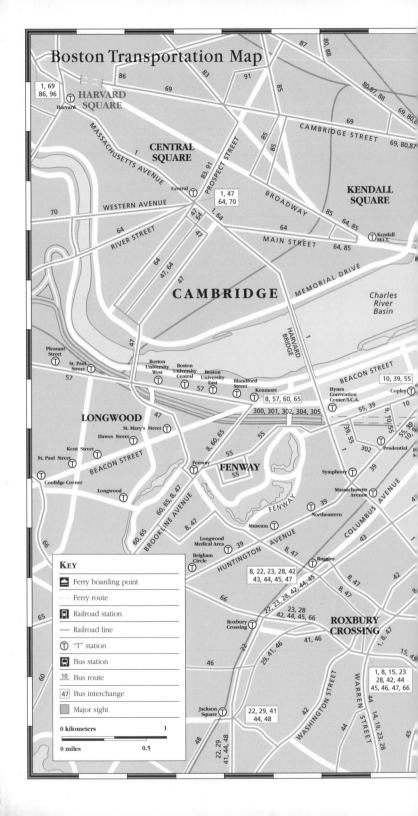